# Bumper Book of Simplex Crosswords

# BUMPER BOOK OF SIMPLEX CROSSWORDS

**Mary O'Brien**

Gill Books

Gill Books
Hume Avenue, Park West, Dublin 12
Gill Books is an imprint of M.H. Gill & Co.
www.gillbooks.ie

© Mary O'Brien 2008
978 07171 4384 9
Print origination by O'K Graphic Design, Dublin
Printed by Clays, Elcograf, UK

This book is typeset in 9/10 pt Zurich Condensed.

The paper used in this book comes from the wood pulp of managed
forests. For every tree felled, at least one tree is planted, thereby
renewing natural resources.

A CIP catalogue record for this book is available from the British
Library.

In memory of
Eileen Scully
our favourite crossword fan

# The Puzzles

# 1

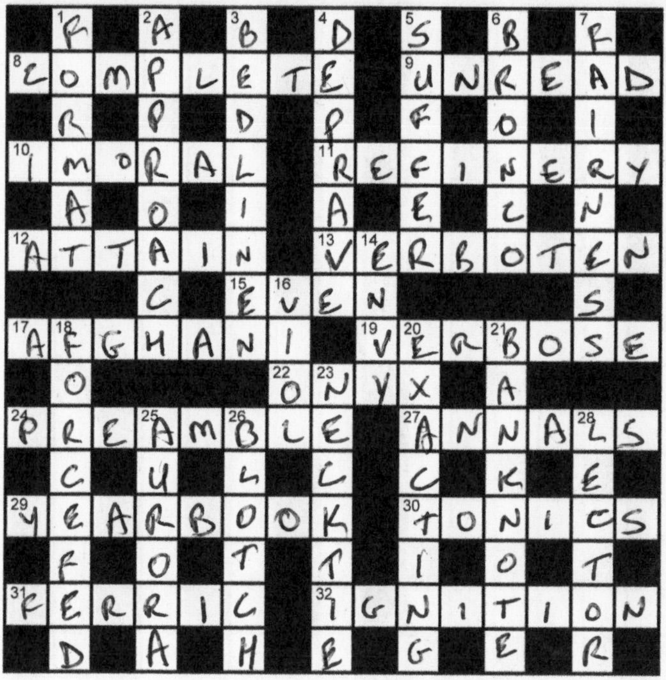

**ACROSS**

8 Whole and entire (8)
9 Not perused (6)
10 Without standards or principles (6)
11 An industrial plant for purifying a crude substance (8)
12 Gain with effort (6)
13 It's forbidden in Germany (8)
15 Type of number divisible by two (4)
17 I fan hag for a native of Kabul, say (7)
19 Using too many words (7)
22 Quartz with alternating bands of colour (4)
24 Preliminary introduction to a document (8)
27 Chronological records (6)
29 Reference book that's published annually (8)
30 Medicines that strengthen and invigorate (6)
31 Relating to iron (6)
32 Initiation of combustion (8)

**DOWN**

1 The general appearance, layout (6)
2 Move towards (8)
3 Sheets, pillowcases etc. (3,5)
4 Corrupt morally (7)
5 Endure pain (6)
6 An unbroken mustang, bucking perhaps (6)
7 Ability to make judgments free from discrimination or dishonesty (8)
14 The green-eyed monster (4)
16 Family of instruments that preceded the violin (4)
18 Compelled to eat (8)
20 Strict and demanding (8)
21 Piece of paper money (4,4)
23 It's worn under the collar (7)
25 Goddess of the dawn (6)
26 Irregularly shaped spot (6)
28 Reader at certain universities (6)

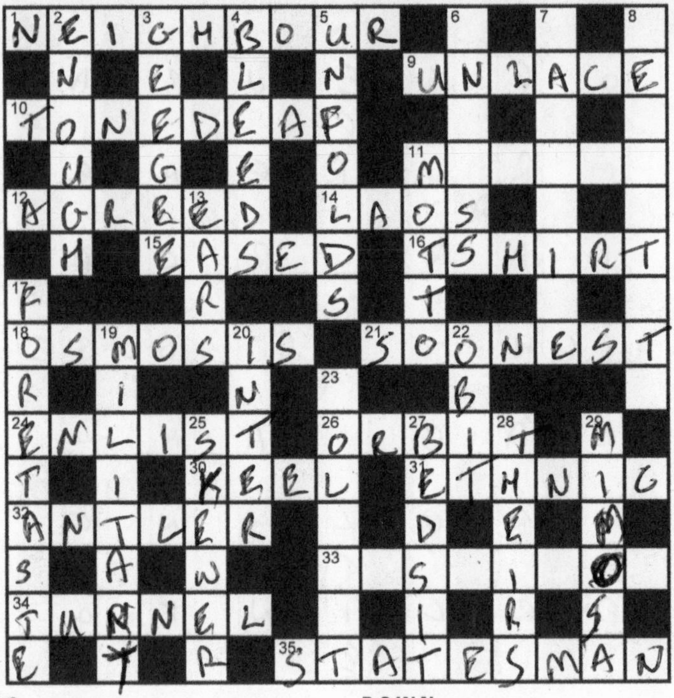

## 2

**ACROSS**

1 Person who lives near you (9)
9 Undo the ties (6)
10 Unable to appreciate music (4-4)
11 Tell 'im about the grain (6)
12 Had the same opinion (6)
14 Republic in southeastern Asia (4)
15 Alleviated (5)
16 Close-fitting pullover shirt (1-5)
18 O, is moss a gradual absorption or assimilation? (7)
21 With the least delay (7)
24 Join the military (6)
26 The path of a celestial body (5)
30 One of the main beams of a vessel (4)
31 Describes a distinctive group (6)
32 The part of the stamen that contains pollen (6)
33 A receptacle for expectorations (8)
34 Underground passage (6)
35 Respected leader in national or international affairs (9)

**DOWN**

2 Sufficient (6)
3 Child's word for horse (3-3)
4 Loses blood (6)
5 Stretches out to the full length (7)
6 A laminated metamorphic rock similar to granite (6)
7 Small flat implement for paring (8)
8 Indigent (9)
11 Catchword, slogan (5)
13 Auricles (4)
17 Flavour of something about to happen (9)
19 Showing a fighting disposition (8)
20 Place in a grave or tomb (5)
22 Biography after death, in short (4)
23 Skunk (7)
25 Long meat-pin (6)
27 Living-room with sleeping accommodation, in short (6)
28 Belonging to them (6)
29 Tropical shrub with fragrant yellow flowers (6)

**3**

## ACROSS

1. Slowly and gracefully in music (6)
5. Abundance of material possessions (6)
10. Applies badly or incorrectly (7)
11. Dampen (7)
12. Mormon state (4)
13. Stage whisper (5)
15. Festival (4)
17. Enclosure for swine (3)
19. Laugh nervously or foolishly (6)
21. Systematic plan of action (6)
22. Boat with a flat bottom for carrying loads (7)
23. Boost (6)
25. Heart or clock (6)
28. Money risked on a gamble (3)
30. Contest of speed (4)
31. Public meeting or assembly for open discussion (5)
32. ... Lang Syne (4)
35. The stalks of this vegetable/fruit are edible, but the leaves poisonous (7)
36. Glitter (7)
37. Get back, recover the use of (6)
38. One or the other (6)

## DOWN

2. Far apart in space or time (7)
3. Short sharp intake of breath (4)
4. Be fully and persistently preoccupied with something (6)
5. Medicine or therapy that cures (6)
6. Elegant and stylish (4)
7. Furthest or highest degree of something (7)
8. Quantity (6)
9. Involuntary expulsion of air from the nose (6)
14. More fidgety or restless (7)
16. Extremely cold (5)
18. Pungent, biting (5)
20. Tear violently (3)
21. Group of things of the same kind (3)
23. Sudden outburst, uproar (6)
24. Discourse on some subject, to a class say (7)
26. Joint of a finger (7)
27. Blush (6)
28. Reel, spool (6)
29. Rough-and-tumble (6)
33. Thanks, to a child perhaps (2-2)
34. Small, pointed missile (4)

**4**

## ACROSS

1 Quibbles (6)
4 A 'wannabe' found in past rain (8)
9 Type of shrub or tree (6)
10 Flatter to get something (6,2)
12 Style of speech of a specific group (5)
13 Military or hospital attendants (9)
15 Have, possess (3)
16 Transfer a train to another track (5)
17 Modest and shy (6)
22 Noisy fight (6)
24 Give personal assurance (5)
27 ... polloi, the common people (3)
28 Repeat again (9)
31 Sound (5)
32 In a way that minimises suffering (8)
33 Franklin ... Roosevelt (6)
34 Military personnel (8)
35 Cuts off (6)

## DOWN

1 Maddest (8)
2 Eucharist given to dying Roman Catholics (8)
3 Melodic phrase that accompanies the reappearance of a person on stage (9)
5 Smallest army unit (5)
6 Former title of junior certificate, in short (5)
7 Quick or skilful (6)
8 Operator of a machine that prints one character at a time (6)
11 Large bird of prey (6)
14 Large flightless bird (3)
18 Violent disturbance (6)
19 Wandering ocular organ (6,3)
20 Gluey substance secreted by plants (8)
21 So then Pa goes for large open cars with folding tops (8)
23 Evergreen tree for Irish men? (3)
25 Curved shapes that span openings (6)
26 Depressing in character or appearance (6)
29 Boredom (5)
30 More capable (5)

**5**

Crossword grid solution:

Row 1: M Y S T E R I E S _ K _ L _ H
Row 2: E _ R _ X _ S A L I V A
Row 3: C O L O N I Z E _ R _ B _ R
Row 4: _ M _ O _ S _ _ S A L A A M
Row 5: S A M P L E _ T A C T _ T _ O
Row 6: N _ S I D L E _ R E G I O N
Row 7: S _ E _ D _ A _ O _ I
Row 8: T R A I N E D _ A P P E N D S
Row 9: A _ T _ N _ E _ E
Row 10: M O R A L S _ R A T E D _ C
Row 11: M _ O _ A U R A _ E L I C I T
Row 12: E N C O R E _ U _ L _ R
Row 13: R _ I _ A N N O U N C E
Row 14: E N T R E E _ I _ I _ T _ L
Row 15: D Y R _ F L U S T E R E D

**ACROSS**

1 They're beyond understanding or explanation (9)

9 Liquid secreted in the mouth (6)

10 Form a settlement in a foreign country (8)

11 Eastern greeting (6)

12 Part representing the whole (6)

14 Diplomacy, discretion (4)

15 Move like a crab (5)

16 Area, neighbourhood (6)

18 Instructed (7)

21 Adds to the end (7)

24 Ethical motives (6)

26 Estimated the value, assigned a ranking (5)

30 Distinctive atmosphere (4)

31 Draw out (6)

32 Once more (6)

33 Make known, declare (8)

34 Right of admission (6)

35 Hot and bothered (9)

**DOWN**

2 Old officer in the bodyguard of the British monarch (6)

3 Bodies of soldiers (6)

4 Lifted up or nurtured (6)

5 Made a great physical effort (7)

6 Japanese system of unarmed combat (6)

7 A serving of an alcoholic beverage (8)

8 Combine notes to make chords (9)

11 Fight for a small fragment? (5)

13 Right to retain property until a debt is paid (4)

17 Spoke haltingly (9)

19 Act of shocking cruelty (8)

20 Follow as a consequence (5)

22 Rind of a fruit (4)

23 Excessive labour (7)

25 Food cupboard (6)

27 Game played with a racket (6)

28 Add liquid to lessen strength (6)

29 Curved closed line (6)

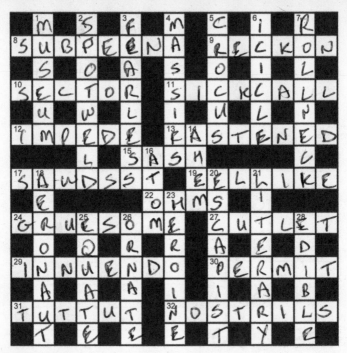

**6**

## ACROSS

8 Legal writ compelling attendance (8)
9 Consider or calculate (6)
10 Group of businesses that form part of an economy (6)
11 A visit to the ill (4,4)
12 Obstruct, hold up progress (6)
13 Buttoned, secured (8)
15 Broad band, the one me father wore? (4)
17 Fine particles of wood (7)
19 Resembling a type of fish, long, thin and sinuous (7)
22 Units of electrical resistance (4)
24 Shockingly repellent (8)
27 Thin piece of rib-meat (6)
28 An indirect implication (8)
30 Allow (6)
31 Exclamation of rebuke (3-3)
32 Slit Ron's nose parts badly (8)

## DOWN

1 Depository to display objects of interest (6)
2 Join metals with single fusings (8)
3 Resolute in facing danger (8)
4 Geological formations that make mountain peaks (7)
5 Plant from which saffron is taken (6)
6 Pendent spear of frozen water (6)
7 Type of turned-down collar (8)
14 Half-cough to draw attention (4)
16 Particle of matter (4)
18 Someone who operates an aircraft (8)
20 Inclination to retreat from unpleasant realities through diversion (8)
21 Of good writing (8)
23 Main female character in a story (7)
25 Consider analogous (6)
26 Rich in decorative detail (6)
28 Fit to eat (6)

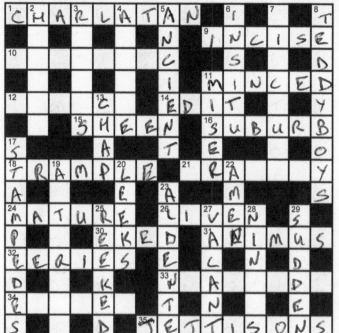

## ACROSS

1 Quack, flamboyant deceiver (9)
9 Cut into (6)
10 Representing something else (8)
11 Cut into small pieces (6)
12 Refuse to accept (6)
14 Prepare for publication (4)
15 Lustre (5)
16 Residential district on the outskirts of a city (6)
18 Tread underfoot (7)
21 Ornamental openwork in Gothic architecture with strange car tyre (7)
24 Fully developed (6)
26 Animate (5)
30 ... out, made to last through frugality (4)
31 A feeling of ill will or hostility (6)
32 Lofty nests of birds of prey (6)
33 It occurs between the first and third quarters of the moon (4,4)
34 Short-range guided missile (6)
35 Throws goods overboard (9)

## DOWN

2 Tomboy (6)
3 Hydrophobia (6)
4 Remove a bodily structure by surgery (6)
5 Of times long past (7)
6 In the original position (2-4)
7 Alcoholic solution of medicine (8)
8 Youth of 1960s, wore Edwardian clothes (9)
11 Hoarder of money and possessions (5)
13 Leather legging worn by cowboys (4)
17 Headlong rush of crowds (9)
19 Located before, in time or place (8)
20 Welsh vegetables? (5)
22 So be it (4)
23 Cooked so as still to be firm when bitten (2,5)
25 Smelled to high heaven (6)
27 Without an incumbent (6)
28 Seven of these parts in 63 (6)
29 Happening without warning (6)

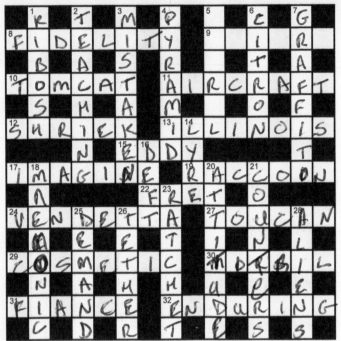

Grid answers (handwritten):

Row 1 (Down clue letters): K T M P | C G
Row 2: 8 FIDELITY | 9 ... I R
Row 3: B A S R | T A
Row 4: 10 TOMCAT | 11 AIRCRAFT
Row 5: S M A M | O F
Row 6: 12 SHRIEK | 13/14 ILLINOIS
Row 7: N 15/16 EDDY | T
Row 8: 17 IMAGINE | 19 20/21 RACCOON
Row 9: A | 22/23 FRET | O
Row 10: 24 VENDETTA | 27 TOUCAN
Row 11: A E F T | I N L
Row 12: 29 COSMETIC | 30 MORBIL
Row 13: N A H H | U E E
Row 14: 31 FIANCE | 32 ENDURING
Row 15: C D R T E S S

## ACROSS

**8** Faithfulness (8)
**9** Place where bees are kept (6)
**10** Male feline (6)
**11** Learjet, say (8)
**12** Sharp piercing cry (6)
**13** The state capital is Springfield (8)
**15** Miniature whirlpool (4)
**17** Form a mental picture (7)
**19** American nocturnal mammal (7)
**22** Worry about doing woodwork? (4)
**24** Murderous feud (8)
**27** A pair would be able for this bird, by the sound of it (6)
**29** Preparation designed to beautify the body (8)
**30** Small tasty bit of food (6)
**31** He's engaged to be married (6)
**32** Putting up with something (8)

## DOWN

**1** Put this on something and stop it from happening (6)
**2** Imparting skills or knowledge (8)
**3** Wrong (8)
**4** Massive Egyptian memorial (7)
**5** Does Al rule this bush? (6)
**6** Large lemon-like fruit (6)
**7** Defacement on public surface (8)
**14** A harp used by ancient Greeks (4)
**16** Quick and skilful in movement (4)
**18** Device to aid the memory (8)
**20** Mental orientation (8)
**21** Horizontal surfaces on which business is transacted (8)
**23** Toothed wheel (7)
**25** Peremptory request (6)
**26** Tie up an animal (6)
**28** Saline mix for foreigners (6)

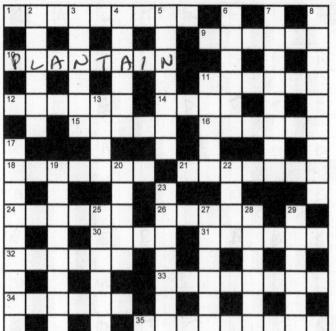

**ACROSS**

1 Prove to be right (9)
9 Excessively ornate style (6)
10 Coarse banana (8)
11 It was part of Yugoslavia (6)
12 Change to ice (6)
14 Lake of the North (4)
15 Chair carried by two (5)
16 Deepest within (6)
18 Emotionally hardened (7)
21 Meeting for an exchange of ideas (7)
24 Dwarfed tree or shrub (6)
26 Express mirth (5)
30 Drink containing carbonated water (4)
31 Foul vapours or unwholesome air (6)
32 Accomplish (6)
33 Mechanical cage in a vertical shaft (8)
34 Throughout the time (6)
35 Support through grants (9)

**DOWN**

2 They don't like work (6)
3 Refuses to grant or recognise (6)
4 Went after with the intent to catch (6)
5 Straight line that touches but doesn't intersect a curve (7)
6 Unlawfully distilled whiskey (6)
7 Old Spanish gold coin (8)
8 Residence of a religious community (9)
11 Sneering, supercilious (5)
13 Nought (4)
17 Sheaths for swords or daggers (9)
19 For a relatively extended period (4-4)
20 Organisation of employees formed to bargain with the employer (5)
22 The sages who visited the stable at Bethlehem (4)
23 A flat highland (7)
25 Natives of China, say (6)
27 Plants in which the individual flower stalks arise from the same point (6)
28 A source of danger (6)
29 Raise in a relief (6)

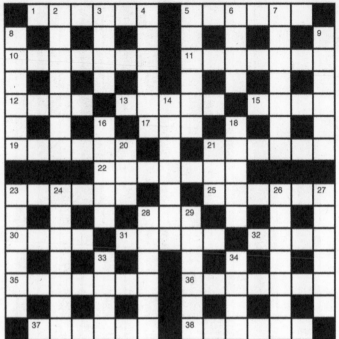

## ACROSS

**1** In the arms of Morpheus (6)
**5** Types of stockings (6)
**10** Offensive or indecent (7)
**11** Underground rootstock of a plant (7)
**12** Team to man a ship, say (4)
**13** Relating to people (5)
**15** Asian title for a prince (4)
**17** Drunkard (3)
**19** Short sharp noise on the door (3-3)
**21** Pick out (6)
**22** Failures to face difficulties squarely (3-4)
**23** Narrow channel of the sea joining two larger bodies of water (6)
**25** Gives in (6)
**28** Deed (3)
**30** Boisterous practical jokes by college students (4)
**31** Keep away from (5)
**32** Cut metal with acid (4)
**35** Contrary to or forbidden by law (7)
**36** Tediously repetitious or lacking in variety (7)
**37** Hairdresser (6)
**38** Reptile with a bony shell (6)

## DOWN

**2** Imagine to be true (7)
**3** Level or straight (4)
**4** Solar ..., network of nerves behind the stomach (6)
**5** Declaration of intention to harm (6)
**6** Facial expression showing amusement or pleasure (4)
**7** To cheer about the poetic metre (7)
**8** Association football (6)
**9** Ante up for the hard fruit (6)
**14** Country of fine leather (7)
**16** Implied, understood (5)
**18** Rinse out this substance from trees (5)
**20** Add up (3)
**21** Inflammation on the eyelid (3)
**23** Seamy, squalid (6)
**24** Paraphernalia indicative of high office (7)
**26** Situated at or extending to the side (7)
**27** Ordered system (6)
**28** Manifestation of a Hindu deity in visible form (6)
**29** Protective helmet once worn by construction and mine workers (3,3)
**33** Someone who works during a strike (4)
**34** Arabian ruler (4)

**11**

## ACROSS

**1** Contests in which teams pull opposite ends of a rope (4-2-3)
**9** Tall vertical upright (6)
**10** Logical and lucid (8)
**11** Small appetising savoury (6)
**12** Make a hole in (6)
**14** Public act of violence by an unruly mob (4)
**15** Twilled woollen fabric (5)
**16** Humble, lowly, work say (6)
**18** Cul-de-sac (7)
**21** Fairy who puts children to sleep (7)
**24** City in central Spain famous for swords (6)
**26** Socio-economic group (5)
**30** Reverse an action (4)
**31** Sign that represents something else (6)
**32** Directions for cooking (6)
**33** Ball game (8)
**34** National song (6)
**35** Device for observing events at a distance and transmitting the information back to the observer (9)

## DOWN

**2** Thomas More's perfect society (6)
**3** Large scissors with strong blades (6)
**4** Tentative suggestion designed to elicit the reactions of others (6)
**5** Clothed (7)
**6** Turn on or around an axis (6)
**7** Doctrine that rejects religion and the supernatural (8)
**8** Give extra weight to (9)
**11** Punctuation mark (5)
**13** Surrender or relinquish possession (4)
**17** Newspaper opinion piece (9)
**19** Distribute according to a plan (8)
**20** Not a single person (2-3)
**22** Offensively curious or inquisitive (4)
**23** Whip, flagellate (7)
**25** Apartment with rooms on two floors (6)
**27** Take to be the case (6)
**28** Blemish made by dirt (6)
**29** Gruff, husky (6)

**ACROSS**

1 Supernatural forces, events and beings (6)
5 Structure manufactured in one place and placed elsewhere, in short (6)
10 Sanction (7)
11 Pretentious or silly talk (7)
12 Highly excited (4)
13 Get hitched (5)
15 Sign of something about to happen (4)
17 Sign of assent (3)
19 Mentally ill (6)
21 Communication that encodes a message (6)
22 Exposes pretentious or false claims (7)
23 Shorebird with pointed wings (6)
25 Solution applied to wounds as an antiseptic (6)
28 Number not divisible by two (3)
30 ... Saint Laurent (4)
31 Plait (5)
32 Look at with amorous intentions (4)
35 Excessively agitated (7)
36 Fully developed person (7)
37 Iced, as creme de menthe perhaps (6)
38 Symbol, representation (6)

**DOWN**

2 Large in number or quantity (7)
3 Abreast of, au fait with (2,2)
4 Surgical instrument used to remove sections of bone from the skull (6)
5 Explosive device used to break down a wall (6)
6 Set of questions to evaluate (4)
7 Region of the body between the thorax and the pelvis (7)
8 Highly seasoned sausage (6)
9 Shelter for a dog (6)
14 Circular building with a dome (7)
16 Alphabetical listing of names, topics and page numbers (5)
18 Large shaggy-maned animal (5)
20 Ever, to the poet (3)
21 Narrow runner for the snow (3)
23 Recompense for worthy acts (3-3)
24 Out of doors (4,3)
26 Artless innocent young girl on stage (7)
27 Not subject to, taxation say (6)
28 Authoritative person who divines the future (6)
29 Small wooded hollow, in Kerry? (6)
33 Cease (4)
34 Place of burial (4)

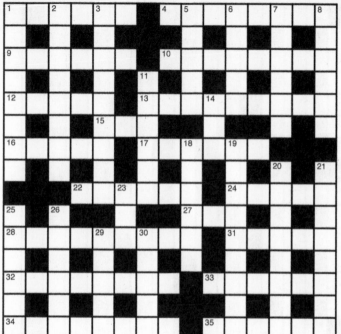

## ACROSS

**1** Bring to the latest state of the art (6)
**4** Formal jacket for men (8)
**9** Someone who pays rent (6)
**10** Well below average height (4-4)
**12** Cuban folk dance (5)
**13** Instrument or artefact that performs a service (9)
**15** Mixed breed of dog (3)
**16** Pertaining to a number system based on eight (5)
**17** Toughen by gradually heating and cooling (6)
**22** Stage whispers (6)
**24** Orange-yellow colour (5)
**27** Woollen cap of Scottish origin, in short (3)
**28** State of dishonour (9)
**31** Chap, fellow (5)
**32** Indicates by signs (8)
**33** Bring in from abroad (6)
**34** Sole, lone (8)
**35** African fly that transmits sleeping sickness (6)

## DOWN

**1** Beneath the surface, deliberately concealed (8)
**2** Powerful explosive (8)
**3** Flexible organs on the head of some animals (9)
**5** Adios (5)
**6** Ease off (3,2)
**7** The boy who wanted more (6)
**8** A score (6)
**11** Person who announces important news (6)
**14** Frozen water (3)
**18** Inhabited an egg-laying place (6)
**19** Weapons that release enormous energy by nuclear fission (4,5)
**20** Gunfight (5-3)
**21** The drink causing sorrow to be forgotten, poetically (8)
**23** Mischievous fairy (3)
**25** Changes to suit a new purpose (6)
**26** Pertaining to the stars (6)
**29** Construct, build (5)
**30** Below or beneath (5)

## ACROSS

**1** Not transmitting or reflecting light (6)
**5** Sleeveless and collarless jacket (6)
**10** Island state in the West Indies (7)
**11** Not in any place (7)
**12** Professional cook (4)
**13** Single-masted sailing vessel (5)
**15** Beat severely with a whip (4)
**17** Make a mistake (3)
**19** Work lightly (6)
**21** Morally bad or wrong (6)
**22** Pain in an aural appendage (7)
**23** Female domestic servant who does all kinds of menial work (6)
**25** Go higher than another at an auction (6)
**28** Printer's medium (3)
**30** Destroy completely (4)
**31** Arise out of (5)
**32** Not far (4)
**35** Recreation (7)
**36** Tending to occur among members of a family (7)
**37** Be about to happen (6)
**38** Duct that carries urine (6)

## DOWN

**2** Rule of conduct or doctrine (7)
**3** Dock, wharf (4)
**4** Render capable (6)
**5** Younger or lower in rank (6)
**6** Angry disputes (4)
**7** It's applied to cool or reduce swelling (3,4)
**8** Small receptacle for a breakfast dish (6)
**9** Way of doing (6)
**14** Decrees and admits to holy orders (7)
**16** Annoy, get at, irritate (5)
**18** Secure with ropes (3,2)
**20** Column of light (3)
**21** What person (3)
**23** Round shape formed by concentric circles (6)
**24** Heavy brittle metallic element (7)
**26** Inhale and exhale air (7)
**27** Guide, actors in a play say (6)
**28** In truth (6)
**29** Chinese martial art (4,2)
**33** Hexahedron with six equal faces (4)
**34** One time (4)

## ACROSS

1 Clandestine (6)
4 Actions disadvantageous to those who carry them out (3,5)
9 Take away, dispose of (6)
10 Judge the worth of something (8)
12 Fencing swords (5)
13 Misadventure, mishap (9)
15 Substance for staining or colouring (3)
16 Woodland deity, attendant on Bacchus (5)
17 Strip for take-off and landing of aircraft (6)
22 Earnest request (6)
24 Stupid foolish person (5)
27 Proprietary brand of beef cube (3)
28 He comes between producer and consumer (9)
31 Belonging to you (5)
32 Use again after reprocessing (8)
33 Capital of Turkey (6)
34 Lacking zest or vivacity (8)
35 Remove, erase (6)

## DOWN

1 Desist, refrain from (8)
2 Remarks (8)
3 Listen without the speaker's knowledge (9)
5 Men's marriage partners (5)
6 A narrow gorge with a stream running through it (5)
7 Begone, in Shakespearian times (6)
8 Turnips (6)
11 Come into view (6)
14 Female of domestic cattle (3)
18 Women's stockings made from a sheer material (6)
19 Irritation, vexation (9)
20 Hatch (8)
21 Visor worn by card-players (8)
23 Dish baked in pastry-lined pan (3)
25 Free-living (6)
26 Decrees, orders (6)
29 Anaesthetic that numbs only one area of the body (5)
30 Encounters (5)

## ACROSS

**8** Old coin, one twentieth of a pound (8)
**9** Man or beast (6)
**10** Walk leisurely (6)
**11** Large table centrepieces with branching holders (8)
**12** Roman Catholic devotion over nine days (6)
**13** Cut Rufus up about this legal right to use another's property (8)
**15** A court proceeding (4)
**17** Tightly twisted woollen yarn (7)
**19** Betting for a win or a place (4,3)
**22** Inquires (4)
**24** Hardened area of skin (8)
**27** Watery fluid of blood (6)
**29** Hired killer (8)
**30** Property consisting of houses and land (6)
**31** Rumple, dishevel (6)
**32** Midday meal (8)

## DOWN

**1** Residential district of a city in which one class of people are required to live (6)
**2** Underpants or flowers (8)
**3** Channel for water that turns a grinder (8)
**4** Produced under conditions involving intense heat (7)
**5** French boat (6)
**6** Digit (6)
**7** City in eastern Spain on the Mediterranean (8)
**14** Try to locate or discover (4)
**16** Said to be the progenitor of the human race (4)
**18** The time of a particular event (8)
**20** Painkillers for 21dn say (8)
**21** A pain in the brain (8)
**23** Beatific (7)
**25** Pass, as time (6)
**26** Removed from office (6)
**28** Manner, technique (6)

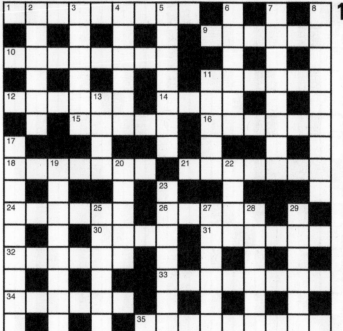

**17**

## ACROSS

**1** Sitting a lot and taking little exercise (9)
**9** Scattered about (6)
**10** Court of justice or arbitration (8)
**11** Ocean trip taken for pleasure (6)
**12** Instruct with authority (6)
**14** Walk heavily, trudge (4)
**15** Small shelters for doves (5)
**16** Name of the writer on an article (2-4)
**18** Strive to imitate (7)
**21** Acutely insightful and wise (7)
**24** The greatest possible degree (6)
**26** Relating to the nose (5)
**30** The other one from that (4)
**31** Not having the necessary means or know-how (6)
**32** Pay no attention to (6)
**33** They're also called Wellingtons (8)
**34** Treatise resulting from research (6)
**35** According to law (9)

## DOWN

**2** Short trip for a message (6)
**3** En masse (6)
**4** Lessee (6)
**5** Fall back into bad health (7)
**6** Strong and stout (6)
**7** Womanly (8)
**8** Pastimes, hobbies (9)
**11** Venomous snake (5)
**13** Ninth letter of the Greek alphabet (4)
**17** Renounce, disown (9)
**19** Lacking a crew (8)
**20** Levy of one tenth (5)
**22** Method for accomplishing something (4)
**23** Clear or deep perception of a situation (7)
**25** Pass through a filter (6)
**27** Refer for judgment or consideration (6)
**28** Array, presentation (6)
**29** Long, loose overcoat from the province (6)

## ACROSS

**1** Ineffectual or indolent (6)
**5** Credit to a source or cause (6)
**10** Short-tailed burrowing rodent (7)
**11** Word that can be exchanged for another (7)
**12** Poke or spur (4)
**13** Gem, say (5)
**15** Sour and sullen (4)
**17** Deplete, drain of resources (3)
**19** Departs (6)
**21** Keeper of the net (6)
**22** Cattle thief (7)
**23** From what place (6)
**25** Hard rock (6)
**28** Wooden pin (3)
**30** Tart spiciness (4)
**31** Assuage, ease (5)
**32** Long narrative poem telling of a hero's deeds (4)
**35** Sea-water flowing out (7)
**36** Attribute (7)
**37** Failing in what duty requires (6)
**38** Lay to rest in an underground vault (6)

## DOWN

**2** Lottery in which tickets are drawn from a revolving drum (7)
**3** Profane or obscene expression (4)
**4** Eagles' nests (6)
**5** Arch of the foot (6)
**6** Panel of glass (4)
**7** Very thin and flexible sheet of aluminium (7)
**8** Place of worship (6)
**9** Become visible (6)
**14** Person who dissipates resources (7)
**16** Imperial measure of fish? (5)
**18** Sudden short attack (5)
**20** The girl to take to court (3)
**21** Precious stone (3)
**23** Shrivel up, shrink (7)
**24** Lend dignity or honour to (7)
**26** Christian sacrament signifying rebirth (7)
**27** Go beyond (6)
**28** Gripping tool (6)
**29** Building for cars (6)
**33** Pacific island, capital Suva (4)
**34** Type of jazz singing (4)

## ACROSS

**1** Long cluster of flowers along a main stem (6)
**4** Drew out (8)
**9** Room in a church where sacred vessels and vestments are kept (6)
**10** Ancient war engine for hurling large stones (8)
**12** Goodbye to the French (5)
**13** Dishes made with beaten eggs (9)
**15** Peace to the old Romans (3)
**16** Tedium (5)
**17** Financial gain (6)
**22** Pestilence (6)
**24** Court proceedings (5)
**27** It remains after burning (3)
**28** Alpine plant (9)
**31** Smell (5)
**32** Thin tube to withdraw fluids from the body (8)
**33** Bushes or trees with large fragrant flowers (6)
**34** XIX (8)
**35** Three-dimensional sound effect (6)

## DOWN

**1** Disclosed (8)
**2** Lessens the impact (8)
**3** Pouched mammal (9)
**5** Let for money (5)
**6** Large long-necked wading bird (5)
**7** Worthy of being relied on (6)
**8** Dislike intensely (6)
**11** Fighting with the fists (6)
**14** W.C. (3)
**18** Wrinkle (6)
**19** Member of Wesleyan religion (9)
**20** Extinct reptile (8)
**21** In the open air (8)
**23** A serve that the receiver is unable to reach (3)
**25** Rank of clergy (6)
**26** Part of fruit used in making fruit jellies and jams (6)
**29** Cereal crop (5)
**30** Girl of peace (5)

## ACROSS

**8** Keep in a certain state (8)
**9** Tap, faucet (6)
**10** It qualifies the predicate (6)
**11** Made a musical sound by blowing through a small opening (8)
**12** Showing extreme courage (6)
**13** Bridge-builder, for instance (8)
**15** Bone in the arm (4)
**17** Official who ensures fair play (7)
**19** They're surrounded by water (7)
**22** Aquatic bird (4)
**24** Commercial or industrial enterprise (8)
**27** Make possible (6)
**29** Imaginary, not based in reality (8)
**30** Discharging a debt (6)
**31** Wise and trusted advisor (6)
**32** Showing sound judgment (8)

## DOWN

**1** Stick of wax with a wick (6)
**2** One leapt badly on the graceful ruminant (8)
**3** Cook-out (8)
**4** Figures in white in winter (7)
**5** Inquiring (6)
**6** Once this, twice shy (6)
**7** Space between the eyes (8)
**14** Thin pointed fastener (4)
**16** Lower limbs (4)
**18** Schooled (8)
**20** Dormant (8)
**21** Any sails resulting from the investigation? (8)
**23** Having no beneficial function (7)
**25** Urge, instigate (6)
**26** Exertion, endeavour (6)
**28** Lacking companions (6)

**21**

## ACROSS

**1** Abstruse (6)
**4** Protection from the rain (8)
**9** Prayer beads (6)
**10** News report (8)
**12** Sand at the side of the sea (5)
**13** Normally, not artificially (9)
**15** Misery, great suffering (3)
**16** Annoy good-naturedly (5)
**17** Sagely (6)
**22** Remained (6)
**24** Inside horizontal surface (5)
**27** Scottish river (3)
**28** It transmits speech over a distance (9)
**31** Gives support to (5)
**32** Young frogs (8)
**33** Grown up (6)
**34** Excited anticipation of an approaching climax (8)
**35** The way something appears (6)

## DOWN

**1** Circus tumblers (8)
**2** Robinson Crusoe was one (8)
**3** Mayo and Donegal are here (9)
**5** Climb, stairs say (5)
**6** Strip used for drawing straight lines (5)
**7** In the recent past (6)
**8** Irritates, bothers (6)
**11** Allowing travel in one direction only (3-3)
**14** Function (3)
**18** Unexpected, no warning (6)
**19** Crafts for rescue at sea (9)
**20** Decide by reasoning or draw to a close (8)
**21** Outlook (8)
**23** Remainder of fire (3)
**25** Declares (6)
**26** Slips, slithers (6)
**29** Lying face downward (5)
**30** Carries out orders (5)

## ACROSS

**8** Large extinct creature (8)
**9** Utilitarian (6)
**10** Cuban capital (6)
**11** Equivalence, par (8)
**12** Look up to (6)
**13** One of the expenses of maintaining property (8)
**15** A form of wrestling (4)
**17** Imbiber, toper (7)
**19** Close-fitting casual tops (1-6)
**22** Developed, matured (4)
**24** Differ in opinion (8)
**27** Taking in food (6)
**29** Authoritative (8)
**30** Warning, menace (6)
**31** Quick look (6)
**32** The person who pays (8)

## DOWN

**1** Reptile with two pairs of legs (6)
**2** Calling, career (8)
**3** Person from Tokyo, say (8)
**4** Power to act without restraint (7)
**5** Time yet to come (6)
**6** Affluence, riches (6)
**7** Deduct (8)
**14** Ballot (4)
**16** Exhort, press (4)
**18** Water falling in drops (8)
**20** 'Success is counted ... by those who ne'er succeed' (Dickinson) (8)
**21** Inside (8)
**23** Put back or substitute (7)
**25** Strangers or extraterrestrials (6)
**26** Made a sudden surprise attack on (6)
**28** Closer (6)

## ACROSS

**8** Available reserve (8)
**9** Unbalanced (6)
**10** Animating force in living things (6)
**11** In the open air (8)
**12** Me, emphatically (6)
**13** Assaulted (8)
**15** Lacking in beauty (4)
**17** Brown bison (7)
**19** Outcomes (7)
**22** Falsehoods (4)
**24** It's a strange fair cart to fly in (8)
**27** Aromatic trees (6)
**29** Strange ballot of the game (8)
**30** Remove any contamination from (6)
**31** Take in, eat (6)
**32** Each year (8)

## DOWN

**1** Profoundly (6)
**2** This clover is lucky (4-4)
**3** Thankful, appreciative (8)
**4** Of the thighbone (7)
**5** Disapproving noises (3-3)
**6** Dauntless (6)
**7** Most jolly (8)
**14** Rubber cushion on a wheel (4)
**16** Flog the game badly (4)
**18** Coins run off these imaginary creatures (8)
**20** Getting away from confinement (8)
**21** In motion, making progress (8)
**23** A Latin I turn up in Tuscany, say (7)
**25** Urban areas (6)
**26** Adjusts for a new use (6)
**28** Lottery with tickets (6)

## ACROSS

**8** Person who holds public office (8)
**9** Struck lightly (6)
**10** Long fruit (6)
**11** Constituent parts (8)
**12** Tie rod to newspaper head (6)
**13** Numbers (8)
**15** Reproductive bodies (4)
**17** Short-bodied canine (7)
**19** Does he sling out the language? (7)
**22** Freedom from difficulty (4)
**24** In these times (8)
**27** Is the brown bird daft? (6)
**29** Food of the gods (8)
**30** Carelessly dropped rubbish (6)
**31** Late meal (6)
**32** Enfolds, confines (8)

## DOWN

**1** Frightened (6)
**2** Sudden great misfortune (8)
**3** Take issue with (8)
**4** Pasting (7)
**5** Flow of liquid (6)
**6** Become visible (6)
**7** Cold-blooded vertebrates (8)
**14** Functions (4)
**16** Midway between white and black (4)
**18** Extraordinarily large (8)
**20** Adornment of chain or cord (8)
**21** Place (8)
**23** Mortified (7)
**25** Short, sharp or sudden (6)
**26** Suck up (6)
**28** Followed commands (6)

**ACROSS**

**8** Desire for food (8)
**9** Fruit and colour (6)
**10** Outcome (6)
**11** Periods before nightfall (8)
**12** Area, location (6)
**13** Rough idea (8)
**15** Masticate (4)
**17** Carry out surgery (7)
**19** Writers, originators (7)
**22** Chunk, clod (4)
**24** Grows (8)
**27** For certain (6)
**29** Occurring at a particular time of the year (8)
**30** Grants (6)
**31** Purloined (6)
**32** Strained (8)

**DOWN**

**1** Solid figure with every point equidistant from the centre (6)
**2** Odd, rum (8)
**3** Separate and clear-cut (8)
**4** Umpire (7)
**5** Take what's offered (6)
**6** Means of communication (6)
**7** Emitting more light (8)
**14** Travelled through water (4)
**16** Assist (4)
**18** Keeps from happening (8)
**20** On a higher floor (8)
**21** Non-toxic (8)
**23** Having no function (7)
**25** Artists' stands (6)
**26** Possessing (6)
**28** Attorney (6)

## ACROSS

**8** Look after the upkeep (8)
**9** They take on workers (6)
**10** Assimilate (6)
**11** Ironed (8)
**12** Of the smallest piece of matter (6)
**13** Fastened together (8)
**15** Nasty-looking (4)
**17** Covering that provides protection from the weather (7)
**19** Shoving (7)
**22** One thing on a list (4)
**24** Paper container (8)
**27** Let lab open up for dance (6)
**29** Protection for a wheel (8)
**30** Goes in (6)
**31** To this document, in legal jargon (6)
**32** Made bigger (8)

## DOWN

**1** Burrowing animal (6)
**2** Casual (8)
**3** Meal cooked outdoors (8)
**4** Not common or ordinary (7)
**5** Passage to the stomach and lungs (6)
**6** Professional analyst of art (6)
**7** With no constraints (4,4)
**14** Classification (4)
**16** Grasp, hold firmly (4)
**18** Conferred with laurels (8)
**20** Lure lamb under it out of the rain (8)
**21** Sheaths for handguns (8)
**23** Children's toy bears (7)
**25** Young bird of prey (6)
**26** Public speaker (6)
**28** Acquired through effort (6)

## ACROSS

**1** Dignified and sombre (6)
**4** Annoy, bother (8)
**9** Consider, view (6)
**10** Equalises, offsets (8)
**12** Hidden drawback (5)
**13** Power to exercise control (9)
**15** ... Wiedersehen, goodbye to the Germans (3)
**16** Fabric from flax plant (5)
**17** Blazes (6)
**22** Landed property (6)
**24** Periods of time (5)
**27** Knock, tap (3)
**28** Artificial (9)
**31** Entire amount (5)
**32** Asked about (8)
**33** Root vegetable (6)
**34** The funds of a government (8)
**35** Analyses to determine properties (6)

## DOWN

**1** Rigorously (8)
**2** Starting a fire (8)
**3** Traders (9)
**5** Show a response (5)
**6** State capital is Boise (5)
**7** Polar region (6)
**8** Literary compositions (6)
**11** Palm leaf fibres used to make mats (6)
**14** Low continuous sound (3)
**18** Punish by imposing a fine (6)
**19** Natives of Cairo, say (9)
**20** Organisms at weird ice-bar (8)
**21** Keeps apart from others (8)
**23** Join, link (3)
**25** Lend a hand (6)
**26** Without equal (6)
**29** Inheritors (5)
**30** Belonging to them (5)

**ACROSS**

**8** Client (8)
**9** Likenesses (6)
**10** Concern, matter (6)
**11** Ugly terrifying creatures (8)
**12** Stable, immobile (6)
**13** Increased, augmented (8)
**15** Prefix for against (4)
**17** Completely accurate (7)
**19** Floor-coverings (7)
**22** Grows old (4)
**24** Appropriate, apt (8)
**27** Found the solution (6)
**29** Most content (8)
**30** Shaped hollows for wax (6)
**31** Seal we turn into a long thin mammal (6)
**32** Balderdash (8)

**DOWN**

**1** Set of clothing (6)
**2** Strange Latin cat to be found in the ocean (8)
**3** Continents, north and south (8)
**4** Brass musical instrument (7)
**5** Gesture of communication (6)
**6** Physical substance (6)
**7** Most fatigued (8)
**14** City in southern France (4)
**16** Orderly and clean (4)
**18** Substitutes, supplants (8)
**20** Inferring (8)
**21** Contaminated (8)
**23** Obtaining (7)
**25** Act against (6)
**26** Standards sailed away (6)
**28** Oldest (6)

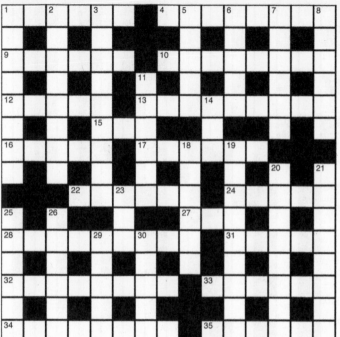

## ACROSS

**1** Word added to the end of another (6)
**4** Particular, explicit (8)
**9** From side to side (6)
**10** Special purpose or social affair (8)
**12** Tall structure (5)
**13** Express strong disapproval (9)
**15** Append (3)
**16** A synthetic fabric (5)
**17** Middle part of the foot (6)
**22** Add flavour (6)
**24** Number with no factor except itself and 1 (5)
**27** Ocean (3)
**28** Eat char up for something to break your fall (9)
**31** Carer of the sick (5)
**32** Edge of thoroughfare (8)
**33** One only (6)
**34** Wealth stored up (8)
**35** Organisation that provides a service (6)

## DOWN

**1** Leaning, sloping (8)
**2** Leave-taking (8)
**3** Promise of reimbursement in the case of loss (9)
**5** Full and rounded (5)
**6** Go by bicycle (5)
**7** Pay-day for some (6)
**8** Malignant growth and sign of the zodiac (6)
**11** Small whirlpools off the main stream (6)
**14** Decay, decompose (3)
**18** End of day (6)
**19** Enlarging, extending (9)
**20** N (8)
**21** Harshly, gravely (8)
**23** Grey-barked tree (3)
**25** Life-force (6)
**26** Bring into existence (6)
**29** Barrel-shaped containers for liquids (5)
**30** Mammary gland of cows (5)

## ACROSS

**1** In accordance with convention (9)
**9** In the direction of (6)
**10** Separating into parts (8)
**11** Mysterious or secret (6)
**12** Unfurl (6)
**14** Facial twitches (4)
**15** Regal, majestic (5)
**16** Building material (6)
**18** Fulfil the requirements (7)
**21** Legal counsels (7)
**24** Large African antelopes (6)
**26** Single parts of a whole (5)
**30** Individual unit in a list (4)
**31** Act or power of selecting (6)
**32** Tries to provoke good-naturedly (6)
**33** Had a leaning (8)
**34** Fellow-members, confederates (6)
**35** Concord, harmony (9)

## DOWN

**2** Employees' organisations (6)
**3** Maker of garments (6)
**4** Chiefly, principally (6)
**5** Justly, honestly (7)
**6** Unprocessed (6)
**7** From the land of the rising sun (8)
**8** Call attention to (9)
**11** Capital of Ghana (5)
**13** Items for auction (4)
**17** Basic or necessary (9)
**19** Labours, exertions (8)
**20** Hands with fingers clenched (5)
**22** Accompanying (4)
**23** Leaping, bounding (7)
**25** See lid for the engine (6)
**27** Spear of frozen water (6)
**28** Bluish-white alkaline metal (6)
**29** Examine for suitability, sift (6)

**ACROSS**

**8** I bar Gaul from the country (8)
**9** The inventor is strangely onside (6)
**10** Not faint or feeble (6)
**11** Prohibit (8)
**12** Take back something said (6)
**13** Despite the fact that (8)
**15** Rim (4)
**17** Field suitable for grazing (7)
**19** Nerve cells (7)
**22** Consumes (4)
**24** Distinctive dress worn by particular groups (8)
**27** Secret or hidden (6)
**29** Unit of a spoken word (8)
**30** Ceremonial procession (6)
**31** Think up, create (6)
**32** Predilection (8)

**DOWN**

**1** Flurry, fuss (6)
**2** Unaware (8)
**3** More brilliant (8)
**4** Container for money etc. (7)
**5** Room with sleeping accommodation, in short (6)
**6** Island in Venice with famous bridge (6)
**7** Flat-bottomed sled (8)
**14** From Ash Wednesday to Holy Saturday (4)
**16** Consider, regard (4)
**18** Disturbing, irritating (8)
**20** Breaking out (8)
**21** Absent-minded waking dreams (8)
**23** Facets (7)
**25** Made a movie (6)
**26** Automatons (6)
**28** Cut down (6)

## ACROSS

**1** Contemporary, up-to-date (6)
**4** Document to allow entry to another country (8)
**9** Pleasantly (6)
**10** Professional who solves practical problems (8)
**12** Person who does business on behalf of another (5)
**13** Models to be emulated (9)
**15** Not well (3)
**16** Long-noosed rope (5)
**17** Tiny baby (6)
**22** Effective (6)
**24** Alphabetical listing (5)
**27** Site of an archaeological exploration (3)
**28** Compare readings with an accurate standard (9)
**31** Dwelling, living quarters (5)
**32** Not derived from something else (8)
**33** Oral cavities (6)
**34** Ridicule with irony (8)
**35** Relative positions or degrees (6)

## DOWN

**1** In the mind (8)
**2** Diminish (8)
**3** People connected by blood or marriage (9)
**5** Inane musical drama? (5)
**6** Stint, scrimp (5)
**7** So pare back the shows (6)
**8** Push forcefully (6)
**11** Alleviation (6)
**14** Extinct bird of New Zealand (3)
**18** Bent over or doubled up (6)
**19** Person who lives near another (9)
**20** Altered slightly for accuracy (8)
**21** Reimbursed money spent in the course of work (8)
**23** Organ of hearing (3)
**25** Reverberations (6)
**26** Cry of sorrow and grief (6)
**29** Prickly woody stem (5)
**30** Collect or gather (5)

**33**

## ACROSS

**8** Chat Clio up to be universal (8)
**9** Restore to good condition (6)
**10** Carbohydrate from plants (6)
**11** Accepted as true (8)
**12** Word that modifies another (6)
**13** Recurring with regularity (8)
**15** Guitarist on the brink? (4)
**17** Hard igneous rock (7)
**19** Items inserted in a written record (7)
**22** Competent (4)
**24** Height above the sea (8)
**27** Type of worker employed occasionally (6)
**29** Case for magnetic tape (8)
**30** Outer reaches (6)
**31** Protect against attack (6)
**32** Showing lack of skill in handling delicate situations (8)

## DOWN

**1** Moved rapidly and lightly (6)
**2** Baker's dozen (8)
**3** Set of letters (8)
**4** Large floating mass of frozen water (7)
**5** By word of mouth (6)
**6** Oral communication (6)
**7** In addition, similarly (8)
**14** Back of the foot (4)
**16** Devoid of life (4)
**18** Freed, discharged (8)
**20** Piece of jewellery (8)
**21** Appear to be like (8)
**23** At a lower place (7)
**25** Important questions, in a dispute say (6)
**26** Slovenly, unkempt (6)
**28** Is tart creative? (6)

**34**

## ACROSS

**8** Exhaustive, complete (8)
**9** Crusty, tufty growth on trees and stones (6)
**10** Substance that curdles milk (6)
**11** Becomes joined or linked (8)
**12** Very light gas (6)
**13** Means or place of going in (8)
**15** Sicilian volcano (4)
**17** Book repository (7)
**19** Animals that suckle their young (7)
**22** Riverside grass (4)
**24** Performs surgery (8)
**27** Comes by, drops in (6)
**29** Capital of South Carolina (8)
**30** More adjacent (6)
**31** Sewing implement (6)
**32** Components (8)

## DOWN

**1** Pressed curd of milk (6)
**2** International boundary (8)
**3** Purchaser (8)
**4** Keep the creature in check, wrongly (7)
**5** Celestial body (6)
**6** Skin condition (6)
**7** Perpendicular (8)
**14** Appellation (4)
**16** Wheel-covering (4)
**18** Grew or made better (8)
**20** Moves forward (8)
**21** Misguided (8)
**23** Absconds (7)
**25** Drinks for everyone (6)
**26** Bleats about furniture (6)
**28** XX (6)

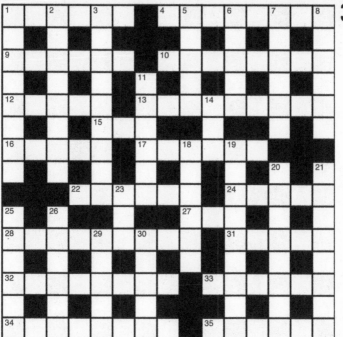

**35**

## ACROSS

**1** Written version of a drama (6)
**4** Examining, for accuracy say (8)
**9** Die or go out of date (6)
**10** Case, example (8)
**12** Striped equine animal (5)
**13** Animals from the palest hen, strangely (9)
**15** Racing tip that professes to be a certainty (3)
**16** Din (5)
**17** Sets seeds in the ground (6)
**22** Floor in a building (6)
**24** Confined to a limited area (5)
**27** Raw mineral (3)
**28** Periodic passage of animals from one place to another (9)
**31** Small biting flies (5)
**32** Felon (8)
**33** Soldier trained to serve at sea (6)
**34** More curious or unfamiliar (8)
**35** Sings in one tone (6)

## DOWN

**1** Explosively expelling air from the nose (8)
**2** Pub relic found in a type of government (8)
**3** Lasting, unchangeable (9)
**5** It follows from that fact (5)
**6** Fastener on door or window (5)
**7** Period of play in baseball or cricket (6)
**8** Smeared with fat (6)
**11** Pungent condiment (6)
**14** Greek god of fields and woods (3)
**18** Any person (6)
**19** It's used for communications over wires (9)
**20** Time of an event (8)
**21** Groups, bunches (8)
**23** Choose (3)
**25** Slaps (6)
**26** Less pleasing to look at (6)
**29** Foreign (5)
**30** Representation (5)

## ACROSS

**8** Fleshy fungus (8)
**9** But ran out for the headdress (6)
**10** Go without food (6)
**11** Of regions north and south of the Equator (8)
**12** Not uneven (6)
**13** In conjunction, combined (8)
**15** Highest point (4)
**17** The tale of one who is very fit (7)
**19** Got away from (7)
**22** Female relation (4)
**24** Predict (8)
**27** Sad emu was strangely pleased (6)
**29** Perfect, complete (8)
**30** Large soup dish (6)
**31** Heaviness (6)
**32** System of words used by a group (8)

## DOWN

**1** Accepted practice (6)
**2** Stick for the artist (8)
**3** To a moderate degree (8)
**4** Copy (7)
**5** Mighty, powerful (6)
**6** Painter or sculptor, say (6)
**7** Ape jeans of this nationality (8)
**14** Bovine animals (4)
**16** Edible seeds (4)
**18** Difficulties, worries (8)
**20** Beginning (8)
**21** Fish tank (8)
**23** Thoroughly, wholly (7)
**25** Adequate amount (6)
**26** Keenness of perception (6)
**28** Capacity for activity (6)

## ACROSS

1 Even if, although (6)
5 Where the current runs very fast (6)
10 Letters slanting to the right (7)
11 Trailer with living quarters (7)
12 Fellows, chaps (4)
13 Small fruit (5)
15 Likewise (4)
17 Unhappy, sorry (3)
19 Andrew, strangely, is in prison (6)
21 Assisted (6)
22 Vessel with a handle and spout (7)
23 Upshot (6)
25 Field of grass (6)
28 Cooking vessel (3)
30 Dismal, dour (4)
31 Last (5)
32 Second-hand (4)
35 Rotating windstorm (7)
36 Trifling objects, baubles (7)
37 Standards of perfection (6)
38 Make certain (6)

## DOWN

2 Hero's beloved in Greek mythology (7)
3 Way out (4)
4 Throws carelessly (6)
5 Best sporting performance ever (6)
6 Area for recreation in a town (4)
7 Grow, progress (7)
8 Tree of the Salix family (6)
9 Take cargo off (6)
14 Con Cora into getting the furry American animal (7)
16 Answer (5)
18 Goddess of agriculture (5)
20 Egg of parasitic insect (3)
21 Border of a garment (3)
23 They're due by law (6)
24 Moved very slightly (7)
26 State of no hope (7)
27 Broadest (6)
28 They guide ships in and out of harbours (6)
29 Ravel, snarl (6)
33 Funny type of ditch? (2-2)
34 Low-lying wetlands (4)

**38**

## ACROSS

**8** Take unawares (8)
**9** Coloured stick (6)
**10** Able to withstand attack (6)
**11** Information presented to a court (8)
**12** Unveil (6)
**13** Lacking knowledge (8)
**15** Not in favour of (4)
**17** One can paint a thousand words, it's said (7)
**19** Admiration or esteem (7)
**22** In good health (4)
**24** Despairing (8)
**27** Adequate amount (6)
**29** Large church building (8)
**30** Oh rent out this seat (6)
**31** Refrain from (6)
**32** Massive (8)

## DOWN

**1** Elusive, delicate (6)
**2** Adversary (8)
**3** Denoting one (8)
**4** Something that aids (7)
**5** Deed (6)
**6** Progression through working life (6)
**7** Relating to eruption in earth's surface (8)
**14** Young female (4)
**16** Fresh information (4)
**18** Kept apart from others (8)
**20** Poll (8)
**21** Sequences of instructions to computers (8)
**23** Flees (7)
**25** Draw out a response (6)
**26** Orders, fiats (6)
**28** Exceptional ability (6)

## ACROSS

1 Send into custody or put on bail while waiting for trial (6)
4 Wind generator (8)
9 Cause harm to (6)
10 A shift or stirring (8)
12 Place to dance to recorded music (5)
13 Looks like (9)
15 Operate (3)
16 Ways out (5)
17 Analyses for chemical substances (6)
22 Marine mollusc (6)
24 Portion, allotment (5)
27 Select (3)
28 Evening before All Saints' Day (9)
31 Noteworthy happening (5)
32 Liquefy, melt (8)
33 Have high regard for (6)
34 Anxiety (8)
35 Recurring series of events (6)

## DOWN

1 Animal with large antlers (8)
2 Royal, regal (8)
3 Edgily, uneasily (9)
5 Clubs with metal heads (5)
6 Reverie or nightmare (5)
7 Models (6)
8 Most recent (6)
11 Bosom (6)
14 Period of history (3)
18 Loose skirt of the South Pacific (6)
19 Day before (9)
20 Tangible substance (8)
21 Plumages (8)
23 Plant seeds (3)
25 Protected from heat or light (6)
26 Embraces, hugs (6)
29 Scent (5)
30 Mischievous fairies (5)

## ACROSS

**1** Private or police investigator (9)
**9** Blade to propel (6)
**10** Study in order to discover (8)
**11** Stand firm (6)
**12** Of teeth (6)
**14** Box or outer covering (4)
**15** Expand (5)
**16** Form of industrial action (6)
**18** Break down to study the parts (7)
**21** Protection from harm (7)
**24** More profound or more intense (6)
**26** Limb hinge (5)
**30** A ... Called Henry (Roddy Doyle) (4)
**31** Absence of interest or emotion (6)
**32** Determines the number (6)
**33** Strong drive for success (8)
**34** Sounds like fuel for the bird (6)
**35** Spur on, inspire (9)

## DOWN

**2** Hole for a shoe-lace (6)
**3** Expels, forces out (6)
**4** Reptile with a bony shell (6)
**5** Structure for transporting (7)
**6** Device that attracts iron (6)
**7** Calculation of the sum (8)
**8** They profess great sensitivity to art and beauty (9)
**11** Publish, bring out (5)
**13** Distant (4)
**17** Expanse of scenery (9)
**19** Enough to meet the need (8)
**20** Segregates items into groups (5)
**22** A complete failure (4)
**23** Absolutely sure (7)
**25** High regard (6)
**27** Tropical grass (6)
**28** Server at table (6)
**29** Large gathering of people (6)

**41**

## ACROSS

**8** Travel document (8)
**9** Early counting-frame (6)
**10** European principality (6)
**11** I lecture about the old drawstring handbag (8)
**12** Putting a question (6)
**13** Sir, cheer about the fruit (8)
**15** Lowest female singing voice (4)
**17** Conjure up in the mind (7)
**19** Left out (7)
**22** Strip for measuring (4)
**24** Any living entity (8)
**27** General principles (6)
**29** Flying machine (8)
**30** Most recent (6)
**31** Pay no attention to (6)
**32** Everything that exists everywhere (8)

## DOWN

**1** No swag on these vehicles (6)
**2** Breaking loose (8)
**3** Narrow sledge (8)
**4** Draw, captivate (7)
**5** Let rat make the sound (6)
**6** East Indian sailor (6)
**7** Centre of the target (8)
**14** Arch used in croquet (4)
**16** Allows (4)
**18** Periods between dawn and noon (8)
**20** Relating to shiny chemical element (8)
**21** Centres for dramatic art (8)
**23** Nonprofessional (7)
**25** Device to hold a ship in place (6)
**26** Mental representations (6)
**28** Withstand a force (6)

## ACROSS

**8** At the earliest stage of development (8)
**9** XI (6)
**10** Legal possessors (6)
**11** Most blessed with good fortune (8)
**12** Drink in (6)
**13** Giving permission (8)
**15** A length without breadth or thickness (4)
**17** Bet (7)
**19** Earnest requests (7)
**22** Deposit of valuable ore (4)
**24** Manifestation of mirth (8)
**27** Written announcement (6)
**29** Dependable (8)
**30** Identifying, citing (6)
**31** Strict, harsh (6)
**32** Between birth and death (8)

## DOWN

**1** Filaments made by a spider (6)
**2** Container for paper (8)
**3** Reasonable, judicious (8)
**4** Native of Sicily, say (7)
**5** Writing implement (6)
**6** New appraisal (6)
**7** Particular to an individual (8)
**14** Travel in front to guide (4)
**16** Inactive (4)
**18** Roused from sleep (8)
**20** Small cutting tool for the pocket (8)
**21** Calculate approximately (8)
**23** Systematic, not haphazard (7)
**25** They show the way (6)
**26** Pill (6)
**28** Movie theatre (6)

**43**

## ACROSS

1 Informal (6)
4 Reached with effort (8)
9 Figure found in inn, yet (6)
10 Resentfully, rancorously (8)
12 Under, lesser (5)
13 Contamination with micro-organism (9)
15 Finish in first place (3)
16 Powder from cacao seeds (5)
17 Eagerly (6)
22 Make reference (6)
24 Sound of a sheep (5)
27 Lyric poem (3)
28 Of significance or value (9)
31 Melon is another fruit (5)
32 Gathering together to the point of overflowing (8)
33 Noisy winged insect (6)
34 Doubt someone's honesty (8)
35 Expressed willingness (6)

## DOWN

1 Strife, friction (8)
2 Slices of bread with filling (8)
3 At a later time (9)
5 Robber (5)
6 Room at the top (5)
7 Relating to Scandinavian language (6)
8 Removing the moisture (6)
11 Concluding part of a performance (6)
14 Bring to a close (3)
18 In entirety (2,4)
19 Putting identifying slips on (9)
20 Imbue, spread through (8)
21 Touchstone, benchmark (8)
23 Examine carefully (3)
25 Sticky, gluey (6)
26 Protective garments (6)
29 Traveller on horseback (5)
30 Female relatives (5)

**44**

## ACROSS

**8** Citizen of the Union (8)
**9** Relating to nerves (6)
**10** Large edible fish, worn on the feet? (6)
**11** Burn slowly without a flame (8)
**12** Edible plant (6)
**13** Businesses (8)
**15** Annoy, nettle (4)
**17** Boiled, with anger perhaps (7)
**19** Feeling the need to drink (7)
**22** Comfort (4)
**24** Contest in which teams pull a rope (3-2-3)
**27** Grasslike plants in wet places (6)
**29** Albeit (8)
**30** Spoke (6)
**31** Looked fixedly (6)
**32** Official record of names (8)

## DOWN

**1** Crackpot bird? (6)
**2** Compare differences (8)
**3** Strand, beach (8)
**4** Out of the ordinary (7)
**5** Catnap (6)
**6** Open to everyone (6)
**7** Lowest floor (8)
**14** Acquires (4)
**16** Thought (4)
**18** Parity (8)
**20** Property or culture passed down (8)
**21** Unable to relax (8)
**23** Experts with bow and arrow (7)
**25** Not the ones already mentioned (6)
**26** Lesions, injuries (6)
**28** Prime number (6)

**45**

## ACROSS

**8** Edible fungus (8)
**9** Subjects, themes (6)
**10** Warmest season (6)
**11** Collected in one place (8)
**12** Remove cargo (6)
**13** Item of jewellery (8)
**15** Follow orders (4)
**17** Time for relaxation and pleasure (7)
**19** Having no limit (7)
**22** As well as (4)
**24** Blood-sucking insect (8)
**27** Wisely (6)
**29** Vacations (8)
**30** Go or come back (6)
**31** Small amount (6)
**32** Amplified (8)

## DOWN

**1** Season of mists and mellow fruitfulness (6)
**2** O Ma shops for the soaps (8)
**3** Passageway (8)
**4** Envisage (7)
**5** Immobile (6)
**6** Plea, petition (6)
**7** Chemistry, biology etc. (8)
**14** Organs of sight (4)
**16** Rhythmic musical unit (4)
**18** Relating to organisms and their environment (8)
**20** Nasal cavities (8)
**21** It binds to restrict blood flow (8)
**23** Marine crustacean (7)
**25** Padded bedspreads (6)
**26** Effigies (6)
**28** Food store-room (6)

**ACROSS**

**8** Bony covering on some animals (8)
**9** Free from a liability (6)
**10** Flat-bottomed boats for carrying loads (6)
**11** Divulged (8)
**12** Superior of two alternatives (6)
**13** Improbable (8)
**15** Small island (4)
**17** Control, machinery say (7)
**19** Before, earlier (7)
**22** Intangible quality surrounding a person (4)
**24** Bunches of flowers (8)
**27** Gave a gratuity (6)
**29** Game played in the sable lab (8)
**30** Principles, beliefs (6)
**31** Covering for arm (6)
**32** Unexpectedly, abruptly (8)

**DOWN**

**1** Public procession (6)
**2** Female offspring (8)
**3** Ancient language of India (8)
**4** Frightened, apprehensive (7)
**5** Evil we find in a beetle (6)
**6** Comment (6)
**7** Took a case to higher court for review (8)
**14** Close to (4)
**16** Place to sit (4)
**18** Having a good chance of happening (8)
**20** Imaginary line around the earth (8)
**21** Excised, struck out (8)
**23** Having no function (7)
**25** Lines of waiting people (6)
**26** Implement for deleting (6)
**28** Praises, lauds (6)

## ACROSS

**1** Medical institutions (9)
**9** Tropical fruit with yellowish flesh (6)
**10** Extreme commitment, to a god say (8)
**11** Not very bright (6)
**12** Expresses mirth (6)
**14** Old Russian ruler (4)
**15** Pen for small animals (5)
**16** Too numerous to be counted (6)
**18** Intoxicating liquor (7)
**21** Cupboard of ministers? (7)
**24** Mad bird? (6)
**26** Physically weak (5)
**30** Short light gust of air (4)
**31** Handwear (6)
**32** More extended (6)
**33** Get a cost for the small houses (8)
**34** Designations of honour or office (6)
**35** Weaponry (9)

## DOWN

**2** Dramas are, er, soap (6)
**3** Farm tool for cutting furrows (6)
**4** The need to drink (6)
**5** Distances from end to end (7)
**6** Dough of flour, water and shortening (6)
**7** Crusade, drive (8)
**8** Applicant (9)
**11** Group of volcanic islands in the S. Pacific (5)
**13** Be quiet (4)
**17** Compute, reckon (9)
**19** No stucco on these hard fruits (8)
**20** Olfactory sensation (5)
**22** Security to guarantee appearance of prisoner (4)
**23** Person with authority in the forces (7)
**25** Exposed (6)
**27** ... Christie (author) (6)
**28** Herb made from a glove (6)
**29** Sorrowful through loss (6)

## ACROSS

**8** Conjuror, wizard (8)
**9** Coolness and composure (6)
**10** Hand-gun (6)
**11** Demanding, onerous (8)
**12** Finding the sum (6)
**13** Agitating a liquid (8)
**15** Sound reflection (4)
**17** Return to original condition (7)
**19** Large cattle farms (7)
**22** Slope, slant, lean (4)
**24** Foreshadow or presage (8)
**27** Drumbeat or design on skin (6)
**29** Rain came to this nationality (8)
**30** Herb and horse (6)
**31** Cliques that control governments (6)
**32** Preliminary drawings (8)

## DOWN

**1** Different, diverse (6)
**2** Territorial division (8)
**3** Denizen of a small settlement (8)
**4** Let loose (7)
**5** Italian sausage (6)
**6** Nine counties (6)
**7** Distinction, high status (8)
**14** Rocky hills (4)
**16** Basic unit of all organisms (4)
**18** Colossal (8)
**20** Certified, vouched (8)
**21** Eye complaint and waterfall (8)
**23** Malady, sickness (7)
**25** White herons (6)
**26** Absolve (6)
**28** Carried out orders (6)

**49**

## ACROSS

**8** Consisting of many (8)
**9** Irregular (6)
**10** This servant works for the state (6)
**11** Stimulated to excellence (8)
**12** Arrangement of parts functioning together (6)
**13** Approximate calculation (8)
**15** Strange cure for a colour (4)
**17** Crater (7)
**19** Preserves in writing or sound (7)
**22** At what time? (4)
**24** Learn by heart (8)
**27** Label showing price (6)
**29** Stone or gem in which the shape is hollowed out (8)
**30** Part of a river with very fast current (6)
**31** Companion or associate (6)
**32** Meaningless words (8)

## DOWN

**1** Great comfort or extravagance (6)
**2** Fit and active (8)
**3** Example regarded as typical of its class (8)
**4** Bring to a destination (7)
**5** When daylight is dying (6)
**6** Intermediary between the living and the dead (6)
**7** Abandoned (8)
**14** Certain (4)
**16** Bovine animals (4)
**18** Flowering shrub from olden era, oddly (8)
**20** Going in (8)
**21** Inhabited (8)
**23** Woman of courageous achievements (7)
**25** One believed to give divinely-inspired answers (6)
**26** Relatives by marriage (2-4)
**28** Firstborn (6)

## ACROSS

**1** District, colony (9)
**9** Hue, tint (6)
**10** Difficulties that need to be resolved (8)
**11** Russian vehicle pulled by three horses (6)
**12** Make up one's mind (6)
**14** Flying saucers (4)
**15** Gustatory sensation (5)
**16** Give up a job (6)
**18** Group of fruit trees (7)
**21** Agrees, complies (7)
**24** Not unusual (6)
**26** Happen (5)
**30** Move along as a stream (4)
**31** Fully-grown animals (6)
**32** Bosses, heads (6)
**33** '... in Blue' (Gershwin) (8)
**34** Foreign and striking (6)
**35** Moving staircase (9)

## DOWN

**2** Gained by work (6)
**3** Floppy-eared animal (6)
**4** Subjects, topics (6)
**5** Delivered from danger (7)
**6** A score can be crude (6)
**7** Act of will (8)
**8** Outstanding importance or grandness (9)
**11** Metal neck or arm bands worn by ancient Celts (5)
**13** Items of information (4)
**17** Linked, related (9)
**19** Indoor passage (8)
**20** Small rounded breads (5)
**22** Potato (4)
**23** In the direction of (7)
**25** Business or love matter (6)
**27** Part of North America (6)
**28** Eastern European state (6)
**29** Room to make radio or television programme (6)

**51**

## ACROSS

**8** Save Jean from the Indonesian islander (8)
**9** Reflections of sound (6)
**10** Express dissent (6)
**11** Farm vehicles (8)
**12** Pratie (6)
**13** Coffee-producing country (8)
**15** Accessible to all (4)
**17** Aversion, antipathy (7)
**19** Green vegetable with dense head of leaves (7)
**22** Historic periods (4)
**24** Wetness (8)
**27** Sibling (6)
**29** Soonest (8)
**30** Sheds skin (6)
**31** Bar in a compass (6)
**32** Prime number (8)

## DOWN

**1** Giant tropical grass (6)
**2** American team game (8)
**3** Reading matter for school or college (8)
**4** Salad green (7)
**5** Recollect (6)
**6** Beat of a piece of music (6)
**7** Discovering, finding out (8)
**14** At one time (4)
**16** Juicy fruit (4)
**18** Cut off from others (8)
**20** Believing to be fact (8)
**21** Small flat sweet cakes (8)
**23** Acquiring (7)
**25** Food mixtures including greens (6)
**26** Irregular, not smooth (6)
**28** ... / or (6)

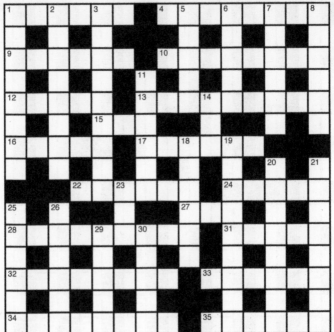

**52**

## ACROSS

1 Brittle (6)
4 Taught, instructed (8)
9 Films (6)
10 Conveying, transporting (8)
12 One sixteenth of a pound (5)
13 Space traveller (9)
15 Show agreement (3)
16 Occurrence (5)
17 Facilitate (6)
22 Mug spy made from this mineral (6)
24 Relating to principles of right and wrong (5)
27 Decorate a cake (3)
28 The general state of things (9)
31 Bitten, by a bee say (5)
32 Acknowledged to be true (8)
33 Drinking glass with base and stem (6)
34 Psychological suffering (8)
35 Lethal (6)

## DOWN

1 Beethoven or Brahms, say (8)
2 Created, dreamt up (8)
3 Before long (9)
5 Preliminary version or sketch (5)
6 Goods carried by a vehicle (5)
7 Of the clan (6)
8 Numbers (6)
11 Military trainees (6)
14 Steal from (3)
18 Equipping with weapons (6)
19 A sedimentary rock (9)
20 Bothered, perturbed (8)
21 To a small degree (8)
23 Large deep hole in the ground (3)
25 Land surrounded by water (6)
26 Receipts for postal fees (6)
29 Change (5)
30 Thoughts, concepts (5)

**53**

## ACROSS

**8** Highly decorated glazed earthenware (8)
**9** Distinctive periods in history (6)
**10** Hairy aromatic herb (6)
**11** Extinct creature (8)
**12** Reach a goal (6)
**13** Height above the earth's surface (8)
**15** In which birds or animals may be kept (4)
**17** One more (7)
**19** Area for exhibiting works of art (7)
**22** Fe (4)
**24** Defensive fence of stout posts (8)
**27** It takes over other birds' nests (6)
**29** Not excessive (8)
**30** Edible bulbs (6)
**31** Fight, combat (6)
**32** Stored-up wealth (8)

## DOWN

**1** Not occupied (6)
**2** Low in spirits (8)
**3** Old tanner (8)
**4** Case for personal items (7)
**5** Substance to curdle milk (6)
**6** Mollycoddle (6)
**7** Take a burden on this joint (8)
**14** Toy with plastic bricks (4)
**16** Desiccated (4)
**18** Of a country (8)
**20** Grounded, fixed firmly (8)
**21** Most fortunate (8)
**23** States again (7)
**25** Generate (6)
**26** Astounded (6)
**28** Proprietors (6)

## ACROSS

1 Straight, without deviation (6)
4 Praises loudly (8)
9 Undoubtedly (6)
10 All that is (8)
12 Go upwards (5)
13 Find out for sure (9)
15 One of 12 curved arches of bone (3)
16 Musical play (5)
17 A swallow-tailed flag (6)
22 Male, female (6)
24 Mental picture (5)
27 Finish (3)
28 Capacity to become something (9)
31 Leave out, vowels say (5)
32 Having no intelligible meaning (8)
33 Exploits, feats (6)
34 Catastrophe (8)
35 Covering for organ of sight (6)

## DOWN

1 Controller (8)
2 Came to understand (8)
3 Have a party (9)
5 One who believes that the motives of others are always selfish (5)
6 Bar for prising (5)
7 Encroachment (6)
8 Perceiving by eye (6)
11 Arrested, collared (6)
14 Ovum (3)
18 Seldom (6)
19 Apparently or obviously (9)
20 Based on reason (8)
21 Dead (8)
23 Egg of parasitic insect (3)
25 Revealed (6)
26 Unbroken periods of work (6)
29 Is in want of (5)
30 Important topic (5)

## ACROSS

**1** Most odd (9)
**9** Musical interval of eight notes (6)
**10** Salacious (8)
**11** Obsolete unit of distance (6)
**12** Raises or hauls up (6)
**14** Stated (4)
**15** Horizontal surface for holding objects (5)
**16** Closer at hand (6)
**18** Reduces in size (7)
**21** Obscure, nameless (7)
**24** Fall (6)
**26** Performances without words (5)
**30** Notion (4)
**31** Marriages (6)
**32** Areas in airfields for manoeuvres (6)
**33** Selection by ballot (8)
**34** British schools' examination (1,5)
**35** Sailboats with three parallel hulls (9)

## DOWN

**2** No part for this large fish (6)
**3** One side to the other (6)
**4** Thick fatty oil (6)
**5** Satiate (7)
**6** Agree to a request (6)
**7** Would oak groan under this animal? (8)
**8** Adverting (9)
**11** Fabric made from flax (5)
**13** At that time (4)
**17** Capital of Pakistan (9)
**19** Gave back (8)
**20** Categories, sorts (5)
**22** Enthusiastic (4)
**23** Unpaid performer (7)
**25** Cut into small pieces (6)
**27** Building for historical objects (6)
**28** Relative in hospital? (6)
**29** Issue an injunction (6)

## ACROSS

**8** Matrimony (8)
**9** Generator (6)
**10** Yellow fruit (6)
**11** Elucidates, accounts for (8)
**12** He was thrown into a den of lions (6)
**13** Commonplace and ordinary (8)
**15** Fencing sword (4)
**17** Run loaf through the milky mixture (7)
**19** Bringing up (7)
**22** Old ballads (4)
**24** Travellers to sacred places (8)
**27** Emits vapour (6)
**29** All one's days (8)
**30** Contemporary, present day (6)
**31** Open shoe (6)
**32** Naturally gifted (8)

## DOWN

**1** Tomorrow in Spain (6)
**2** Any living thing (8)
**3** Going in the same direction but always the same distance apart (8)
**4** Adjudicator (7)
**5** Specimen (6)
**6** Constant, regular (6)
**7** Artificial jet of water (8)
**14** To a high degree (4)
**16** Tropical tree with large leaves (4)
**18** Not copied from something else (8)
**20** Get together in one place (8)
**21** Travelling rapidly (8)
**23** Declares to be true (7)
**25** Avaricious (6)
**26** Hanging ice (6)
**28** Weasel-like animal (6)

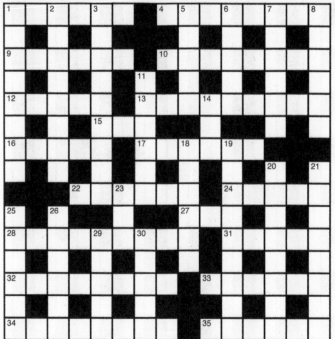

**57**

## ACROSS

**1** Small animal with six legs (6)
**4** Particular, explicit (8)
**9** Baby's bed (6)
**10** Act of making up one's mind (8)
**12** This bread is soon forgotten (5)
**13** Put in or set up for use (9)
**15** Lacking clarity or distinctness (3)
**16** Meaning (5)
**17** Indicates a direction (6)
**22** Acquiescence (6)
**24** Once more (5)
**27** Termination (3)
**28** Unsure (9)
**31** Located inside (5)
**32** Rodent with bushy tail (8)
**33** Relating to the gods (6)
**34** Firm in purpose (8)
**35** Horse's head in chess (6)

## DOWN

**1** Make bigger (8)
**2** Leaning, sloping (8)
**3** Lyrics end strangely in round containers (9)
**5** Compositions, usually in metrical feet (5)
**6** Hi, can this make a porcelain? (5)
**7** Evenhandedly (6)
**8** North American nation (6)
**11** Uncomplicated (6)
**14** 2240 lbs (3)
**18** Have as a purpose (6)
**19** Inherited custom (9)
**20** Artistic composition (8)
**21** Most furious (8)
**23** Heavy tippler (3)
**25** Treasurer at a college (6)
**26** Comes to pass (6)
**29** Relating to country life (5)
**30** Showing skill or aptitude (5)

## ACROSS

**8** Evenly, with no difficulties (8)
**9** Person with knowledge, skill (6)
**10** Happen to (6)
**11** Each year (8)
**12** Light-hearted raillery (6)
**13** Allotted (8)
**15** Other than (4)
**17** Erupting hole in the earth's crust (7)
**19** Eternal (7)
**22** A stitch in time saves it (4)
**24** Marriage ceremonies (8)
**27** Combinations of notes sounded together (6)
**29** Cabaret I attend with the life-forms (8)
**30** Acquires knowledge or skills (6)
**31** Austere, grim (6)
**32** Making a choice (8)

## DOWN

**1** Tiny one-celled animal in water (6)
**2** Lovey-dovey (8)
**3** Sons and daughters (8)
**4** Jam a spy into these at night (7)
**5** Life forms (6)
**6** Leaped forward (6)
**7** Shopping baskets on wheels (8)
**14** Observed or perceived (4)
**16** Extending far (4)
**18** Overcome with wonder (8)
**20** Piece of jewellery (8)
**21** ... da Vinci (8)
**23** Land masses with water on all sides (7)
**25** Obligations, responsibilities (6)
**26** Takes care of the sick (6)
**28** Eating dinner (6)

**59**

## ACROSS

**8** Bury fear at this time of the year (8)
**9** Paid attention to (6)
**10** Abrasion or mischievous escapade (6)
**11** Flight transport depots (8)
**12** Respect highly (6)
**13** Convoke (8)
**15** For fear that (4)
**17** Infant food in the US (7)
**19** Versus (7)
**22** Uncommon (4)
**24** The ... of Venice (Shakespeare) (8)
**27** Outline drawing (6)
**29** Funfair (8)
**30** Improvement, in business say (6)
**31** Softwood tree with catkins (6)
**32** Performance spaces (8)

## DOWN

**1** Received stolen goods (6)
**2** Any life form (8)
**3** Goodbye and good luck (8)
**4** Sleeping suit (7)
**5** Regular tasks (6)
**6** Change for the better (6)
**7** Fabrics, materials (8)
**14** Point of light in the heavens (4)
**16** Gain by effort (4)
**18** Machine manipulator (8)
**20** Motions to convey messages (8)
**21** One's singularity (8)
**23** Person trained to compete in sports (7)
**25** Better to light one than curse the darkness (6)
**26** Modifier (6)
**28** Outer covering of the eye (6)

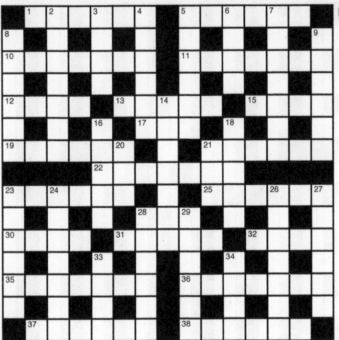

## ACROSS

**1** Is equivalent to (6)
**5** Careless, messy (6)
**10** Denser (7)
**11** Bolster or back up (7)
**12** Receive willingly (4)
**13** Alleviated (5)
**15** Not present (4)
**17** Habitation of wild animals (3)
**19** Travelling company of entertainers (6)
**21** Addressed God (6)
**22** Half woman, half fish (7)
**23** Elude, dodge (6)
**25** Sudden outburst of anger (6)
**28** Social insect (3)
**30** Fill to satisfaction (4)
**31** Theatrical performer (5)
**32** Streaks of electrical discharges (4)
**35** Young frog (7)
**36** Contribute to progress or growth (7)
**37** Dry red wine (6)
**38** Join the military (6)

## DOWN

**2** Faster (7)
**3** Inquires about (4)
**4** Strew or distribute over an area (6)
**5** Hidden (6)
**6** Finishing line for a race (4)
**7** Room access, threshold (7)
**8** Inert (6)
**9** Remained (6)
**14** One part of a whole (7)
**16** Moves fluid or gas by pressure or suction (5)
**18** Command (5)
**20** Observe (3)
**21** Quarry (3)
**23** Artificial and inferior (6)
**24** Fort, fastness (7)
**26** Brightly-coloured tropical birds (7)
**27** More imprudent, at breakfast? (6)
**28** Distinctive manner of speaking (6)
**29** Fall, tumble (6)
**33** Fibre from coconut husk (4)
**34** Hood (4)

## ACROSS

**8** Energetic, strenuous (8)
**9** With greater volume (6)
**10** Light evening meal (6)
**11** Replied (8)
**12** Word that qualifies another (6)
**13** Reckon the cost (8)
**15** Mislaid (4)
**17** Eternally (7)
**19** A group of them can form an atoll (7)
**22** Care about the land measure (4)
**24** Look like (8)
**27** Sedately, with self-possession (6)
**29** Most direct (8)
**30** Recompense for worthy act (6)
**31** Tags, brands (6)
**32** Stretched out (8)

## DOWN

**1** Substance in a fluid state (6)
**2** Entire, uncut (8)
**3** Ghastly, grisly (8)
**4** Eludes (7)
**5** Small compartment for clothing (6)
**6** Repository for historical objects (6)
**7** Abandoned, forsook (8)
**14** Move very slightly, or agitate (4)
**16** By word of mouth (4)
**18** Hear dove badly aloft (8)
**20** Protection or surety (8)
**21** Permitting (8)
**23** Places where particular activities are concentrated (7)
**25** Merited through effort (6)
**26** Bust (6)
**28** Bigger, greater (6)

## ACROSS

**1** Show, portray (6)
**4** Frozen dessert (3,5)
**9** Loud and disturbing noise (6)
**10** Aspiration (8)
**12** Soft limestone (5)
**13** Band of musicians (9)
**15** Encountered (3)
**16** Madame Butterfly, for one (5)
**17** Temper, steel say (6)
**22** Rubble, detritus (6)
**24** Token of victory (5)
**27** Ailing (3)
**28** Area surrounded by walls or buildings (9)
**31** Different, disparate (5)
**32** Job opportunities (8)
**33** Most pleasing (6)
**34** Differ in opinion (8)
**35** Business that acts for other businesses (6)

## DOWN

**1** Board member (8)
**2** Parcels (8)
**3** Victory in chess (9)
**5** Professional joke-teller (5)
**6** Act punishable by law (5)
**7** Is extant (6)
**8** Hand-book (6)
**11** Discommode, annoy (6)
**14** Possessed (3)
**18** Dwell (6)
**19** Travelling in unknown territories (9)
**20** Age of eligibility to vote (8)
**21** On the QT (8)
**23** Indentation in a shoreline (3)
**25** Resounded (6)
**26** Monarchs (6)
**29** Object (5)
**30** Present reasons for or against (5)

**63**

## ACROSS

**8** Prevailing (8)
**9** Whole and complete (6)
**10** Not faint or feeble (6)
**11** Clapping (8)
**12** Great fright (6)
**13** Reckoning, estimating (8)
**15** Aces (4)
**17** Hair cleaner (7)
**19** Language of the shingle? (7)
**22** Left or right (4)
**24** Building blocks of a language (8)
**27** Section of a legal document (6)
**29** Relating to overseas dominions (8)
**30** 'I wandered ... as a cloud' (Wordsworth) (6)
**31** French cake (6)
**32** Fruits of a tropical palm tree (8)

## DOWN

**1** Glass or plastic vessel (6)
**2** Unit of mass (8)
**3** Leaping marsupial (8)
**4** Odd (7)
**5** Human beings (6)
**6** Takes without the owner's consent (6)
**7** Gifts (8)
**14** Hand-me-down (4)
**16** Olfactory organ (4)
**18** How alloy becomes the site of an English prison (8)
**20** Ornamental chain (8)
**21** Absorbing knowledge (8)
**23** Slanting typeface (7)
**25** Horny ends of some animals' feet (6)
**26** Lebanese capital (6)
**28** Military gesture (6)

## ACROSS

**8** Of lesser quality (8)
**9** The second of two (6)
**10** Device for taking pictures (6)
**11** Painstakingly careful (8)
**12** One of a group or club (6)
**13** Provides protection against the weather (8)
**15** Reflection of sound (4)
**17** Angry dispute (7)
**19** Large farms in the US (7)
**22** Uncle's wife (4)
**24** Crabwise (8)
**27** Go tune up what's in the mouth (6)
**29** Medical institution (8)
**30** Hard limestone (6)
**31** Fishing boats (6)
**32** Jewish Sabbath (8)

## DOWN

**1** Take on, hire (6)
**2** Last month (8)
**3** Take issue with (8)
**4** Hits rib of this nationality (7)
**5** Small recess in a room (6)
**6** The greatest possible degree (6)
**7** Dish of rice, eggs and fish (8)
**14** Brass instrument (4)
**16** Soft wet earth (4)
**18** Liveries (8)
**20** Endeavours (8)
**21** Exact opposition (8)
**23** Having no purpose (7)
**25** Consider probable (6)
**26** Painter, say (6)
**28** Take cargo off (6)

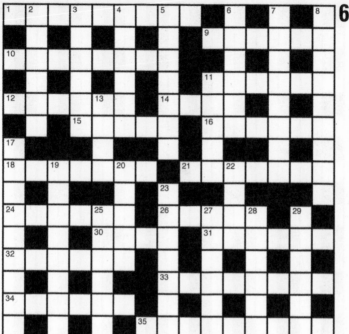

**65**

## ACROSS

1 Hearten, foster (9)
9 Substance used in dyeing (6)
10 Recipient of a degree (8)
11 Closed curve (6)
12 Large-grained or rough to the touch (6)
14 Instrument, implement (4)
15 Marsh plant (5)
16 The colour of ripe cherries (6)
18 Make an effort (7)
21 Highest (7)
24 Man, say (6)
26 Light carried in the hand (5)
30 Go it alone (4)
31 Card suit (6)
32 Distance from top to bottom (6)
33 Really (8)
34 Close-fitting pullover shirt (1-5)
35 Winners in competition (9)

## DOWN

2 Not wide (6)
3 Dictates, commands (6)
4 Bellowed, thundered (6)
5 Said hello (7)
6 Lacking depth, argument say (6)
7 Write upon, formally perhaps (8)
8 Activities, pursuits (9)
11 Late-night drink (5)
13 Appear, look (4)
17 Device for making a descent from an aircraft (9)
19 Dusk (8)
20 Aviator (5)
22 Open-weave fabric (4)
23 Does Mac host this organ? (7)
25 As hero leaves the sea and goes here (6)
27 Musical beat (6)
28 The Aloha State (6)
29 Pinched (6)

## ACROSS

**8** Requiring tact and discretion (8)
**9** Straight sword with narrow blade (6)
**10** Glowing with heat (3-3)
**11** Unofficial (8)
**12** Extreme alarm (6)
**13** Took into custody (8)
**15** Lied about doing nothing (4)
**17** Iron lever for prising (7)
**19** The people born in a particular place (7)
**22** Swallows food (4)
**24** Small migratory birds (8)
**27** Free from danger (6)
**29** Ulster or Munster (8)
**30** Shapes (6)
**31** Small ball of shot (6)
**32** Inclination, propensity (8)

## DOWN

**1** Rigid, serious (6)
**2** Highly cultured or educated (8)
**3** Tiny organisms that can cause disease (8)
**4** System based on ten (7)
**5** Like better (6)
**6** Momentary flashes of light (6)
**7** Native of Beirut, say (8)
**14** Tenant's payment (4)
**16** Made lines on a surface (4)
**18** Gave something in recognition of achievement (8)
**20** Presupposing (8)
**21** Takes in (8)
**23** Views (7)
**25** Full of zest and energy (6)
**26** Richly decorated (6)
**28** Boil down or cut back (6)

**67**

## ACROSS

1 Assortments, diversities (9)
9 Sadness, regret (6)
10 Passageway with rooms off (8)
11 Social event or sexual relationship (6)
12 Severely trying experience (6)
14 Border (4)
15 Welsh vegetables? (5)
16 Area, territory (6)
18 No longer in use (7)
21 The celestial sphere (7)
24 Save from harm (6)
26 Play cricket here with the peers (5)
30 Festive celebration (4)
31 Regard, respect (6)
32 Short high-pitched noise (6)
33 Egalitarianism, sameness (8)
34 Improves, corrects (6)
35 Equipped with tables, chairs etc. (9)

## DOWN

2 On ship, train or plane (6)
3 Lear is to be found in this state (6)
4 Walk unsteadily, as a small child (6)
5 Sincere, heartfelt (7)
6 Popular beverage (6)
7 Set up, co-ordinate (8)
8 Consciousness (9)
11 Concur (5)
13 Division of geological time (4)
17 Spoke to (9)
19 Long narrow openings (8)
20 Squeaking sound (5)
22 Finds the sum (4)
23 Flat highland (7)
25 Kampala is its capital (6)
27 Profit (6)
28 Fashions, modes (6)
29 Boil with anger (6)

**68**

## ACROSS

**8** Registered, entered (8)
**9** Loathes (6)
**10** Experience distress (6)
**11** Early parts of nights (8)
**12** Belonging to them (6)
**13** Ben talks about the bedclothes (8)
**15** Instance (4)
**17** One who eats to excess (7)
**19** Of times long gone (7)
**22** Naked (4)
**24** Despot, tyrant (8)
**27** Crawls silently (6)
**29** Plan of activities (8)
**30** Wee (6)
**31** Disclose (6)
**32** Position (8)

## DOWN

**1** Ample (6)
**2** Confrontation, discord (8)
**3** Out of doors (8)
**4** Modifying words (7)
**5** Light-proof box (6)
**6** Reduce in size (6)
**7** Cause fear (8)
**14** Heavy grey metal (4)
**16** The name's the same, either way (4)
**18** Sets in motion, a ship say (8)
**20** Item of jewellery (8)
**21** Who one is (8)
**23** Completely and without qualification (7)
**25** Took orders from (6)
**26** Monetary unit of Russia (6)
**28** Cushion for sleep (6)

**69**

## ACROSS

**8** Correct, precise (8)
**9** Refrain of a song (6)
**10** Colour between red and blue (6)
**11** Lift up the tea-lover (8)
**12** Account book (6)
**13** Creator of music (8)
**15** Time out for the unit (4)
**17** Flat highland (7)
**19** Pressing (7)
**22** Pace (4)
**24** Chance event (8)
**27** Toxin (6)
**29** Small town, with only one quadruped? (3-5)
**30** Lustrous, shining (6)
**31** Fervent proponent (6)
**32** Cutting implement (8)

## DOWN

**1** Not passive (6)
**2** Solar rays (8)
**3** Race a bit with the tiny living things (8)
**4** Act of keeping safe from danger (7)
**5** Sharp piercing cry (6)
**6** Edible tuber (6)
**7** Of the continent (8)
**14** Leave out (4)
**16** Bend, move round (4)
**18** Authorised officially (8)
**20** This type of government is an epic blur (8)
**21** Making the most sound (8)
**23** Person who denies the existence of God (7)
**25** Breathe in (6)
**26** Mistakes in printed matter (6)
**28** Different ones (6)

**ACROSS**

1 Turn of phrase for an angel (6)
4 Tumblers (8)
9 Procedure (6)
10 Watcher, spectator (8)
12 More awful or unwell (5)
13 Unconventional or unusual (9)
15 Quantity of money (3)
16 Regions (5)
17 Come into sight (6)
22 Slumbering (6)
24 Dish out food (5)
27 Foot of an animal (3)
28 Abode (9)
31 Symbolic bird of the US (5)
32 Slowly moving ice-masses (8)
33 Moral excellence (6)
34 Foot levers (8)
35 Type of business (6)

**DOWN**

1 To some extent (8)
2 Came back (8)
3 Procedures (9)
5 Having three dimensions (5)
6 Great sea (5)
7 Allude (6)
8 Piercing (6)
11 Woman, girl (6)
14 'Cast a cold ... on life, on death' (Yeats) (3)
18 Small doll on strings (6)
19 Replying (9)
20 Cause fear (8)
21 Harshly, gravely (8)
23 Prevaricate (3)
25 Frank Lloyd ... (aviator) (6)
26 Tea-set for the large demesne (6)
29 Removed moisture (5)
30 Care for the sick (5)

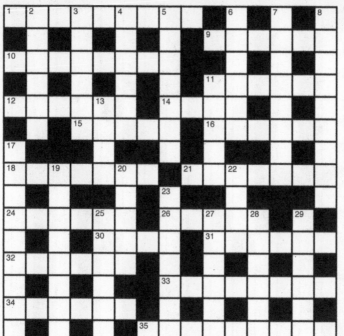

**71**

## ACROSS

**1** Strewn about (9)
**9** Improve (6)
**10** Recants (8)
**11** Cooking by dry heat (6)
**12** Associations of people with common interests or purposes (6)
**14** Morally reprehensible (4)
**15** Misplaces (5)
**16** Hold on to (6)
**18** Abandons, forsakes (7)
**21** Ecclesiastical assembly or subdivision of a written work (7)
**24** IDA inn provides for this nationality (6)
**26** Momentary brightness (5)
**30** Ego (4)
**31** Wandered about aimlessly (6)
**32** Slumbers (6)
**33** Small one-storied houses (8)
**34** Figure that's longer in one direction with opposite sides parallel (6)
**35** Carried out or rehearsed (9)

## DOWN

**2** Written order directing a bank to pay money (6)
**3** Exhilarate, excite (6)
**4** More than is needed (6)
**5** Requiring least effort (7)
**6** Feed or entertain well (6)
**7** Having the qualities or effects of a poison (8)
**8** Not based on fact (9)
**11** Nativity (5)
**13** Portal (4)
**17** Acknowledgment of the truth of something (9)
**19** Abruptly (8)
**20** Melodies (5)
**22** Additionally (4)
**23** One with military authority (7)
**25** Quivering poplars (6)
**27** Icy area (6)
**28** The 50th US state (6)
**29** Hard to endure (6)

**ACROSS**

**1** Joins together as one (6)
**5** Of blossoms (6)
**10** Broke free from (7)
**11** Meet a demand (7)
**12** Decorates with frosting (4)
**13** Hollow cylindrical shapes (5)
**15** Spoken (4)
**17** Married female (3)
**19** Be unable to remember (6)
**21** Body parts and musical instruments (6)
**22** Projectile (7)
**23** Gait of a horse (6)
**25** Dashed (6)
**28** Scenery for play or film (3)
**30** 4840 square yards (4)
**31** Overturn or unsettle (5)
**32** In addition (4)
**35** Less cloudy, more easily understood (7)
**36** Wanting (7)
**37** Emblem, sign (6)
**38** Snow vehicle (6)

**DOWN**

**2** Of atomic energy (7)
**3** Gratuities (4)
**4** Metallic element, burns with a yellow flame (6)
**5** Angles (6)
**6** Chooses (4)
**7** The capital is Vienna (7)
**8** Faith (6)
**9** Series, rounds (6)
**14** Minor encounters, with the law say (7)
**16** Acidic fruit (5)
**18** Bar me from the freshwater fish (5)
**20** Indication of potential opportunity (3)
**21** Aged (3)
**23** Look briefly (6)
**24** For the most part (7)
**26** Informing (7)
**27** Blueprint (6)
**28** Corkscrew shape (6)
**29** Sent in to play the game (6)
**33** Dull, dreary (4)
**34** Surrender, give up (4)

## ACROSS

**8** Exercising influence or control (8)
**9** Rubber (6)
**10** Mighty, powerful (6)
**11** Of artistic writing (8)
**12** Not so far away (6)
**13** Accomplished (8)
**15** Finished (4)
**17** Soap for hair (7)
**19** The quality to do something (7)
**22** Hollow cylinder (4)
**24** Sample (8)
**27** Deep red jewels (6)
**29** The collarbone (8)
**30** Looted the Spanish city badly (6)
**31** Break loose (6)
**32** Cells underground (8)

## DOWN

**1** Vessel for liquids (6)
**2** Metric weight (8)
**3** Oak or nag the animal (8)
**4** Sportsperson (7)
**5** Relating to teeth (6)
**6** Infertile (6)
**7** Most cheerful (8)
**14** Native of North Africa (4)
**16** Poll (4)
**18** Certain to fail (8)
**20** Rebuking severely (8)
**21** Tagged (8)
**23** Relaxes from tension (7)
**25** Roe of sturgeon (6)
**26** Derided, scoffed at (6)
**28** Concluding (6)

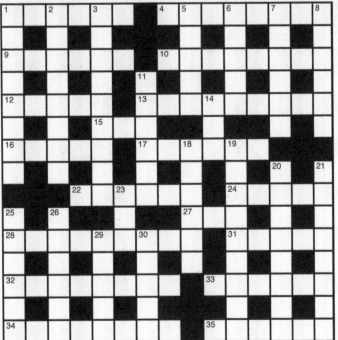

**74**

## ACROSS

1 It's as good as a rest, they say (6)
4 Accentuated (8)
9 Existing in fact (6)
10 Condescending (8)
12 Bedtime drink (5)
13 Lasting from dusk to dawn (9)
15 Short sleep (3)
16 Adroit (5)
17 Immature forms of invertebrates (6)
22 Inclined, tilted (6)
24 Subdivision of a play (5)
27 Consume (3)
28 Investigator (9)
31 Bellows (5)
32 Mastering a subject (8)
33 Plane supported by air (6)
34 Students (8)
35 Praised (6)

## DOWN

1 Black carbon material (8)
2 Things, objects (8)
3 Pledge or assurance (9)
5 Motif, subject (5)
6 He removed marbles from the Parthenon (5)
7 Confidence tricks by the bee? (6)
8 Fingers and toes (6)
11 Type of fabric (6)
14 Motor rotation, in short (3)
18 Buy back, or convert into cash (6)
19 A US lariat can be found in the country (9)
20 Requested forcefully (8)
21 Determined the dimensions (8)
23 Appropriate (3)
25 Mature animals (6)
26 Conjoin (6)
29 Man-made waterway (5)
30 Inside (5)

## ACROSS

**8** Processions of camels travelling in single file (8)
**9** Overwhelming fear (6)
**10** Possessing, owning (6)
**11** Aroused (8)
**12** Popular wood for furniture (6)
**13** Albert ... (physicist) (8)
**15** Ceases (4)
**17** State clearly, announce officially (7)
**19** Taking a siesta (7)
**22** Wags, quipsters (4)
**24** Flaw, failing (8)
**27** Drink of beer and lemonade (6)
**29** Australian capital (8)
**30** Avenge the Swiss city (6)
**31** Round black hat with brim (6)
**32** Putting on clothes (8)

## DOWN

**1** Country, canal and hat (6)
**2** Consistent with logic (8)
**3** Member of a criminal group (8)
**4** Analysed the chemical substances (7)
**5** Stress, tension (6)
**6** Ordained minister (6)
**7** Professional teller of jokes (8)
**14** Was not, in the present (4)
**16** Fresh information (4)
**18** US lift (8)
**20** Ascribed (8)
**21** Most unembellished (8)
**23** Lad sins when surrounded by water (7)
**25** Crush or grind grain coarsely (6)
**26** Mistakes (6)
**28** Of the gods (6)

**ACROSS**

**8** Pinkish-brown colour (8)
**9** Out of the country (6)
**10** Numbers of associated individuals (6)
**11** Arriving at (8)
**12** We send out to the country (6)
**13** Officer presiding at meetings (8)
**15** Remain (4)
**17** The more, the ... (7)
**19** Device that provides energy to perform a task (7)
**22** The relation is a nut, oddly (4)
**24** In these times (8)
**27** Spoke (6)
**29** Brolly (8)
**30** Ripe (6)
**31** Ineffectual, unavailing (6)
**32** Able to read and write (8)

**DOWN**

**1** Hole in the ground made by an animal (6)
**2** Between the neck and the arm (8)
**3** Gibberish (8)
**4** Continent (7)
**5** Tropical oblong fruit (6)
**6** Expert with bow and arrow (6)
**7** Keep in good condition (8)
**14** Song of praise (4)
**16** Flat surface for carrying something (4)
**18** Huge (8)
**20** Tries (8)
**21** Holders for handguns (8)
**23** Under normal conditions (7)
**25** Quick or skilful (6)
**26** Dormant (6)
**28** Greets the herons (6)

## ACROSS

**8** Drawn vehicle (8)
**9** Allowable margin, latitude (6)
**10** Furry burrowing animal (6)
**11** Answer, reply (8)
**12** Prepared wood (6)
**13** Final, extreme (8)
**15** Inert (4)
**17** Liquid used as condiment or food preservative (7)
**19** Feeling guilt or remorse (7)
**22** Bad tuna for the relative (4)
**24** Slight suggestions, intimations (8)
**27** Send back (6)
**29** Captious (8)
**30** Observe (6)
**31** Except on condition that (6)
**32** Regularly, constantly (8)

## DOWN

**1** It was formerly known as Nyasaland (6)
**2** Likely but not certain (8)
**3** Cite Arab about the organisms (8)
**4** Frightened, apprehensive (7)
**5** US wardrobe (6)
**6** Give up bad old ways (6)
**7** Case test for tapes (8)
**14** Incline, bend (4)
**16** Pull against a resistance (4)
**18** Uninformed (8)
**20** Truth can be ... than fiction (8)
**21** One's position on a matter (8)
**23** Serving no purpose (7)
**25** Metric units of capacity (6)
**26** Most agreeable (6)
**28** Lavishly, luxuriously (6)

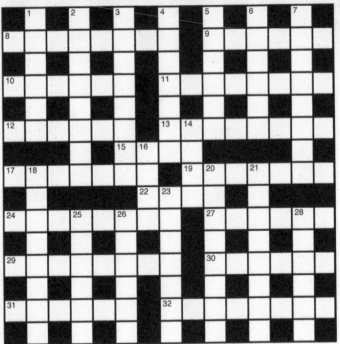

**78**

### ACROSS

**8** Intimidated, bullied (8)
**9** From the subcontinent (6)
**10** Not engaged (6)
**11** Most enraged (8)
**12** Pauper who seeks alms (6)
**13** Makes right (8)
**15** One on a list (4)
**17** Flat raised land (7)
**19** Wounded (7)
**22** Short letter (4)
**24** Is Tom Cruise a client? (8)
**27** Fabric woven from plant fibres (6)
**29** Offspring (8)
**30** Citrus fruits (6)
**31** Make visible (6)
**32** Arousing strong feeling (8)

### DOWN

**1** Argument, discussion (6)
**2** With no deviations (8)
**3** Reference points, standards (8)
**4** Bring forward (7)
**5** Vocalist (6)
**6** Suggest (6)
**7** For audio or video tape (8)
**14** Neglect to do (4)
**16** Air (4)
**18** The sound of amusement (8)
**20** Adornment for the throat (8)
**21** Utmost or extreme (8)
**23** Gear son up for fruit (7)
**25** Speaker (6)
**26** Only, and nothing more (6)
**28** Possessing (6)

## ACROSS

**1** Grassland (6)
**5** Animals (6)
**10** Stayed clear of (7)
**11** Decorated, bedecked (7)
**12** Den of an animal (4)
**13** Residue of fires (5)
**15** Small shelter, for doves say (4)
**17** Weight equivalent of 20 cwts (3)
**19** Ball-game (6)
**21** Bags for money (6)
**22** Wants (7)
**23** It's cast by blocked light (6)
**25** Term of office (6)
**28** At a great distance (3)
**30** Rescue (4)
**31** Single thickness, tier (5)
**32** Regretted (4)
**35** Least difficult (7)
**36** Long-tentacled creature (7)
**37** Director of published content (6)
**38** Group of countries under a single authority (6)

## DOWN

**2** The wearing away by weather (7)
**3** Fathers, informally (4)
**4** Most encompassing (6)
**5** Defeated (6)
**6** Particle of matter (4)
**7** Cords of tissue connecting muscle to bone (7)
**8** Story danced to music (6)
**9** Small vipers (6)
**14** Vacation (7)
**16** Woman whose husband is dead (5)
**18** Louse turned out to be a thrush (5)
**20** Make stitches (3)
**21** Loved domestic animal (3)
**23** Female relation (6)
**24** Counselled (7)
**26** One who illegally supplants another (7)
**27** First in age (6)
**28** Quicker (6)
**29** Distant in time or space (6)
**33** Caused to go somewhere (4)
**34** Halt (4)

**80**

## ACROSS

8 Elevation above sea level (8)
9 Book and prophet of the Old Testament (6)
10 Edible tuber (6)
11 Bring to a close (8)
12 Courage, heart (6)
13 Breaking free (8)
15 Land measurement (4)
17 It emits lava (7)
19 In opposition to (7)
22 Lazy (4)
24 It's taken to treat disease (8)
27 Council in a Communist country (6)
29 Case for tape (8)
30 Disordered, disarranged (6)
31 Unit of instruction (6)
32 They keep everything spotless (8)

## DOWN

1 Recess in a room or wall (6)
2 Exceedingly large (8)
3 The continental is a pure one (8)
4 Instructor (7)
5 Alfresco meal (6)
6 All at GPO go at this rate (6)
7 Brightly coloured neckerchief (8)
14 Marine mammal (4)
16 Metal money disc (4)
18 Performed surgery (8)
20 Gesticulations (8)
21 Requesting the pleasure of (8)
23 Arguments against an accusation (7)
25 Take a firm stand (6)
26 Purpose, plan (6)
28 Bear with courage (6)

## ACROSS

1 Set up, bring about (9)
9 Cheap and vulgar tastelessness (6)
10 Find out, detect (8)
11 Type of bean (6)
12 Marked by pomp or ceremony (6)
14 Centre around which something rotates (4)
15 Stiff, inflexible (5)
16 Leave (6)
18 Day for sea duty? (7)
21 Steady, even (7)
24 Gained (6)
26 Relating to city life (5)
30 Vessel for carrying blood (4)
31 Stunned (6)
32 Forfeited, relinquished (6)
33 Not based on fact, dubious (8)
34 Visual perceptions (6)
35 Investing with priestly authority (9)

## DOWN

2 Mariner (6)
3 One who uses a bow (6)
4 Having great affection for (6)
5 Distributes widely (7)
6 Part of a sentence (6)
7 All in RAF can get wet (8)
8 Geographical region (9)
11 Long narrow hilltop (5)
13 Moderate, temperate (4)
17 Or else (9)
19 Items of jewellery (8)
20 Appended (5)
22 Metric unit of weight (4)
23 More amusing (7)
25 Incidents (6)
27 Yellow fruit (6)
28 Body of people under one government (6)
29 Put down, degrade (6)

**ACROSS**

**8** Up to now (8)
**9** Sounds (6)
**10** Design of small pieces of coloured stone or glass (6)
**11** Particular time (8)
**12** Seasoned sausage (6)
**13** Towards the rising sun (8)
**15** Nocturnal birds (4)
**17** Fate, destiny (7)
**19** Rapped on the door (7)
**22** Facility (4)
**24** Evolves (8)
**27** Carvings in relief on stone (6)
**29** Forbearance (8)
**30** Undo, make less tight (6)
**31** Container or courage (6)
**32** Undertaking, dealing with (8)

**DOWN**

**1** Flower of Maoism? (6)
**2** Game bird (8)
**3** Small piece forming part of a whole (8)
**4** No cello for the officer (7)
**5** Light meals (6)
**6** Tool for cutting curved outlines (6)
**7** Available supply (8)
**14** Poses a question (4)
**16** Shed tears (4)
**18** Is the handler a trooper? (8)
**20** Does the jewellery make the EEC clank? (8)
**21** Usually, normally (8)
**23** Vistas (7)
**25** Is (6)
**26** Sixteen to a lb (6)
**28** Great seas (6)

## ACROSS

1 Scraped, scored (9)
9 Sheep's coat (6)
10 Demolishes, ruins (8)
11 'Every little breeze seems to whisper ...' (old song) (6)
12 Water down (6)
14 Imitated (4)
15 Tracks or paths (5)
16 Facet (6)
18 Recondition (7)
21 Betwixt (7)
24 Spider's gossamer (6)
26 Peruses (5)
30 Company emblem (4)
31 Hold, keep back (6)
32 Broadsheet or tabloid, say (6)
33 Arctic animal (8)
34 Type of sports bat (6)
35 Exhibiting strong feelings (9)

## DOWN

2 Time given to pay for goods (6)
3 Giving a false appearance of frankness (6)
4 Split, hoof say (6)
5 State of elated bliss (7)
6 Large flows of water (6)
7 Breed of small dog (8)
8 Saying or doing again (9)
11 Depart (5)
13 Mexican rolled pancake (4)
17 Shaped like a cross (9)
19 Take away (8)
20 Automaton (5)
22 Periodic rise and fall of the sea (4)
23 Sequence of instructions for a computer (7)
25 Exhilarated (6)
27 Creative person (6)
28 Workroom for 27 down (6)
29 Movie theatre (6)

**84**

## ACROSS

**8** Commonplace (8)
**9** Deep distress (6)
**10** Surpassingly good (6)
**11** Individuality (8)
**12** Motionless (6)
**13** Assailed (8)
**15** Displeasing to the senses (4)
**17** Barricade (7)
**19** Hurrying (7)
**22** One thing on a list (4)
**24** Postal wrapper (8)
**27** It gives the name of the writer of a report (2-4)
**29** Forgave (8)
**30** Takes part in (6)
**31** Strike and bounce off (6)
**32** Augmented (8)

## DOWN

**1** Marcel ..., French novelist (6)
**2** One on board (8)
**3** Meal outside (8)
**4** Characteristic (7)
**5** Agreement (6)
**6** Region around the North Pole (6)
**7** These lights form the aurora borealis (8)
**14** Rubber covering (4)
**16** Grasp, clutch (4)
**18** Per annum (8)
**20** Protection from sun or rain (8)
**21** Awkwardly slots her guns into them (8)
**23** Undergarments and children's toys (7)
**25** Completion (6)
**26** Small weights, about 28g each (6)
**28** Cared for a patient (6)

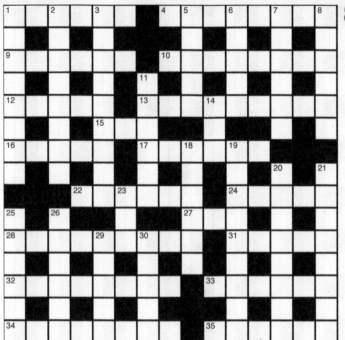

**85**

## ACROSS

**1** Crust for pies, tarts etc. (6)
**4** Express discontent (8)
**9** Acquire (6)
**10** Insisting on sticking strictly to the rules (8)
**12** Becomes less interesting (5)
**13** Realisation (9)
**15** Silvery metal (3)
**16** Court of the papal see (5)
**17** Nevertheless (6)
**22** Annul, rescind (6)
**24** A or e, say (5)
**27** Strong caustic solution (3)
**28** Bring in something or someone new (9)
**31** Lists of names of members (5)
**32** Widespread outbreak of disease (8)
**33** Unmarried (6)
**34** Was present at (8)
**35** Demises (6)

## DOWN

**1** Future possibility (8)
**2** Pioneers, homesteaders (8)
**3** Restore to previous position (2-7)
**5** Musical drama (5)
**6** Repose, tranquillity (5)
**7** Horn of the deer (6)
**8** Most pleasing (6)
**11** Small appetiser (6)
**14** Angry dispute (3)
**18** Shouted out (6)
**19** Publicise (9)
**20** Just after sunset (8)
**21** Bunches, clumps (8)
**23** Seed container (3)
**25** The Savoy in Dublin, for instance (6)
**26** Severe (6)
**29** Atlantic (5)
**30** Become one (5)

## ACROSS

**8** Mythical monster with the head of a bull and the body of a man (8)
**9** Open shoe (6)
**10** Rob (6)
**11** Complete a degree successfully (8)
**12** Repeated pattern of sound (6)
**13** I cue Dean for the spectators (8)
**15** ... and the Man (Shaw) (4)
**17** Erupting mountain (7)
**19** Does a bunk (7)
**22** Endure (4)
**24** Adverted, cited (8)
**27** Craggy and sturdy (6)
**29** Tabular array of days (8)
**30** Responsible for a reprehensible act (6)
**31** Abhor, execrate (6)
**32** Scatterings of liquid (8)

## DOWN

**1** Half quarter (6)
**2** Relating to home (8)
**3** He sells lean mass, strangely (8)
**4** Set of commands for a computer (7)
**5** Tory or Clare, say (6)
**6** Uncertain (6)
**7** Small piece of matter (8)
**14** Purposes (4)
**16** Part to play (4)
**18** Person who controls, a machine perhaps (8)
**20** Laboured effort (8)
**21** Most exasperated (8)
**23** Location of a building (7)
**25** Occurrences (6)
**26** Long, narrow ranges of hills (6)
**28** Tie her up to one or the other (6)

## ACROSS

**1** Observation (6)
**5** Depends (6)
**10** Base, post (7)
**11** Condemns, excoriates (7)
**12** Has a meal (4)
**13** Give permission to (5)
**15** Stand for a coffin (4)
**17** Affirmative (3)
**19** Informal meal outside (6)
**21** Premeditated killing (6)
**22** Has import, counts (7)
**23** It attracts iron (6)
**25** Hollow tubes for drinking (6)
**28** Fasten with needle and thread (3)
**30** Small quantity of liquid (4)
**31** Small mouselike animal (5)
**32** Largest continent (4)
**35** Agitated (7)
**36** Intended (7)
**37** Concurs (6)
**38** Pushed against gently (6)

## DOWN

**2** Springing back to shape after stretching (7)
**3** Passage in a mine (4)
**4** Good-hearted, charitable (6)
**5** Exhibitions of cowboy skills (6)
**6** Deficiency, want (4)
**7** Enlightened (7)
**8** See, pal is not awake (6)
**9** Moneylender who charges excessive interest (6)
**14** Tanned animal skin (7)
**16** Directed, targeted (5)
**18** Zest, relish (5)
**20** Feline mammal (3)
**21** She's married (3)
**23** Humble, meek (6)
**24** Developing, maturing (7)
**26** It's said to make the heart grow fonder (7)
**27** Structures where people sit to watch, oddly (6)
**28** Hues, colours (6)
**29** With which to cause harm (6)
**33** Consistent with fact (4)
**34** Poet of old (4)

**ACROSS**

8 Strong, hard, building material (8)
9 Directed one's gaze (6)
10 Dishes of lettuce etc. (6)
11 Above ground floor (8)
12 Pattern (6)
13 Logical about the Latin oar (8)
15 Old (4)
17 '..., ... little star' (song) (7)
19 Let fall (7)
22 Not only but ... (4)
24 Enjoyment, delight (8)
27 Technique (6)
29 Business, trade (8)
30 Female relatives (6)
31 Show a revel (6)
32 Aimlessly wandering from place to place (8)

**DOWN**

1 Reverent regard (6)
2 Big event (8)
3 Pertaining to oneself (8)
4 Need (7)
5 Cupboard (6)
6 Spud (6)
7 Lessen (8)
14 Appends (4)
16 Toothed wheel that interlocks with another (4)
18 Cordially received (8)
20 Soppy, mushy (8)
21 They require medical care (8)
23 Stories handed down (7)
25 Military land forces (6)
26 Unfurl (6)
28 Bodies of salt water (6)

**ACROSS**

**1** Utters a loud cry (6)
**4** Perplexed, befuddled (8)
**9** Rough (6)
**10** Distressing, perturbing (8)
**12** Precisely correct (5)
**13** Concord, harmony (9)
**15** Adult males (3)
**16** In that place (5)
**17** Sew with the lee end (6)
**22** Noise caused by electrical interference (6)
**24** Hidden treasure (5)
**27** Wrath (3)
**28** Emollients, unguents (9)
**31** Rustic (5)
**32** Gives, a speech say (8)
**33** Groups of ships or aircraft (6)
**34** Calamity (8)
**35** Went by bicycle (6)

**DOWN**

**1** Sent dust to the learners (8)
**2** Nervously amazed (8)
**3** Handling, management of something (9)
**5** Stench (5)
**6** Powerful effect or influence (5)
**7** Thin fragment or slice (6)
**8** Numerals (6)
**11** Is not in a position to (6)
**14** Conclusion or purpose (3)
**18** Expunge the tax? (6)
**19** Actually, really (9)
**20** Ring it for access (8)
**21** Became aware (8)
**23** Chopping tool (3)
**25** Prodded, needled (6)
**26** Small hillocks (6)
**29** Changes location (5)
**30** Relating to ancient Scandinavia (5)

## ACROSS

**8** Declare publicly (8)
**9** Outsmart (6)
**10** Wild and menacing (6)
**11** Questioned closely (8)
**12** Meticulous (6)
**13** Ideas (8)
**15** Reverberation of sound (4)
**17** Cyclone (7)
**19** Occidental (7)
**22** Lubricates (4)
**24** It's thrown in winter fun (8)
**27** Moves upwards (6)
**29** Drive to achieve (8)
**30** Venom, toxin (6)
**31** Unobserved (6)
**32** Rays from the source of light (8)

## DOWN

**1** Tiny tot (6)
**2** Whereabouts (8)
**3** Originated, created (8)
**4** This heaven is the most exalted state of happiness (7)
**5** El ..., place of fabulous wealth or great opportunity (6)
**6** Light cord (6)
**7** One on board (8)
**14** Loud emotional utterance (4)
**16** Moderately cold (4)
**18** Soothing cream (8)
**20** Absconding (8)
**21** When the sun is just below the horizon (8)
**23** Indisposition, ailment (7)
**25** Remained in readiness (6)
**26** They're from another world (6)
**28** Shouting in disapproval (6)

## ACROSS

**1** Absolutely essential (9)
**9** Sheepdog (6)
**10** Put on paper or tape (8)
**11** Sign of the fish (6)
**12** It has canals instead of streets (6)
**14** Object of devotion (4)
**15** Small light boat (5)
**16** Acquired knowledge or skill (6)
**18** Tightest (7)
**21** Dried leaves for smoking (7)
**24** Strongly opposed (6)
**26** Angela's ... (Frank McCourt) (5)
**30** Shellfish with pincers (4)
**31** Bowed, curved (6)
**32** This national rang me up (6)
**33** Came to consciousness (8)
**34** Spoken language (6)
**35** Verse line with six metrical feet (9)

## DOWN

**2** English cathedral city and county town of Devon (6)
**3** Strikingly strange (6
**4** Impulsive (6)
**5** Redder in complexion (7)
**6** Gentle and biddable (6)
**7** Of a form of energy (8)
**8** Feeling (9)
**11** Acute viral disease (5)
**13** Walking stick (4)
**17** Most peculiar (9)
**19** Not gained by labour (8)
**20** Forbidding, austere (5)
**22** Alcoholic beverage (4)
**23** Beg a cab to take the vegetable (7)
**25** Hard to find (6)
**27** Aha, van in Cuba (6)
**28** Connive, intrigue (6)
**29** Spartan, strict (6)

**ACROSS**

**8** More peevish (8)
**9** Astonished (6)
**10** Ring (6)
**11** Creeping or grovelling (8)
**12** Variety of polecat (6)
**13** Jumping lightly (8)
**15** Frank, not secret (4)
**17** Rebuke formally (7)
**19** Interminable (7)
**22** Measure of a 2-dimensional surface (4)
**24** Dampness (8)
**27** Striped cats (6)
**29** Changed direction, deviated (8)
**30** Yield (6)
**31** Hire for work (6)
**32** '... in Blue' (Gershwin) (8)

**DOWN**

**1** Acclaim (6)
**2** Imaginary horned creatures (8)
**3** One sits on board (8)
**4** Exact (7)
**5** Hunting expedition in Africa (6)
**6** Fast gait (6)
**7** Imports, messages, senses (8)
**14** Leg joint (4)
**16** Fruit that sounds like two (4)
**18** Feelings (8)
**20** Countrywide (8)
**21** Least heavy (8)
**23** Causes to become (7)
**25** Piece of playground equipment (6)
**26** Unfastened (6)
**28** Circuits of the golf course (6)

## ACROSS

**1** Foretold (9)
**9** Seek (6)
**10** Fragments of transparent quartz (8)
**11** Rubbed out (6)
**12** Journey by air (6)
**14** Irish Republic (4)
**15** Structures for egg-laying (5)
**16** Delineate again (6)
**18** Hired hands in the old West (7)
**21** Design style, popular in the 1920s and 1930s (3,4)
**24** Fowl and country (6)
**26** Coarse files (5)
**30** Performance by one person (4)
**31** Worked hard (6)
**32** Lives (6)
**33** Rebel, deserter (8)
**34** Numbers for rowing crews (6)
**35** Place stress on (9)

## DOWN

**2** Not often (6)
**3** Create, make out a plan (6)
**4** Seashores (6)
**5** Most lenient (7)
**6** Legally-binding decision (6)
**7** Prevent from rotting (8)
**8** Go through punching motions but without an opponent (6-3)
**11** Blunder (5)
**13** Exceptionally courageous person (4)
**17** Strewn about (9)
**19** Words of caution (8)
**20** Playthings with spool and reel (2-3)
**22** Mistake in printed matter, in short (4)
**23** Software to control operations (7)
**25** Group of suburban houses (6)
**27** Unpleasant odour (6)
**28** Persistent attacks on fortified places (6)
**29** Elevated open grasslands in southern Africa (6)

## ACROSS

**8** Nice, satisfying (8)
**9** Outlined or tracked back (6)
**10** King's fighting man in the middle ages (6)
**11** Addendum (8)
**12** Great dread (6)
**13** The mathematics of points, lines and surfaces (8)
**15** Something imagined (4)
**17** Learned person (7)
**19** Cover, protection (7)
**22** 'For ... us a child is born' (Handel's Messiah) (4)
**24** Envy, resent (8)
**27** Engines (6)
**29** One always tends to take a favourable view of things (8)
**30** Habitual (6)
**31** Acceptance (6)
**32** Storehouses for weapons (8)

## DOWN

**1** Thrust or dive into (6)
**2** Large Australian mammal (8)
**3** I bet a car against the little living thing (8)
**4** Unknown (7)
**5** Artist's workroom (6)
**6** Baby's plaything (6)
**7** Asset (8)
**14** Orient (4)
**16** It's used as a medicine or narcotic (4)
**18** Least expensive (8)
**20** Words that sound the same, though with different meanings (8)
**21** Of writing with artistic merit (8)
**23** Impartial (7)
**25** Made a sudden, surprise attack (6)
**26** Small and pretty (6)
**28** Roved (6)

## ACROSS

1 Punctuation marks (6)
5 Dissimilar (6)
10 Unpaid or unskilled (7)
11 Stirs up, rouses (7)
12 Exclude (4)
13 Member of a nomadic people (5)
15 Footwear (4)
17 Articulate (3)
19 Transmitter (6)
21 Smoothed with heat (6)
22 Destroying completely (7)
23 Rule, control (6)
25 Country, state (6)
28 Keep secret from Mother? (3)
30 Imperial measurement (4)
31 Aviator (5)
32 Bring to a close (4)
35 Lived (7)
36 Money spent in the course of work (7)
37 Stamina (6)
38 Laugh nervously (6)

## DOWN

2 Loud applause (7)
3 Encounter (4)
4 Jets of vapour (6)
5 Anxious, restless (6)
6 Chance, fate, fortune (4)
7 Room with cooking facilities (7)
8 Shavers (6)
9 Go up (6)
14 Aching, hurtful (7)
16 Full of fun and gaiety (5)
18 Air-powered instrument (5)
20 Move fast or manage (3)
21 Public house (3)
23 Loose fragments of rock (6)
24 Account from one point of view (7)
26 Extreme or deeply felt (7)
27 See it and die, they say (6)
28 Twelve noon (6)
29 Instant (6)
33 Asterisk (4)
34 Expectorate (4)

**ACROSS**

**8** Ended, over (8)
**9** Dull sounds of heavy blows (6)
**10** River of S. America (6)
**11** Circus performers (8)
**12** Liveliness of mind or spirit (6)
**13** Fruits with hard stones (8)
**15** Brainwave (4)
**17** West Indian island (7)
**19** Musical beats (7)
**22** Travel on the back of animal (4)
**24** Alongside (8)
**27** Concedes (6)
**29** Short official statement (8)
**30** Refuse to acknowledge (6)
**31** Plain, unadorned (6)
**32** Parts, portions (8)

**DOWN**

**1** Acid turns it red (6)
**2** Shop for Italian pie (8)
**3** Relating to speech sounds (8)
**4** Payment ahead of due date (7)
**5** Deprive of food (6)
**6** Dressed timber (6)
**7** Against the current (8)
**14** Difficult or firm (4)
**16** Have the courage to try something (4)
**18** Very early calculators (8)
**20** Audiences in a court of law (8)
**21** Gifted (8)
**23** Sickness (7)
**25** Fellow-members, confederates (6)
**26** Chair or bed carried on two poles (6)
**28** Sensation caused by heat (6)

## ACROSS

**1** Pressure or strain (6)
**4** Takes to be the case (8)
**9** Win victory over (6)
**10** Aspiration, dream (8)
**12** Incident (5)
**13** Journeyed (9)
**15** Epoch (3)
**16** At a future time (5)
**17** More orderly (6)
**22** They avoid work (6)
**24** Frolic, prank (5)
**27** Fruiting head of a cereal (3)
**28** Mentions, references (9)
**31** Tall, strong, evergreen plant (5)
**32** Woods of fruit trees (8)
**33** Thwart, hinder (6)
**34** Knitted upper garments (8)
**35** Aphrodite's beloved (6)

## DOWN

**1** Abruptly (8)
**2** Thinks over (8)
**3** Broke into many pieces (9)
**5** Dance in Burma? (5)
**6** River of France (5)
**7** For the most part (6)
**8** Council to discuss ecclesiastical business (6)
**11** Position or posture (6)
**14** Size up (3)
**18** Judge the worth of (6)
**19** Converted into code (9)
**20** Example regarded as typical of its class (8)
**21** Idealists or wishful thinkers (8)
**23** Hawaiian necklace of flowers (3)
**25** No swag on these vehicles (6)
**26** Commonplace remark, banality (6)
**29** Bright or dapper (5)
**30** Command (5)

**ACROSS**

**8** The region inside (8)
**9** Belonging to them (6)
**10** Audacious, bold (6)
**11** Growing stronger (8)
**12** Rupture in muscle tissue (6)
**13** Recognise, name (8)
**15** Stem of bamboo (4)
**17** Applies the mind to learning (7)
**19** Comes into sight (7)
**22** Put to death (4)
**24** Any living entity (8)
**27** Real, existing (6)
**29** Most concise and full of meaning (8)
**30** Compulsory force or threat (6)
**31** Two or more (6)
**32** Determined the sum (8)

**DOWN**

**1** Draw into the lungs (6)
**2** Planned or created (8)
**3** Dishonour (8)
**4** Combination of amino acids in living matter (7)
**5** Fast (6)
**6** Fabric with soft pile (6)
**7** Move from one place to another (8)
**14** Hand out playing cards (4)
**16** Inquires (4)
**18** Awful, dire (8)
**20** Enthusiastic approval (8)
**21** Wholly, completely (8)
**23** Ape, copy (7)
**25** Leave the water and go badly hoarse (6)
**26** Highest standards (6)
**28** Passages between seats (6)

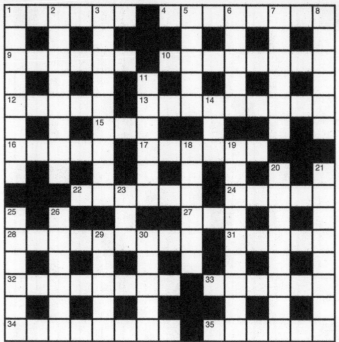

## ACROSS

**1** Mat has strange respiratory disorder (6)
**4** Tiny speck (8)
**9** Thinly scattered (6)
**10** Decoration, adornment (8)
**12** The lowest point (5)
**13** Publication on folded sheets (9)
**15** Is plural (3)
**16** Explosive weapon (1-4)
**17** Become larger (6)
**22** Make visible (6)
**24** Formula believed to have magical force (5)
**27** Go for (3)
**28** Conspicuous in position or importance (9)
**31** Caper, prank (5)
**32** Fancy curve in handwriting (8)
**33** Set alight (6)
**34** More regular or constant (8)
**35** Brings up (6)

## DOWN

**1** Strong liquor in the basin? (8)
**2** Hinged opening in floor or ceiling (4-4)
**3** Wretched, doleful (9)
**5** Mark to indicate a direction (5)
**6** Vagrant, drifter (5)
**7** Moves on all fours (6)
**8** Gains entrance (6)
**11** Explosive expulsion of air (6)
**14** Salt water (3)
**18** Aviators (6)
**19** A longing for past times (9)
**20** Sentinels, watches (8)
**21** Slow-moving ice-masses (8)
**23** Commercial vehicle (3)
**25** Aromatic substances (6)
**26** Unrefined (6)
**29** Epic poem by Homer (5)
**30** Draw out, elicit (5)

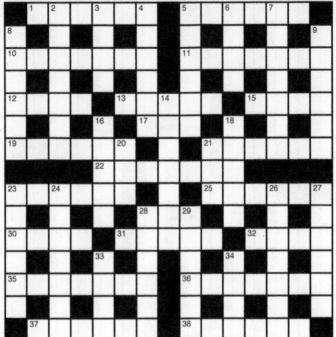

**ACROSS**

1 Credence (6)
5 Worry (6)
10 Buildings for horses (7)
11 Thankless wretch (7)
12 People (4)
13 US ten-cent coins (5)
15 Accessible to all (4)
17 Movable cover (3)
19 Persisted, endured (6)
21 Messengers, emissaries (6)
22 An idler can be found here (7)
23 Power of retaining and recalling past experience (6)
25 Act nervously and indecisively (6)
28 Rigid piece of metal (3)
30 Step on a ladder (4)
31 Reed I make into a duck (5)
32 Cut short the season's yield? (4)
35 Time for a breather (7)
36 Feel din of Kildare town (7)
37 Male relatives (6)
38 Way out (6)

**DOWN**

2 Renders capable (7)
3 Otiose (4)
4 Preserved trace of an ancient plant or animal (6)
5 Travelled by boat (6)
6 Intense anger (4)
7 O Ma hops off the soap (7)
8 Functional (6)
9 Living entities (6)
14 Take someone in the wrong direction (7)
16 Strikingly odd or unusual (5)
18 Reversed an action (5)
20 Arid (3)
21 Finale (3)
23 Just, only (6)
24 Make reference to (7)
26 Leather straps for an animal (7)
27 Where the river runs very fast (6)
28 Animals with two feet (6)
29 Idolise, venerate (6)
33 Animal on target? (4)
34 A long distance away (4)

**ACROSS**

**1** Sculpture representing a human or animal (6)
**5** Place for public worship (6)
**10** Israeli collective farm (7)
**11** Locomotives (7)
**12** Run away (4)
**13** Electronic communication (1-4)
**15** Melody (4)
**17** Deed (3)
**19** Artist's workroom (6)
**21** Brightly coloured tropical bird (6)
**22** Filled beyond capacity (7)
**23** Ought to (6)
**25** Modifier (6)
**28** Printer's liquid (3)
**30** Objectives (4)
**31** Garret (5)
**32** Indonesian island (4)
**35** Framework for climbing plants (7)
**36** Renting (7)
**37** Short-sightedness (6)
**38** Ornamental headdress (6)

**DOWN**

**2** Group arranged as if in a painting (7)
**3** Therefore, hence (4)
**4** Dry skin condition (6)
**5** Money available for borrowing (6)
**6** Try to persuade (4)
**7** Put down by force (7)
**8** Small open boats (6)
**9** Declare, profess (6)
**14** Statement of transactions and costs (7)
**16** Shoulder weapon (5)
**18** Rice-field (5)
**20** Advanced in years (3)
**21** Ape this plant awkwardly (3)
**23** Drowsy (6)
**24** Officer's attendant (7)
**26** Test, probe (7)
**27** Span the card game? (6)
**28** Home of Odysseus (6)
**29** Caused to die (6)
**33** Hen-house (4)
**34** Set of statistics (4)

**ACROSS**

**8** From mare gin I get a severe headache (8)
**9** Zero (6)
**10** Coarse-furred burrowing rodent (6)
**11** Ducks to ride on two wheels? (8)
**12** Hungarian composer (6)
**13** Person connected by blood or marriage (8)
**15** Looked at (4)
**17** Lava-emitting crater (7)
**19** Collects in one place (7)
**22** Employs (4)
**24** Recuperation (8)
**27** Broad bands worn over the shoulder (6)
**29** Misadventure (8)
**30** Measuring instruments (6)
**31** Commonwealth (6)
**32** Imaginary creatures, large and wicked (8)

**DOWN**

**1** Insect with high-pitched drone (6)
**2** Having a strong distinctive fragrance (8)
**3** Incorrect (8)
**4** Determine the dimensions (7)
**5** Unfurl (6)
**6** Sounds of disapproval (3-3)
**7** At whatever place (8)
**14** Boundary (4)
**16** Belonging to you (4)
**18** Defeat, conquer (8)
**20** Supposing (8)
**21** Pause, waver (8)
**23** Arrangements of units that function together (7)
**25** Where something begins (6)
**26** Football team (6)
**28** Bloomers (6)

**ACROSS**

**8** Find fault with (8)
**9** Spain and Portugal (6)
**10** Closed curve (6)
**11** Not derived or copied (8)
**12** Make a rush at (6)
**13** In the direction of the Orient (8)
**15** Titled peer (4)
**17** Use flour, Ma, for the milk substitute (7)
**19** Died by submersion (7)
**22** Hurry or surge (4)
**24** Agitated (8)
**27** Once every 365 days (6)
**29** Showing gratitude (8)
**30** Sincere, upright (6)
**31** Life's work (6)
**32** Cutting implement (8)

**DOWN**

**1** Make smooth and glossy (6)
**2** Crumpets, oddly, can provide the full array of colours (8)
**3** Adieu (8)
**4** Expose, unveil (7)
**5** Musical half notes (6)
**6** Critique, appraisal (6)
**7** Take a different view (8)
**14** Finds the total (4)
**16** Implements of propulsion on water (4)
**18** Operating cost (8)
**20** Rich myth recurs at regular intervals (8)
**21** Frailty, feebleness (8)
**23** Having no purpose (7)
**25** Took care of (6)
**26** Exertion, elbow grease (6)
**28** Brightness from reflected light (6)

**ACROSS**

1 Imagined to be true (9)
9 Daughter of Uranus and Gaia (6)
10 Look similar to (8)
11 Globe, orb (6)
12 Injure the reputation of (6)
14 Variety, kind (4)
15 Holy Book (5)
16 Fills with apprehension (6)
18 People killed, hurt or abused (7)
21 An additional one (7)
24 Reddish brown (6)
26 Existed or dwelt (5)
30 Greek colonnade (4)
31 Source (6)
32 Leaves that bear flowers (6)
33 Busy or inhabited (8)
34 Be indecisive (6)
35 Head of state has a bad red instep (9)

**DOWN**

2 Asymmetrical (6)
3 Building assembled from pre-manufactured parts, in short (6)
4 Spider's fibrils (6)
5 Chose by poll (7)
6 Place of Christian worship (6)
7 Systematic seeking after knowledge (8)
8 Indispensable, essential (9)
11 It pains badly to be there (5)
13 Very short skirt (4)
17 One and all (9)
19 Injured party (8)
20 Gloves worn by fielders (5)
22 Ended (4)
23 Taste (7)
25 Admiration, regard (6)
27 Sounds of people (6)
28 Went down momentarily (6)
29 Town and wood bird (6)

**ACROSS**

8 Easily damaged (8)
9 Recognition given to the source of information (6)
10 Holiday spot (6)
11 Exhaustive, complete (8)
12 More proximate (6)
13 Gathering (8)
15 Inactive (4)
17 Structure of words in sentences (7)
19 Server at tables (7)
22 From where the sun rises (4)
24 Small migratory birds (8)
27 Places frequently visited, hangouts (6)
29 Three-sided figure (8)
30 Person responsible for publication (6)
31 Gain from investment (6)
32 Distorting, turning (8)

**DOWN**

1 Strict (6)
2 Unit of mass (8)
3 Micro-organisms (8)
4 In the middle (7)
5 Resounds (6)
6 Reorganise (6)
7 Extraordinary, exceptional (8)
14 Does needlework (4)
16 Pulled up or behind (4)
18 Offered something for a service or achievement (8)
20 Good at sport (8)
21 Holidaymakers (8)
23 Angles (7)
25 Nautical measure, about 3½ miles (6)
26 Heart and lungs, say (6)
28 Sharp tips on stems (6)

## ACROSS

**1** Impressive displays (6)
**4** Sharp spasms of pain (8)
**9** Unparalleled (6)
**10** A climbing flower, I swear it (8)
**12** Carrying out action (5)
**13** Flapping, hesitating (9)
**15** Lacking in self-confidence (3)
**16** 'She walks in beauty, like the ...' (Byron) (5)
**17** Walked lamely (6)
**22** Jail (6)
**24** Blunder (5)
**27** Portion of a circle (3)
**28** Putting tags on (9)
**31** Leaping amphibians (5)
**32** Limit of settled lands (8)
**33** Perceive (6)
**34** Unexpectedly, abruptly (8)
**35** Compliance (6)

## DOWN

**1** Plentiful, ample (8)
**2** Protective barriers (8)
**3** Child, minor (9)
**5** Contaminate (5)
**6** Lord, sir or doctor, say (5)
**7** Showing extreme courage (6)
**8** Describes thick and poorly groomed hair (6)
**11** Episodes of pastoral or romantic charm (6)
**14** This joint is trendy (3)
**18** Handle, run (6)
**19** Particles with a negative charge (9)
**20** Establish, arrange for (8)
**21** Look for valuable minerals (8)
**23** Sick (3)
**25** Steep rock-faces (6)
**26** Overseas (6)
**29** Metric unit of capacity (5)
**30** One hopes to attain it (5)

**107**

## ACROSS

**8** Expel a devil (8)
**9** Was Medusa pleased? (6)
**10** Subtle difference (6)
**11** Plausible but false (8)
**12** Boredom, ennui (6)
**13** Devastating event (8)
**15** Place of complete bliss (4)
**17** Egg-shaped wind instrument out of Inca oar (7)
**19** Falling to the bottom (7)
**22** Rodents (4)
**24** Evident or seeming to be (8)
**27** Get (6)
**29** N. American petrol (8)
**30** For a short time (6)
**31** Be firm in demands (6)
**32** Removing dirt (8)

## DOWN

**1** Pardon or justify (6)
**2** More stylish, up-to-the-minute (8)
**3** They watch for off-sides and out of bounds (8)
**4** It's by the ocean (7)
**5** Ships of the desert (6)
**6** Students (6)
**7** Light shade of blue (8)
**14** In the present month (4)
**16** Polite euphemism for swear word (4)
**18** Commanders of troops (8)
**20** Quarantined (8)
**21** Would hens tick in these rooms? (8)
**23** At rest or deceased (2,5)
**25** Of minute matter (6)
**26** Has being (6)
**28** Away from the coast (6)

## ACROSS

1 Piece of equipment or a tool (6)
4 Raised flooring or stage (8)
9 Not faint or feeble (6)
10 Holiday (8)
12 'I will ... and go now' (Yeats) (5)
13 Being present at (9)
15 Uncooked (3)
16 It's as strong as its weakest link (5)
17 Untie a relative (6)
22 Counsel (6)
24 Hasten (5)
27 Soluble substance for colouring (3)
28 Latent ability (9)
31 Relative magnitudes of two quantities (5)
32 Soaks, douses (8)
33 Gluey, adhesive (6)
34 Daises (8)
35 Fully developed animals (6)

## DOWN

1 The space between two places (8)
2 Upright (8)
3 Feeling or showing worry or solicitude (9)
5 Lowest or smallest (5)
6 Coach, develop (5)
7 Egyptian god of the underworld (6)
8 Social unit living together (6)
11 US state in the Central Pacific (6)
14 Take food (3)
18 Annoy, tantalise (6)
19 Received from an ancestor (9)
20 Judgmental (8)
21 Interchangeable words (8)
23 A tax (3)
25 Prised out the 8-legged creature (6)
26 Mental or emotional strain (6)
29 More pleasant (5)
30 Part of the small intestine (5)

## ACROSS

**1** Abode (9)
**9** Remember (6)
**10** Boiled oatmeal (8)
**11** Formal, ceremonious (6)
**12** Many and different (6)
**14** Round trip (4)
**15** Lissome (5)
**16** Brilliance (6)
**18** High regard (7)
**21** Went on hands and knees (7)
**24** Voracious sea fish (6)
**26** Verity (5)
**30** Irritating skin sensation (4)
**31** Required (6)
**32** Instructions and ingredients (6)
**33** Relating to the management of wealth (8)
**34** Prime number (6)
**35** Substituting (9)

## DOWN

**2** Unusual, exciting (6)
**3** Jewish state (6)
**4** Most aged (6)
**5** Brings into existence (7)
**6** Defy, withstand (6)
**7** Matter, stuff (8)
**8** Next to (9)
**11** Sweetener (5)
**13** Move upwards (4)
**17** Kept in an unaltered condition (9)
**19** Sought, scoured (8)
**20** Hereditary social class among Hindus (5)
**22** Poker player's stake (4)
**23** Sporting contender (7)
**25** Smoked herring (6)
**27** Unfurl (6)
**28** Bold and brave (6)
**29** Area, neighbourhood (6)

## ACROSS

**8** Shook from fear or cold (8)
**9** Share or allotment, of food say (6)
**10** Cloth, material (6)
**11** Most incensed (8)
**12** Room below ground (6)
**13** Changeless and unceasing (8)
**15** One unit (4)
**17** Smoke out the coat cob (7)
**19** Hurts (7)
**22** Place, location (4)
**24** Weightiest (8)
**27** Moves upwards (6)
**29** Constant and true (8)
**30** Viewed (6)
**31** Less rich (6)
**32** Large oval nuts with fibrous husks (8)

## DOWN

**1** Make (6)
**2** Strangely, a burr elm is a protective covering (8)
**3** Type of energy (8)
**4** Forward movement (7)
**5** Mythological fire-breathing creature (6)
**6** Exacting, rigid (6)
**7** Drivel (8)
**14** Leave out (4)
**16** Throw lightly and casually (4)
**18** Controller, of a camera say (8)
**20** Ornamental chain (8)
**21** Mythical horned creatures (8)
**23** Sloping letters (7)
**25** Electors (6)
**26** Determined attempt (6)
**28** Inhaled and exhaled air (6)

## ACROSS

**8** Time of celebration (8)
**9** US icon for relative (6)
**10** Published (6)
**11** Artist who creates three-dimensional works (8)
**12** Go Nero to the US state (6)
**13** Native of Cairo, say (8)
**15** Feel concern or interest (4)
**17** Der ... (German publication) (7)
**19** Travel depot (7)
**22** ... Curtain (Hitchcock film) (4)
**24** Magician, illusionist (8)
**27** Slanted, angled (6)
**29** Subject to change (8)
**30** Advance information (6)
**31** Exacting (6)
**32** Work-out (8)

## DOWN

**1** The smaller of two (6)
**2** Strenuous effort against odds (8)
**3** Knowledge on which to base belief (8)
**4** Group, clump (7)
**5** Inhabit (6)
**6** Amount produced (6)
**7** Prehistoric creature (8)
**14** Set of equipment (4)
**16** Lowest female singing voice (4)
**18** Certificates declaring wills to be valid (8)
**20** Planned, meant to (8)
**21** Study of government (8)
**23** Issued a command (7)
**25** Liquids from fruits and vegetables (6)
**26** Latex from trees (6)
**28** Expunge the tax? (6)

## ACROSS

**1** Alter, modify (6)
**4** Upriver (8)
**9** XI (6)
**10** Spoke softly or indistinctly (8)
**12** Upper joint of the leg (5)
**13** Scott and Shackleton (9)
**15** Propelling pole (3)
**16** Japanese verse form of three short lines (5)
**17** Coarse, vulgar (6)
**22** Grown-up people (6)
**24** Nascence (5)
**27** Anger (3)
**28** Solvers of practical problems using scientific knowledge (9)
**31** Steps of a ladder (5)
**32** In good spirits (8)
**33** Cursory (6)
**34** Unexpectedly, abruptly (8)
**35** Touch, sight etc. (6)

## DOWN

**1** Swift, long-legged cats (8)
**2** Drink before a meal (8)
**3** Tall, slender canine (9)
**5** Buxom, chubby (5)
**6** Speed of a musical piece (5)
**7** Merited (6)
**8** Humble, unassuming (6)
**11** Morning food in a creel (6)
**14** Item at auction (3)
**18** Stand firm against (6)
**19** Sleep through winter (9)
**20** Words in place of persons, places or things (8)
**21** Sounds of air forced through a small aperture (8)
**23** Put into service (3)
**25** Good ones make good neighbours (6)
**26** Acceded (6)
**29** Look after patients (5)
**30** On a par (5)

**113**

## ACROSS

1 Lend a hand (6)
4 Young frogs (8)
9 Social unit living together, à trois perhaps (6)
10 Forbearance, tolerance (8)
12 Short and to the point (5)
13 Involuntary or mechanical (9)
15 Spanish sun (3)
16 Episode (5)
17 Have a bearing on (6)
22 Appending (6)
24 Oral cavity (5)
27 Jump lightly (3)
28 Apparatus, gear (9)
31 Later on (5)
32 Printer's star (8)
33 Straightforward (6)
34 Unlicensed drinking establishments (8)
35 Imprison without trial (6)

## DOWN

1 Allowed to enter (8)
2 Odds and ends (8)
3 Proposed, recommended (9)
5 Toward the stern of a ship (5)
6 Last king of Troy (5)
7 From end to end (6)
8 Rough drawing (6)
11 A law I'm making up Africa (6)
14 Be indebted to (3)
18 Verbal or physical disputes (6)
19 Person who lives or travels with you (9)
20 Several (8)
21 Baker's dozen (8)
23 Barrier to control the flow of water (3)
25 They eat no animal products (6)
26 Delicate or hardly noticeable (6)
29 Pouch for money (5)
30 German industrial city (5)

## ACROSS

**8** Characteristic of a shiny solid element (8)
**9** Point to aim at (6)
**10** Not rough (6)
**11** Popular resort in the West Indies (8)
**12** Qualifying word (6)
**13** With measured beat (8)
**15** Therefore (4)
**17** Grey rock (7)
**19** Penning (7)
**22** Is Abel capable? (4)
**24** A very desirable feeling (8)
**27** Thin slices of fried potato (6)
**29** Tagged (8)
**30** Uttered (6)
**31** Twos in cards (6)
**32** Relating to Antrim, say (8)

## DOWN

**1** Appeared to be (6)
**2** Bad open loan to the French general (8)
**3** Letters of pale bath (8)
**4** Floating mass of frozen water (7)
**5** Well-built, strong (6)
**6** Failure to follow the rules (6)
**7** Lowering of rank (8)
**14** Cry of a wolf (4)
**16** Back end (4)
**18** Set free (8)
**20** Retrieval (8)
**21** The gloaming (8)
**23** Stooping (7)
**25** Cagney works for this type of business (6)
**26** If not (6)
**28** Literature in metrical form (6)

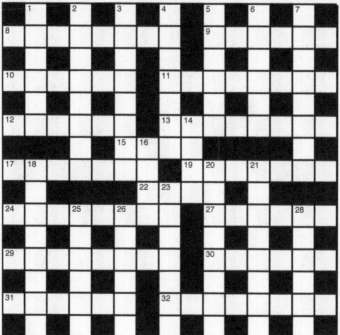

**ACROSS**

**8** Cause to explode (8)
**9** In foreign parts (6)
**10** Soak up, as a sponge (6)
**11** This day's child has far to go (8)
**12** Disastrous (6)
**13** Remembrances of things past (8)
**15** Pre-owned (4)
**17** Passage for water (7)
**19** Conjectures, reckons (7)
**22** Article, of news say (4)
**24** Approximate cost (8)
**27** Is the big one an aircraft? (6)
**29** Regulated activities or showed the way (8)
**30** All assets and liabilities (6)
**31** Roe of sturgeon (6)
**32** Expanded (8)

**DOWN**

**1** One of a group or club (6)
**2** Small sledge for sliding downhill (8)
**3** Curb a bee by cooking with charcoal (8)
**4** Hour to retire (7)
**5** Space containing no matter (6)
**6** With which to rub out (6)
**7** Save Jean from speaking this island language (8)
**14** Fringe (4)
**16** Small narrow opening (4)
**18** Building for the care of the sick (8)
**20** A rum bell to stay dry (8)
**21** As 20dn does (8)
**23** Soft toys (7)
**25** A Brie I made from two countries (6)
**26** Thespians (6)
**28** Hard, aromatic spice (6)

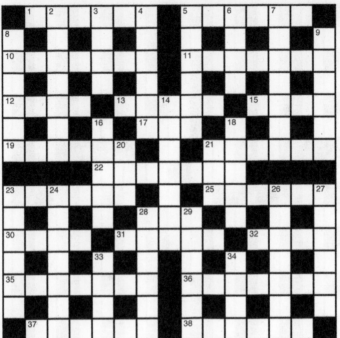

**116**

## ACROSS

**1** Descendants or heirs (6)
**5** Extracting ore etc. from the earth (6)
**10** The reptiles are let rust (7)
**11** State of having lost all hope (7)
**12** Oh, an ark man (4)
**13** The Christian Messiah (5)
**15** Resist, stand up to (4)
**17** Raised edge of a round object (3)
**19** Gangways (6)
**21** Sharp-tasting or resentful (6)
**22** Smallest possible quantity (7)
**23** Young cat (6)
**25** Thin layers of rock for roofing (6)
**28** Light touch or stroke (3)
**30** Strong metal (4)
**31** Wall painting (5)
**32** Military assistant (4)
**35** Emerged from eggs (7)
**36** Type of person who won't take advice (4-3)
**37** Adapt, alter (6)
**38** Withdraw from active participation (6)

## DOWN

**2** Dead body of an animal (7)
**3** Birds of the night (4)
**4** Nurse in charge (6)
**5** Average or intermediate (6)
**6** Prying, snoopy (4)
**7** Closest (7)
**8** Unit of a poem (6)
**9** Act of supplication to a deity (6)
**14** Alike, resembling (7)
**16** Republic on the Arabian Peninsula (5)
**18** Indistinctly (5)
**20** Moral transgression (3)
**21** Public transport vehicle (3)
**23** Chivalrous warrior (6)
**24** Moved at fairly fast gait (7)
**26** Disappear into this and vanish completely (4,3)
**27** Decent, becoming (6)
**28** Learned person (6)
**29** Large cargo ship (6)
**33** You, of old (4)
**34** Size and style of type (4)

**ACROSS**

**1** Seed, source of oil (6)
**4** Liturgical song (8)
**9** Repository for historical objects (6)
**10** Whole formed by two or more elements (8)
**12** Attribute, characteristic (5)
**13** Widenings of arteries (9)
**15** Everything (3)
**16** Frenetic, mad (5)
**17** Leaned to one side (6)
**22** More profound (6)
**24** Softly, in music (5)
**27** Indisposed (3)
**28** Attic hams could make one wheezy (9)
**31** Signs or warnings for the future (5)
**32** Washing or dusting, say (8)
**33** Left at the altar (6)
**34** Yielded a profit (8)
**35** Melt (fat) (6)

**DOWN**

**1** On an indeterminate occasion in the future (8)
**2** Keeps up (8)
**3** Facial hair (9)
**5** Isolated from others (5)
**6** Imbiber (5)
**7** Series of lessons (6)
**8** First in age (6)
**11** Hit hard (6)
**14** Last month, in short (3)
**18** Punctilious (6)
**19** TNT, for example (9)
**20** Gifted (8)
**21** Deem to be (8)
**23** Historical age (3)
**25** East Indian sailor (6)
**26** City thoroughfare (6)
**29** Of lesser importance (5)
**30** Taut, strained (5)

**ACROSS**

**8** Easily recognisable (8)
**9** Clock or heart (6)
**10** Wheel shape (6)
**11** Of 1dn (8)
**12** Demand (6)
**13** Manufacturing enterprise (8)
**15** Long ago (4)
**17** If Ron be outside, is he alight? (7)
**19** Before, earlier (7)
**22** Seldom seen (4)
**24** Kindling (8)
**27** Forms, in wax say (6)
**29** Aloofness (8)
**30** Caught fish and made a clear profit (6)
**31** Conflict, fight (6)
**32** Sleeping spaces (8)

**DOWN**

**1** Country (6)
**2** Devilment, impishness (8)
**3** Could a creditor become a member of the board? (8)
**4** Excessively agitated (7)
**5** Declared (6)
**6** Shovel-like utensils (6)
**7** Excluded, ruled out (8)
**14** Not far away (4)
**16** Barbarous Roman emperor (4)
**18** Master copy (8)
**20** Do enamel the drink (8)
**21** Mathematically, two are equal (8)
**23** Modifying words (7)
**25** One's holdings after death (6)
**26** Light weights (6)
**28** 'We are such stuff / As ... are made on' (The Tempest) (6)

## ACROSS

**1** Precipices (6)
**4** Moves forward (8)
**9** Engage, a lawyer say (6)
**10** Took a loan (8)
**12** This month (5)
**13** Consequently (9)
**15** As well (3)
**16** Not a single person (2-3)
**17** Might Harry work with clay? (6)
**22** Break loose (6)
**24** Roughage (5)
**27** Fury (3)
**28** In need of mending (9)
**31** Projection to tie a rope around (5)
**32** Foolishly fond of one's wife (8)
**33** Side-arm (6)
**34** Had a right (8)
**35** By means of this, legally speaking (6)

## DOWN

**1** Pomp, formality (8)
**2** Inner part (8)
**3** Scares (9)
**5** Male bee for the queen (5)
**6** Concur (5)
**7** Hired hand for cattle-ranch (6)
**8** Abrupt (6)
**11** Place of perfect happiness (6)
**14** Long-tailed rodent (3)
**18** Belonging to them (6)
**19** Efficacious (9)
**20** One not present (8)
**21** Cerebrally (8)
**23** Drinking vessel (3)
**25** Cite evidence for (6)
**26** Accompany to protect (6)
**29** Expel from property (5)
**30** Ill-treatment (5)

**120**

## ACROSS

**1** Most secure (6)
**4** Double-reed instruments (8)
**9** Pieces of playground equipment (6)
**10** Amaze (8)
**12** Over and above (5)
**13** Equipment, gear (9)
**15** Once around the course (3)
**16** Destroy or ruin (5)
**17** Not present (6)
**22** Perfect principles (6)
**24** Male relative (5)
**27** Label (3)
**28** Substitute spread for butter (9)
**31** Inheritors (5)
**32** Get coats from the houses (8)
**33** Short-legged bird (6)
**34** Illness, malady (8)
**35** Communicates by letter (6)

## DOWN

**1** Excited uncertainty (8)
**2** A rubbing between two surfaces (8)
**3** Gestured, signed (9)
**5** So ape the writer of fables (5)
**6** Clean with hard rubbing (5)
**7** Narcotic drug (6)
**8** Split, rift (6)
**11** Tropical fruit with orange flesh (6)
**14** Suddenly cancel (3)
**18** Set-up of parts working together (6)
**19** More badly behaved (9)
**20** Mischance (8)
**21** Tillers of the soil of old (8)
**23** 'Give every man thine ..., but few thy voice' (Hamlet) (3)
**25** Slaps the fishing vessels? (6)
**26** Glacial region (6)
**29** Encore (5)
**30** Articles or units on a list (5)

## ACROSS

**8** Edible fungus (8)
**9** Lustrous structures in oysters (6)
**10** Fast pace (6)
**11** Proclivity (8)
**12** Hidden, private (6)
**13** Hypotheses (8)
**15** Locality (4)
**17** Gleam intermittently (7)
**19** Asks over (7)
**22** In a position to (4)
**24** In any place (8)
**27** Large conurbations (6)
**29** Wonderful, marvellous (8)
**30** Greater in size (6)
**31** Basement (6)
**32** Swap, barter (8)

## DOWN

**1** A truce for the church minister (6)
**2** Little people (8)
**3** The sick person here hails pot (8)
**4** Emulate (7)
**5** No pegs on this substance to soak up (6)
**6** History of a working life (6)
**7** Resulting bruise from a blow to the sight organ (5,3)
**14** Greet or applaud (4)
**16** Hind part (4)
**18** Questioned or marvelled (8)
**20** Throat ornament (8)
**21** Time between (8)
**23** Sandy areas (7)
**25** Heartily, cordially (6)
**26** Exertion (6)
**28** Get-up-and-go, vitality (6)

**122**

## ACROSS

1 Heavy long-handled hammer (6)
4 Mozart or Wagner, say (8)
9 Tot bun up for a fastener (6)
10 Mended, restored (8)
12 Inaccuracy (5)
13 Obtainable (9)
15 Suitable (3)
16 Walk heavily (5)
17 Bird bred for food (6)
22 French secondary schools (6)
24 Sudden burst of flame (5)
27 Rage (3)
28 Eating, using (9)
31 Make cooler (5)
32 Stance (8)
33 Narrow strip of material for decoration (6)
34 Unravelled, stocking say (8)
35 Precious adornments (6)

## DOWN

1 Themes, topics (8)
2 Outside (8)
3 Study of the earth's surface (9)
5 Last Greek letter (5)
6 Jewel from oyster (5)
7 Low, woody perennials (6)
8 Raised bands (6)
11 Neck of a turkey (6)
14 Liquid from a squid (3)
18 Leave office (6)
19 Successful, productive (9)
20 Liable to change (8)
21 Upper limits (8)
23 Rotating mechanism (3)
25 Write carelessly (6)
26 Joined or combined (6)
29 Undo, unlace (5)
30 Empower, endow (5)

## ACROSS

**8** Orchestral music at the beginning of an opera (8)
**9** Long-necked wading birds (6)
**10** Hinder, obstruct, thwart (6)
**11** Vote to select politicians (8)
**12** Rue bin in the sultanate (6)
**13** Lawyer (8)
**15** Declare to be untrue (4)
**17** Outlying or neighbouring area (7)
**19** No longer active in work (7)
**22** Revolving spool (4)
**24** Harvest for sale rather than consumption (4,4)
**27** Most awful (6)
**29** Window for the patriot? (8)
**30** Rue (6)
**31** Staid and sober (6)
**32** Think intently and at length (8)

## DOWN

**1** New embodiment of a familiar idea (6)
**2** Malefactor (8)
**3** Christmas-time (8)
**4** Old hand, ex-service person (7)
**5** Take as true (6)
**6** Integer that can be exactly divided into another integer (6)
**7** Oil used in lamps and heaters (8)
**14** Inflatable covering (4)
**16** Monetary unit (4)
**18** Taken thus, suddenly and unexpectedly (8)
**20** Imaginary place of great wealth and opportunity (2,6)
**21** Pour water on (8)
**23** Typical example, prototype (7)
**25** Laugh of a donkey (3-3)
**26** Smelt strongly (6)
**28** Detective (6)

**124**

## ACROSS

8 Final, extreme (8)
9 Not harmed (6)
10 Viewpoint (6)
11 Unlawful entry (8)
12 Protective covering for battle (6)
13 Imaginative or amorous (8)
15 Individual unit in a list (4)
17 Flat highland (7)
19 Disregarded (7)
22 Relative speed (4)
24 Bases, posts (8)
27 Light meal (6)
29 Percussion instrument (8)
30 Diffident, uncertain (6)
31 Fractured, damaged (6)
32 Auditoriums (8)

## DOWN

1 Nearer in space or time (6)
2 Take to it if the ship is sinking (8)
3 Unicellular life-form (8)
4 Principal film or non-news article (7)
5 Use Mum in the repository (6)
6 No chip on this composer's shoulder (6)
7 High standing, influence (8)
14 Leave out (4)
16 Bend, move round (4)
18 Is this writing art, Riley? (8)
20 Expressive movements (8)
21 Contrary, antithetical (8)
23 Declares to be true (7)
25 Parallel rails (6)
26 Air-powered keyboard instruments (6)
28 High nests of birds of prey (6)

## ACROSS

1 Feeling of heat (6)
4 Uttering (8)
9 Mollusc that clings to rocks (6)
10 Conflict with (8)
12 Is enamoured with (5)
13 Recalls from memory (9)
15 Utilisation (3)
16 'Nothing could be ... than to be in Carolina' (song) (5)
17 Great coolness and composure under strain (6)
22 Acquiescence (6)
24 Lax or at large (5)
27 Organ of sight (3)
28 Examples, illustrations (9)
31 It brings about an effect (5)
32 Unlikely, questionable (8)
33 Spheres (6)
34 Not extreme (8)
35 It's surrounded by water (6)

## DOWN

1 All undomesticated creatures (8)
2 Getting rid of (8)
3 Holds dear, prizes (9)
5 Transparent 3-sided object that separates light into colours (5)
6 Arouse to a sense of danger (5)
7 A serial state (6)
8 Oily or smeared with fat (6)
11 Wrinkle (6)
14 Self (3)
18 Most up-to-date (6)
19 Small particles of matter (9)
20 Capital of South Carolina (8)
21 Turned inside out or upside down (8)
23 Can be mortal or venial (3)
25 Accumulated learning, sagacity (6)
26 Put out, a statement say (6)
29 At a later time (5)
30 Enumerate (5)

## ACROSS

**8** Odd, funny (8)
**9** Power to entice or attract (6)
**10** Find US sari in the country (6)
**11** Highest rankings in the armed forces (3,5)
**12** Older (6)
**13** Words that can be interchanged with others (8)
**15** Resound (4)
**17** Means of communication (7)
**19** Gaping open (7)
**22** Abreast of, au fait with (2,2)
**24** More attractive (8)
**27** One in time can save nine (6)
**29** Surmising (8)
**30** Equip, endue (6)
**31** Five-cent piece (6)
**32** Administrative units of government (8)

## DOWN

**1** Sanctuary, asylum (6)
**2** Interrogative sentence (8)
**3** Gas eider to differ (8)
**4** Rib this nationality (7)
**5** Make moist (6)
**6** Old two-shilling piece (6)
**7** He's a first-year undergraduate (8)
**14** String and reel toy (2-2)
**16** Evidence that helps to solve a problem (4)
**18** Suffering or privation (8)
**20** Responded (8)
**21** Pest (8)
**23** Sequence of instructions for computer (7)
**25** Stems of trees (6)
**26** Tapering piece of ice (6)
**28** Young cattle (6)

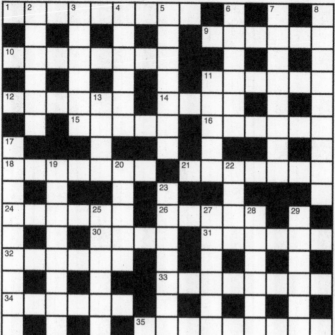

## ACROSS

1 Joy, well-being (9)
9 Ottawa is the capital city (6)
10 Uttered a loud, high-pitched cry (8)
11 Arrived on shore (6)
12 Drenched, soaked (6)
14 Level (4)
15 Alleviates (5)
16 Wide-ranging (6)
18 Akin, associated (7)
21 Okay (7)
24 Where something originates (6)
26 Room on board (5)
30 Against (4)
31 Asiatic wild ass (6)
32 Shouts of approval (6)
33 Unnecessary and unwarranted (8)
34 Drumbeat, or design on skin (6)
35 Becoming aware (9)

## DOWN

2 Grapnel for holding boats (6)
3 Satisfy, gratify (6)
4 People who move about according to the seasons (6)
5 Sorrow, unhappiness (7)
6 Cuban capital (6)
7 Acting as attendant for golfer (8)
8 Contender (9)
11 Straight, even (5)
13 ... of Eden (John Steinbeck) (4)
17 Bring a criminal action (9)
19 Someone honoured for great achievements (8)
20 These are odds, strangely (5)
22 Precipitation (4)
23 Branch of study of the physical world (7)
25 Large bottle for corrosive liquids (6)
27 Of the North wind (6)
28 Planes go awry in Italian port (6)
29 Period of instruction (6)

## ACROSS

**8** Separate and distinct (8)
**9** XXX (6)
**10** Small finch (6)
**11** Archetype (8)
**12** Race for amusement (3,3)
**13** Masses of frozen water (8)
**15** Attractive or cunning (4)
**17** Bore cot out in autumn (7)
**19** Missives (7)
**22** Aquatic bird (4)
**24** Scare (8)
**27** Get-up-and-go, vitality (6)
**29** Sun or rain shade (8)
**30** Names, of books say (6)
**31** Employ (6)
**32** Moves ahead, goes forward (8)

## DOWN

**1** Environmental condition, surrounding (6)
**2** Outline or synopsis of a play (8)
**3** Grammatical string of words (8)
**4** Put into, bank account say (7)
**5** Hit (6)
**6** Godlike (6)
**7** More curious or unfamiliar (8)
**14** Small room for a monk (4)
**16** Exhort, press (4)
**18** Ritual on a solemn occasion (8)
**20** Choice by vote (8)
**21** Areas of operations (8)
**23** Sad, discontented (7)
**25** Teutonic (6)
**26** Higher in stature (6)
**28** Covetous, avaricious (6)

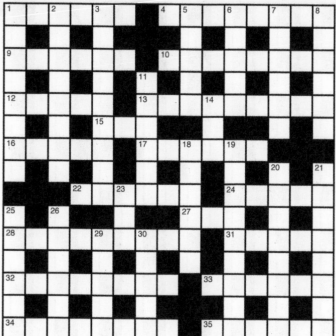

**129**

## ACROSS

**1** Moves stealthily (6)
**4** They train to compete in sports (8)
**9** Writer (6)
**10** Devilment (8)
**12** Freight (5)
**13** Strong fences for defence (9)
**15** Flying saucer (3)
**16** Including everything (3,2)
**17** Metal for the policeman? (6)
**22** Smaller in size or amount (6)
**24** It converts sounds into signals (5)
**27** Sense organ (3)
**28** Inedible fungus (9)
**31** Occasion (5)
**32** Head of the board of directors (8)
**33** Handy (6)
**34** Ceremonial staffs (8)
**35** Grown-ups (6)

## DOWN

**1** Fuel for the barbecue (8)
**2** Wholly and completely (8)
**3** Articulate in a certain way (9)
**5** Examination of evidence in court (5)
**6** Clusters of hair (5)
**7** Chinese secret societies (6)
**8** Most protected (6)
**11** Distinctive periods in history (6)
**14** Mischievous fairy (3)
**18** Wholly, unconditionally (6)
**19** Stated, uttered (9)
**20** Potent, forceful (8)
**21** Cold-blooded vertebrates (8)
**23** Habitual drunkard (3)
**25** These and stones may break my bones (6)
**26** The front of a building (6)
**29** Strap up the small fish (5)
**30** Chicago's main airport (5)

**ACROSS**

**8** Think deeply (8)
**9** Total, sum (6)
**10** Mighty, powerful (6)
**11** The best medicine, it's said (8)
**12** More contiguous (6)
**13** '..., and ..., and ... / Creeps in this petty pace from day to day / to the last syllable of recorded time' (Macbeth) (8)
**15** Overt (4)
**17** Hair cleaner (7)
**19** Conveyed, toted (7)
**22** Aces (4)
**24** Involving more than one (8)
**27** Free from risk (6)
**29** Stretched or forced to the limit (8)
**30** Mobile (6)
**31** Explosion of air from the nose (6)
**32** Magnified (8)

**DOWN**

**1** Glass or plastic vessel (6)
**2** Metric unit (8)
**3** Large Australian mammal (8)
**4** Filled to satisfaction (7)
**5** Space containing no matter (6)
**6** Parent to her Tom (6)
**7** Paper casing (8)
**14** On one occasion (4)
**16** Small lake (4)
**18** Visiting as a ghost (8)
**20** Rally (8)
**21** Healing (8)
**23** Annoys the pointed implements? (7)
**25** Tarred the dealer badly (6)
**26** Attached with pointed piece of metal (6)
**28** Old cooking appliances (6)

## ACROSS

8 Inside part (8)
9 Complied with instructions (6)
10 Preserved trace of an ancient plant or animal (6)
11 Many, multifarious (8)
12 Dive or throw into (6)
13 Walking with regular steps (8)
15 Five- or six-pointed figure (4)
17 Sports contestant (7)
19 Bolts (7)
22 Photograph used in medical diagnosis (1-3)
24 Distinct, discrete (8)
27 Cars (6)
29 Make arrangements for (8)
30 Sounds associated with break-ins (6)
31 Uncover (6)
32 Students or learned people (8)

## DOWN

1 Unfurl (6)
2 Private (8)
3 Most ridiculous (8)
4 Drag man to a relative (7)
5 The first mentioned of two (6)
6 Try to locate (6)
7 Succession, order (8)
14 Tract (4)
16 Written words (4)
18 Theses, possibilities (8)
20 Compassion, fellow-feeling (8)
21 Really (8)
23 Go backwards (7)
25 Flabbergasted (6)
26 Eagerly or greedily (6)
28 Mention, comment (6)

**ACROSS**

**8** Border (8)
**9** Fastener for millinery (6)
**10** Goat with long silky hair (6)
**11** Painstakingly careful (8)
**12** Wine-store (6)
**13** Naming the letters (8)
**15** Sound reflection (4)
**17** Member of the military (7)
**19** Very quickly (7)
**22** Trees of the genus Quercus (4)
**24** Progresses (8)
**27** Poorly (6)
**29** Marked by diversity or difference (8)
**30** High noon (6)
**31** Account, story (6)
**32** Naturally gifted (8)

**DOWN**

**1** Sleep-like state (6)
**2** Unfurled (8)
**3** Rage dies if you differ (8)
**4** Is birth necessary for nationality? (7)
**5** Select (6)
**6** Saunter (6)
**7** Line between opposite corners (8)
**14** Pig meat (4)
**16** Harvest, yield (4)
**18** Ran a machine (8)
**20** Congregation (8)
**21** Event, occurrence (8)
**23** Prospects (7)
**25** Newspaper head (6)
**26** Paths of celestial bodies (6)
**28** Inclined, tilted (6)

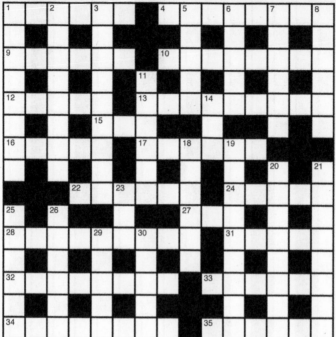

**133**

## ACROSS

1 Stand up to (6)
4 Fastened together (8)
9 Spectres, wraiths (6)
10 In a resentful manner (8)
12 Straight edge for drawing lines (5)
13 Fondness, tenderness (9)
15 Goal, object (3)
16 Occurrence (5)
17 Hairy growths (6)
22 Toward land from the sea (6)
24 Piece of cutlery (5)
27 Groove or furrow (3)
28 Helping to release pent-up emotions (9)
31 To the time that (5)
32 Not a member of the group (8)
33 Bad oar on ship (6)
34 Person holding official authorisation (8)
35 Fully developed animals (6)

## DOWN

1 Considered or deemed to be (8)
2 Take on, blame say (8)
3 Soaks (9)
5 Robber (5)
6 Loft (5)
7 Showing extreme courage (6)
8 Removing the moisture (6)
11 Tall woody plant (6)
14 Part of corn (3)
18 Abstract, synopsis (6)
19 Changed the set arrangement or made uneasy (9)
20 Loft a lob in this game (8)
21 Comprises (8)
23 Belonging to a female (3)
25 Round shape formed by a series of concentric circles (6)
26 Inactive, motionless (6)
29 Foreign (5)
30 In that location (5)

## ACROSS

**1** Dealt with, moved things along (9)
**9** The lowest part (6)
**10** Seeming to be but not necessarily so (8)
**11** Disappear (6)
**12** Employment history (6)
**14** Midday (4)
**15** Sedate, sober (5)
**16** Editions (6)
**18** Possibly but not certainly (7)
**21** Ships or containers (7)
**24** Fight back (6)
**26** Not the same one (5)
**30** You, of old (4)
**31** Quantity (6)
**32** Violent pangs of suffering (6)
**33** Glittered (8)
**34** For making stitches (6)
**35** Helper, aide (9)

## DOWN

**2** Say or do again (6)
**3** Makes sore by friction (6)
**4** Spanish mountain range (6)
**5** Stretches out over a distance (7)
**6** 'Friends, ..., countrymen, lend me your ears' (Julius Caesar) (6)
**7** Perspective, stance (8)
**8** Accentuate (9)
**11** Power of speaking (5)
**13** Sicilian volcano (4)
**17** Directing or controlling, machinery say (9)
**19** Held back or set aside (8)
**20** Ways, routes (5)
**22** Stalk, shank (4)
**23** Series of lessons (7)
**25** Pilfers (6)
**27** The Aloha State (6)
**28** Self-propelled firework or missile (6)
**29** Obscured (6)

## ACROSS

**1** Spite, venom (6)
**4** Aloft, flying (8)
**9** Clear and bright (6)
**10** Bottle with a stopper for wine (8)
**12** Happen as a result (5)
**13** Amuse or take into consideration (9)
**15** Expression of amazement (3)
**16** Cuban folk dance (5)
**17** Adulterated, dirty (6)
**22** Category for sports teams (6)
**24** Large group of fish (5)
**27** Humour or mental capacity (3)
**28** Pasta from tight peas (9)
**31** Inert gas that occurs naturally (5)
**32** Provoking or stirring up (8)
**33** Brownish yellow substance used as pigment (6)
**34** 12-month-old racehorse (8)
**35** U-shaped wire to fasten papers together (6)

## DOWN

**1** Fruit from burry elm? (8)
**2** Single amounts of money (4,4)
**3** Sudden rise in the rate of law-breaking (5,4)
**5** Incompetent and ineffectual (5)
**6** Is the ex-politician a Libra? (5)
**7** Stems of palms used for furniture (6)
**8** Travelling about or going astray (6)
**11** Stitching (6)
**14** Old European currency unit (3)
**18** Does it weep, this bird? (6)
**19** Control, restriction (9)
**20** Period of unusually low temperatures (4,4)
**21** Stretch, pull (8)
**23** One or 11 in cards (3)
**25** Turn to bone with age (6)
**26** Board over house or shop (6)
**29** Travellers' rest (5)
**30** It fits into a mortise (5)

## ACROSS

**8** Notwithstanding (8)
**9** South American river (6)
**10** Relating to teeth (6)
**11** Scope for freedom of action (8)
**12** Armour for the head (6)
**13** Membranes that vibrate to sound (8)
**15** Formerly Persia (4)
**17** Crater in the earth's crust (7)
**19** Nurture, sustain (7)
**22** Coil (4)
**24** Person one doesn't know (8)
**27** Burnish (6)
**29** Bowl or pond dweller (8)
**30** Put one's name to (6)
**31** Alloy of copper and tin (6)
**32** No lariat for the logical (8)

## DOWN

**1** It covers the arm (6)
**2** Metrical (8)
**3** News report (8)
**4** Lace she found in London area (7)
**5** Light, teasing repartee (6)
**6** Gait between a trot and a gallop (6)
**7** Decries (8)
**14** ... Domini, AD (4)
**16** Actor's part (4)
**18** Alfresco (8)
**20** Facing (8)
**21** Institution to express belief in a divine power (8)
**23** Clump of fruit trees (7)
**25** Attaching (6)
**26** Attained, earned (6)
**28** Move up and down on the plaything (6)

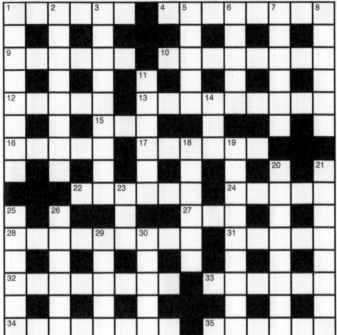

**ACROSS**

**1** Consented (6)
**4** Convene (8)
**9** Branch of the security forces (6)
**10** Well-known (8)
**12** Throw a rope to the show (5)
**13** Litter for ill people (9)
**15** Frozen water (3)
**16** Part of milk (5)
**17** Very distant (3-3)
**22** Mature people (6)
**24** Respond (5)
**27** Greek island (3)
**28** Brought to a destination (9)
**31** Desire strongly (5)
**32** Lacking knowledge or skill (8)
**33** Expression of intention to harm (6)
**34** Concluded from evidence (8)
**35** Relating to milk (6)

**DOWN**

**1** Draw near (8)
**2** Alleviated, eased (8)
**3** Cried out (9)
**5** Step (5)
**6** Be alive (5)
**7** Shining, sunny or clever (6)
**8** Inaccuracies (6)
**11** Serving a purpose (6)
**14** The conscious self (3)
**18** Dwell (6)
**19** A frosty Hi to the shrub (9)
**20** Seeming real but not (8)
**21** Mesmerising (8)
**23** Employ (3)
**25** Advancing sideways (6)
**26** It revolves around the sun (6)
**29** Piece of poetry (5)
**30** Tract of grassy land for livestock (5)

## ACROSS

**1** Showed pleasure (6)
**5** In short supply (6)
**10** Satisfactory, ok (7)
**11** Neck of land between two seas (7)
**12** Single thing (4)
**13** Jokes, japes (5)
**15** Disparaging remark (4)
**17** Diffident (3)
**19** Devices to connect computers to telephone lines (6)
**21** Cure-all potion (6)
**22** Childish, immature (7)
**23** Lessen the strength of (6)
**25** Drum and kitchen utensil (6)
**28** Scottish mountain (3)
**30** Friendly nation (4)
**31** Closing sections of musical compositions (5)
**32** Bullets, say, in short (4)
**35** Designate for a specific purpose (7)
**36** Sudden inclination (7)
**37** Wind in a spiral (6)
**38** Speech in praise (6)

## DOWN

**2** Espoused (7)
**3** Written records of voyages (4)
**4** Obligations, responsibilities (6)
**5** Evasive, devious (6)
**6** Prefix for against (4)
**7** Complicated in structure (7)
**8** It cleans by suction (6)
**9** Loan shark (6)
**14** Avoided dealing with (7)
**16** Urge or force to action (5)
**18** Haemorrhage (5)
**20** Source of light and heat (3)
**21** Large deer (3)
**23** Seal we turn into a mammal (6)
**24** Hypersensitive reaction to certain substances (7)
**26** Delay between actions (4-3)
**27** Short-range guided missile (6)
**28** Turf accountant (6)
**29** Aboriginal (6)
**33** Founder of nihilism (4)
**34** Translucent gem (4)

**ACROSS**

1 Build, make (9)
9 Document granting sole rights to an invention (6)
10 Utter, not limited (8)
11 Godlike (6)
12 Said (6)
14 Stately aquatic bird (4)
15 The more of this, the less speed sometimes (5)
16 Assess or criticise (6)
18 Performance by a soloist (7)
21 Sad reds live here (7)
24 Quality that results from light reflection (6)
26 Kings of the jungle (5)
30 Wide padded seat (4)
31 Character, esteem (6)
32 Scandinavian kingdom (6)
33 Way of thinking about an issue (8)
34 Productivity (6)
35 Church officer in charge of sacred objects (9)

**DOWN**

2 Trajectories (6)
3 Unruffled (6)
4 Charges of ammunition (6)
5 Foods prepared from the pressed curd of milk (7)
6 Of the sea (6)
7 Known for certain (8)
8 In different circumstances (9)
11 Made so bold (5)
13 90 degrees on the compass (4)
17 Exactness, sharpness (9)
19 Accumulates, collates (8)
20 Protective garment (5)
22 Finished or ended (4)
23 Southern American state (7)
25 Effective (6)
27 Rhetorician (6)
28 Sudden forceful flows (6)
29 Sports arenas (6)

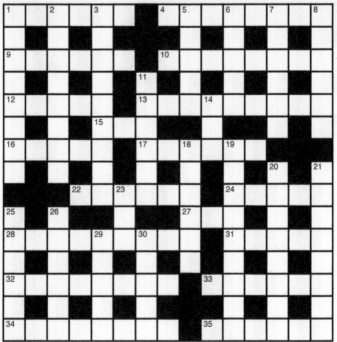

## ACROSS

**1** Most pleasant (6)
**4** Range of colours (8)
**9** Hold back, slow progress (6)
**10** Named, called (8)
**12** Acute anxiety about oneself (5)
**13** Oracle sat on this stairway (9)
**15** 4-wheeled vehicle (3)
**16** Third planet from the sun (5)
**17** Hinged joints (6)
**22** Muddles, confuses (6)
**24** Theatrical work (5)
**27** Hostelry (3)
**28** Exposed, revealed (9)
**31** Noteworthy happening (5)
**32** Projecting through the air (8)
**33** Recommend (6)
**34** Settled a dispute (8)
**35** Rotating series (6)

## DOWN

**1** Recounted (8)
**2** Group or class (8)
**3** Extended, one's limbs perhaps (9)
**5** Overwhelming feeling of fear and anxiety (5)
**6** Sensation of cold or dread (5)
**7** Give a report (6)
**8** Contemporary, up-to-date (6)
**11** Grains as food (6)
**14** Gone, past (3)
**18** Next to (6)
**19** '...'s child is full of woe' (9)
**20** Fabric, cloth (8)
**21** Companions or associates (8)
**23** Female deer (3)
**25** Solid fat churned from milk (6)
**26** Gains points (6)
**29** I or O, say (5)
**30** Remove soap with clean water (5)

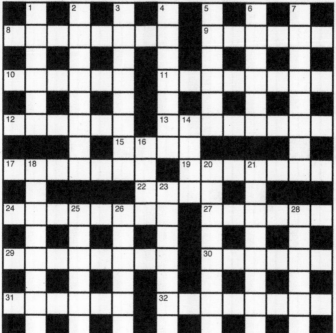

## ACROSS

**8** Biting insect (8)
**9** Entertained, diverted (6)
**10** Of genetically different groups (6)
**11** Holder of office in government or church (8)
**12** University award (6)
**13** Cord worn around the neck to hold a whistle or nautical ties (8)
**15** Celestial body of hot gases (4)
**17** Contaminate (7)
**19** Calamity, disaster (7)
**22** Hurry (4)
**24** Sleeping areas (8)
**27** Uttered a sudden loud cry (6)
**29** Dependable, loyal (8)
**30** Horny ends of some animals' feet (6)
**31** Recall the cold room (6)
**32** Trembled with the cold (8)

## DOWN

**1** Place, situate (6)
**2** Rodent with a bushy tail (8)
**3** Most foolish (8)
**4** Group of symbols to solve a problem (7)
**5** Large, heavy gun (6)
**6** It was once one of the 15 soviet states (6)
**7** Relied (8)
**14** Poetry, music, painting etc. (4)
**16** Limited period of time (4)
**18** Controls machinery (8)
**20** Lilting, regular (8)
**21** Went at a fast gait (8)
**23** Having no beneficial function (7)
**25** Noisy type of snake (6)
**26** Presents for acceptance (6)
**28** Soccer number (6)

## ACROSS

**8** Head of a US state (8)
**9** Ted or I could bring out a newspaper (6)
**10** Malignant growth and sign of the zodiac (6)
**11** Callers (8)
**12** Fearful, timid person (6)
**13** Abandoned (8)
**15** Water pitcher (4)
**17** English, Scottish or Welsh (7)
**19** Attack physically (7)
**22** Old name for Gaelic (4)
**24** Utmost or extreme (8)
**27** Looking at (6)
**29** Container for magnetic tape (8)
**30** It's worn as protection against evil (6)
**31** Life-forms assumed to exist beyond Earth (6)
**32** They were roaring in the last century (8)

## DOWN

**1** Spud (6)
**2** The navy that's commercial (8)
**3** Trespasses (8)
**4** Furnish with (7)
**5** Stops (6)
**6** Resist the relation (6)
**7** A push button for admittance (8)
**14** Epochs, ages (4)
**16** Sharpen, appetite say (4)
**18** Trustworthy (8)
**20** Repeatedly changed between two positions (8)
**21** Satisfactory, enough, (8)
**23** Gives in, softens (7)
**25** Sent out, an announcement say (6)
**26** Creative person (6)
**28** Necessary (6)

**143**

## ACROSS

1 He developed a radiation counter (6)
4 Seep through (8)
9 Noteworthy happenings (6)
10 Unlawfully killed (8)
12 Vapour of boiling water (5)
13 Sets of letters (9)
15 ...-Margret, ... Blyth (old film stars) (3)
16 'She walks in beauty, like the ...' (Byron) (5)
17 Having beautiful natural landscape (6)
22 Episodes of pastoral or romantic charm (6)
24 Area of endeavour (5)
27 Supply with weapons (3)
28 Type of German sausage (9)
31 Path of one body revolving around another (5)
32 Improbable (8)
33 Move out of (6)
34 Absence of light (8)
35 Natural ability (6)

## DOWN

1 Conjecturing, surmising (8)
2 Large masses floating in polar regions (8)
3 Calculated approximately (9)
5 Fit out (5)
6 Mythological Greek princess (5)
7 Concurred (6)
8 Firstborn (6)
11 ... and Gretel (fairy story) (6)
14 Domestic fowl (3)
18 Poor-quality substitute (6)
19 Beloved woman (9)
20 Thin pliable sheet of body tissue (8)
21 Most distant (8)
23 Pronoun (3)
25 Preposterous, nonsensical (6)
26 Seafarer (6)
29 Arouse from sleep (5)
30 Regulations, precepts (5)

## ACROSS

**8** Conversant with the witch's cat? (8)
**9** Appalling (6)
**10** Be owned (6)
**11** Ordinarily (8)
**12** Not productive (6)
**13** Formally arranged gatherings (8)
**15** Game played on opponent's ground (4)
**17** Mathematical expression (7)
**19** Empowered (7)
**22** Travel on the back of animal (4)
**24** Least complex or complicated (8)
**27** Numbers of associated individuals (6)
**29** It forms energy from moving air (8)
**30** Upper garment (1-5)
**31** Coppelia, say (6)
**32** Protecting or concealing (8)

## DOWN

**1** Pale MA has a girl's name (6)
**2** Approximately 2.2lbs (8)
**3** Connecting two nonadjacent corners (8)
**4** Rang dam about a relative (7)
**5** Refuse all food (6)
**6** The 50th state (6)
**7** Discussion between two people (8)
**14** Observed (4)
**16** Armed conflicts (4)
**18** Nail giro to the prototype (8)
**20** Less than zero (8)
**21** Siblings (8)
**23** Are the letters as licit? (7)
**25** Foot levers (6)
**26** Is extant (6)
**28** Mother or father (6)

## ACROSS

**8** Colourful baboon (8)
**9** Bawdy, crude (6)
**10** Discord, conflict (6)
**11** Ensnaring (8)
**12** Of bears (6)
**13** Flying machine (8)
**15** Knock senseless (4)
**17** Decorate a dish (7)
**19** For the most part (7)
**22** Resound (4)
**24** Pensive piece of piano music (8)
**27** By and large (6)
**29** Without curve or bend (8)
**30** Latest, most novel (6)
**31** Symptom of hay fever (6)
**32** Regarding highly (8)

## DOWN

**1** Singer in a synagogue (6)
**2** Increase, augmentation (8)
**3** Radio (8)
**4** A flat highland (7)
**5** Fix, mend (6)
**6** Dealer in clothing (6)
**7** Grateful (8)
**14** Unit of length (4)
**16** At that time (4)
**18** Taking on as one's own (8)
**20** Words that sound the same but have different meanings (8)
**21** Towards the rising sun (8)
**23** Key, pivotal (7)
**25** One who buys and sells (6)
**26** Craggy, sturdy (6)
**28** Misplacing (6)

## ACROSS

1 Symbol of disgrace or infamy (6)
5 Sags, wilts (6)
10 Clever or deceptive device (7)
11 Optical illusions (7)
12 Test, in short (4)
13 Partially melted snow (5)
15 Wise men, visitors to Bethlehem (4)
17 Liquid for writing (3)
19 Workshop of metal worker (6)
21 Small ball of shot (6)
22 Exercises to enhance respiratory efficiency (7)
23 Candied fruit (6)
25 Study of moral values and rules (6)
28 Animal doctor, in short (3)
30 Eat the main meal (4)
31 Ancient city destroyed by God for wickedness (5)
32 Catch sight of (4)
35 If such a strange plant could be a showy flower (7)
36 Entourage, retinue (7)
37 Official order (6)
38 Types of stockings (6)

## DOWN

2 Mini tap for a large drum (7)
3 Dark and depressing (4)
4 It turns litmus blue (6)
5 Linen with a woven pattern (6)
6 Belonging to us (4)
7 Braid of hair (7)
8 Way out (6)
9 Help out (6)
14 Upright, refusing to yield (7)
16 Seat for one (5)
18 Small religious groups (5)
20 Up to the present time (3)
21 Pastry crust with filling (3)
23 Arrange systematically (6)
24 Handcuff (7)
26 Scrutinise, audit (7)
27 Ways of doing (6)
28 Journey over water (6)
29 Male feline (6)
33 Emperor of Russia (4)
34 Boast (4)

**ACROSS**

**8** Car driver (8)
**9** Boisterous and uncontrollable (6)
**10** Force, pressure (6)
**11** Gathering, in an auditorium say (8)
**12** Go back on a promise (6)
**13** Splashes liquid (8)
**15** Strange peas in a church (4)
**17** Brown animal of North America (7)
**19** Water falling in drops (7)
**22** Burden, duty (4)
**24** Collect together (8)
**27** Pulled hard (6)
**29** Part of the main floor of a theatre (8)
**30** Private instructors (6)
**31** Hellenic republic (6)
**32** Hands over (8)

**DOWN**

**1** Moody, glum (6)
**2** 'I'm looking over a ... clover' (song) (4-4)
**3** Relating to the constellations (8)
**4** US stars made the composer (7)
**5** Treeless plain in the Arctic regions (6)
**6** Fervent, impassioned (6)
**7** Elementary particle (8)
**14** Land of the Incas (4)
**16** Small body of water (4)
**18** On an upper floor (8)
**20** In a shrewd manner (8)
**21** Piece of photographic film (8)
**23** Mythological sea nymphs (7)
**25** Old Testament book telling how the Jewish queen of Persia saved her people from massacre (6)
**26** Cask, drum (6)
**28** Howlers (6)

## ACROSS

**1** Physical material (9)
**9** Injure, spoil (6)
**10** Rural settlements (8)
**11** Parameters, limits (6)
**12** Makes a noise like a duck (6)
**14** Smooth, press (4)
**15** Lord or sir, say (5)
**16** Not fertile or productive (6)
**18** Bestows (7)
**21** Unnamed, anonymous (7)
**24** 'O wild west wind, thou breath of …'s being' (Shelley) (6)
**26** Oh, let it take guests (5)
**30** Mental image (4)
**31** Hard substance covering a tooth (6)
**32** Circus performers (6)
**33** Child's play, piece of cake (8)
**34** Incidents (6)
**35** They're beyond understanding (9)

## DOWN

**2** One of a kind (6)
**3** Choose (6)
**4** Majestic month (6)
**5** Employee who deals with money (7)
**6** Tomorrow in Spain (6)
**7** Marsupial (8)
**8** Thinking coherently and logically (9)
**11** Small songbird (5)
**13** Plaything flown in the wind (4)
**17** Abrasions (9)
**19** Does intern go for the inert gas? (8)
**20** Units of money in South Africa (5)
**22** Enthusiastic (4)
**23** Keenly, acutely (7)
**25** Period of time (6)
**27** Cups, saucers etc. (3-3)
**28** Hard work (6)
**29** Exacting (6)

**149**

## ACROSS

**8** Mexican hat (8)
**9** Capacity for rational though (6)
**10** At an oblique angle (6)
**11** Move Bern in this month (8)
**12** Bathing suit for the atoll? (6)
**13** Holds pin for the small whales (8)
**15** Cut into pieces (4)
**17** Hard rock (7)
**19** Oriental (7)
**22** Circle (4)
**24** Smallest room, usually (8)
**27** Brio (6)
**29** Physical force (8)
**30** Domesticated bovine animals (6)
**31** Undergo a change (6)
**32** Internal structure of the body (8)

## DOWN

**1** Art of growing dwarf plants (6)
**2** Cut or scratch (8)
**3** Place limits on (8)
**4** Fierce wind at the tan door (7)
**5** Go on a journey (6)
**6** Sensation caused by heat (6)
**7** Device to control engine speed (8)
**14** Frank, not secret (4)
**16** In Greek mythology, lover of Leander (4)
**18** Converted property into cash (8)
**20** Businesses that serve other businesses (8)
**21** Playhouses (8)
**23** Huge, vast (7)
**25** Not solid (6)
**26** Light weights (6)
**28** Eight pints (6)

**ACROSS**

1 Study of celestial bodies (9)
9 Childless (6)
10 Joins or links (8)
11 Act, conduct oneself (6)
12 Metal bars (6)
14 Organs of hearing (4)
15 Engine (5)
16 Rooms at the top (6)
18 Where the river nears the sea (7)
21 Most profound (7)
24 Representational image (6)
26 Ludicrous act done for fun (5)
30 Car for hire (4)
31 Referring to a tiny particle (6)
32 Soft and watery, swampy (6)
33 Highly valued possession (8)
34 Scrubs (6)
35 Feigned, faked (9)

**DOWN**

2 Pieces of cutlery (6)
3 Haphazard (6)
4 Most agreeable (6)
5 Artists of consummate skill (7)
6 Most guarded (6)
7 Formal exposition (8)
8 Level, degree or magnitude (9)
11 Courageous (5)
13 Garment worn in ancient Rome (4)
17 The feeling that things will turn out badly (9)
19 Day after today (8)
20 Pass along (5)
22 Egress (4)
23 Artist's boat rope? (7)
25 Separate ones (6)
27 Least wild (6)
28 I con us into having a relative (6)
29 Ferocious (6)

## ACROSS

**8** Railcar (8)
**9** Delighted (6)
**10** Jumped forward suddenly (6)
**11** Hitting hard (8)
**12** Higher in rank (6)
**13** Keep up repairs (8)
**15** Ready for business (4)
**17** Hair cleaner (7)
**19** Brass instrument (7)
**22** Lack of difficulty (4)
**24** Commodities offered for sale (8)
**27** Small horses (6)
**29** Unit of a word (8)
**30** Thespians (6)
**31** Affiance (6)
**32** Conjectures (8)

## DOWN

**1** Representative type (6)
**2** Life form (8)
**3** Australian mammal (8)
**4** Small French coin (7)
**5** Traditional Japanese drama (6)
**6** Yield, amount produced (6)
**7** During the intervening period (9)
**14** Social insects (4)
**16** Versifier (4)
**18** Hastening, rushing (8)
**20** Substituted, supplanted (8)
**21** Imaginary frightening creatures (8)
**23** Facets (7)
**25** One hundred cents (6)
**26** Very strong, thick ropes made of steel wire (6)
**28** Acquired through work (6)

## ACROSS

**8** Brontosaurus, for instance (8)
**9** Aquatic or terrestrial reptile (6)
**10** Assimilate (6)
**11** Gathering of onlookers or listeners (8)
**12** Involving grief, death or destruction (6)
**13** Branch of mathematics (8)
**15** Nearly new (4)
**17** Band of broadcasting frequencies (7)
**19** Procuring (7)
**22** Emit the article (4)
**24** Even Opel have the wrapper (8)
**27** Formal march (6)
**29** Indoor shoes (8)
**30** Derivation (6)
**31** Money gained over time (6)
**32** Runs the soap tree (8)

## DOWN

**1** Prepared wood (6)
**2** Sledge (8)
**3** Cook-out (8)
**4** Plan, organise (7)
**5** Artist's workroom (6)
**6** Light wind (6)
**7** Subatomic particle (8)
**14** Perimeter (4)
**16** Small mistake (4)
**18** Dealing with (8)
**20** Hired (8)
**21** Occurring at the end (8)
**23** Stress, tautness (7)
**25** Caveat ..., let the buyer beware (6)
**26** Complied with (6)
**28** Motors (6)

**153**

## ACROSS

**8** Fleshy fungus (8)
**9** Capacity for rational thought (6)
**10** Divides lengthwise (6)
**11** Said or did again (8)
**12** The nationality in a manger (6)
**13** Drapes (8)
**15** Mark left on healed tissue (4)
**17** Area around the altar (7)
**19** Movement to express something (7)
**22** Mental impression (4)
**24** It may contain a letter (8)
**27** Indeed (6)
**29** Of greater rank or quality (8)
**30** A turn at batting (6)
**31** Defeated (6)
**32** A professional, may be civil or electronic (8)

## DOWN

**1** Imperial colour (6)
**2** The officer has an arm chain (8)
**3** Hogwash (8)
**4** Continent (7)
**5** Suitable, right (6)
**6** Tropical fruit (6)
**7** Head of a US state (8)
**14** Exhort, press (4)
**16** Piece of film (4)
**18** Conferred with laurels (8)
**20** Profits, incomes (8)
**21** Prepare for a competition or career (8)
**23** Measures for arcs and angles (7)
**25** Turns inside out (6)
**26** Pungent bulbs (6)
**28** Connected (6)

## ACROSS

1 Arachnid's net (6)
4 Chemistry, biology etc. (8)
9 Get away from the strange EC peas (6)
10 Programme of events (8)
12 Forbidden, proscribed (5)
13 Suite of rooms (9)
15 A longing for money? (3)
16 Gamut (5)
17 Soak, dowse (6)
22 Casual top (1-5)
24 Similar (5)
27 Laid up (3)
28 Vanish (9)
31 Go away from (5)
32 Four-fifths are under water (8)
33 As one (6)
34 Accumulated (8)
35 Received stolen goods (6)

## DOWN

1 Animate being (8)
2 It protects the spinal cord (8)
3 They hire and fire (9)
5 Hot drink (5)
6 Occasion (5)
7 Gives rise to (6)
8 Flat pieces, of cloth or paper say (6)
11 Indian leader (6)
14 Move at speed (3)
18 All (6)
19 Demanding or stimulating situation (9)
20 Exceedingly large (8)
21 Banked on (8)
23 Jump along on one foot (3)
25 Tacking on (6)
26 Prospect, view (6)
29 Bit, part (5)
30 Large bird of prey (5)

**155**

## ACROSS

8 Long-legged, graceful animal (8)
9 Hired hand in the Wild West (6)
10 Soldier at sea (6)
11 Water feature (8)
12 Loop of thread (6)
13 Metrical (8)
15 Military force (4)
17 Perform surgery (7)
19 Artificial (3-4)
22 Female relative (4)
24 Of the cardinal compass point of 0 or 360 degrees (8)
27 Racket and ball game (6)
29 You, emphatically (8)
30 Fully developed (6)
31 Freshest (6)
32 Elected to office (8)

## DOWN

1 Is Nan fit for the child? (6)
2 Enter on an official list (8)
3 To a degree (8)
4 Act, execute (7)
5 Fill or live in (6)
6 Sample piece of cloth (6)
7 Changed or qualified (8)
14 Sacred song (4)
16 Tail-end (4)
18 Put forward for consideration (8)
20 Makes an effort (8)
21 Pecuniary (8)
23 Distinctive dress worn by members of a group (7)
25 Triads, troikas, triplets (6)
26 Occurrences (6)
28 Middle-Eastern state (6)

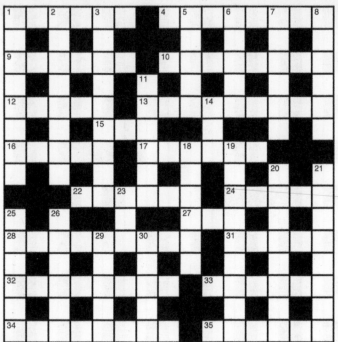

## ACROSS

**1** Adjacent to (6)
**4** ... City (novel by James Plunkett) (8)
**9** Anxious, unquiet (6)
**10** Vagabond, rover (8)
**12** Articulate (5)
**13** Stated (9)
**15** Belonging to us (3)
**16** Appetising (5)
**17** Robbed with the threat of violence (6)
**22** Do tire out the press person (6)
**24** Mistake (5)
**27** Tune, melody (3)
**28** Marking with a name (9)
**31** Lawsuits (5)
**32** Edge, boundary (8)
**33** Guarantee (6)
**34** Unexpectedly, abruptly (8)
**35** The direction a building faces (6)

## DOWN

**1** Bunches of flowers (8)
**2** Most sugary (8)
**3** Damaged irreparably, ruined (9)
**5** Hobo (5)
**6** Beyond normal limits (5)
**7** Group of words without a verb (6)
**8** Prolonged abusive speech (6)
**11** Authorise (6)
**14** Small piece of cloth (3)
**18** For storing vehicles (6)
**19** Muscle movements to promote fitness (9)
**20** It's measured in pascals (8)
**21** Expectation (8)
**23** Under the weather (3)
**25** Escarpments (6)
**26** Out of the country (6)
**29** Unit of liquid measure (5)
**30** Perfect model (5)

## ACROSS

**8** Member of an irregular armed force (8)
**9** Frame with wire and beads for counting (6)
**10** Farm tool for cutting furrows (6)
**11** Reduce (8)
**12** Word that adds information about another (6)
**13** Firedogs (8)
**15** Threshold (4)
**17** Follow as a model (7)
**19** They're in the middle (7)
**22** Puts a question (4)
**24** Arrange by categories (8)
**27** Loving touch (6)
**29** Boeing 747, say (8)
**30** Pale and wan (6)
**31** Brief look (6)
**32** Attend to the needs of others (8)

## DOWN

**1** Early Greek geometrician (6)
**2** Contentious debate (8)
**3** Set of letters (8)
**4** This accessory had bang (7)
**5** Sour, stale (6)
**6** Work path (6)
**7** Pest, pain in the neck (8)
**14** A hard one shows some nerve (4)
**16** Unable to hear (4)
**18** Increase, procreate (8)
**20** Doing a bunk (8)
**21** Indefatigable (8)
**23** Arrangements of units that function together (7)
**25** Boxing match attendant (6)
**26** Visual or mental representations (6)
**28** Black eye (6)

**158**

## ACROSS

**8** Blood-sucking fly (8)
**9** Veiled (6)
**10** Robert Ballagh, say (6)
**11** Rejoined (8)
**12** Accuse formally (6)
**13** First-placed in a competition (8)
**15** Hose for the foot (4)
**17** Come to know (7)
**19** Set free (7)
**22** District (4)
**24** Small amount of liquid causing dampness (8)
**27** ... and Hum (U2) (6)
**29** The killing of a king (8)
**30** Mean to (6)
**31** Unpredictably changeable (6)
**32** Makes a proposal (8)

## DOWN

**1** The Press, the ... estate (6)
**2** Arboreal rodent (8)
**3** Anguish (8)
**4** Leaves for smoking (7)
**5** Sing US airs badly in the country (6)
**6** Dead to the world (6)
**7** Matures (8)
**14** In this place (4)
**16** Perceive sound (4)
**18** Mysterious to all but a chosen few (8)
**20** Remunerations (8)
**21** Authorised (8)
**23** Backtrack (7)
**25** Pieces of wood (6)
**26** Joined as one (6)
**28** Distance from end to end (6)

## ACROSS

1 Groups of birds or sheep (6)
4 Tooth doctors (8)
9 Allotted amount (6)
10 Imaginative (8)
12 Would 'e rail against the spirit in The Tempest? (5)
13 In the direction of Greenland (9)
15 Woodland fairy (3)
16 Fearful expectation (5)
17 Devices to signal danger (6)
22 Demises (6)
24 Double (5)
27 ...dunnit, detective story (3)
28 Severe tropical cyclone (9)
31 Frameworks of torture (5)
32 Of any kind at all (8)
33 State (6)
34 Unsettled (8)
35 Beneficial (6)

## DOWN

1 Sends, dispatches (8)
2 Acquired (8)
3 The result of learning (9)
5 Blunder, slip (5)
6 Impart skills (5)
7 Helical (6)
8 Calm and constant (6)
11 Small baby (6)
14 Old salt or liquid from coal (3)
18 Reply (6)
19 M1 and M50 (9)
20 Impishness (8)
21 One's own business (8)
23 Turn car in a circle (3)
25 Short downpour (6)
26 Publications and instruments (6)
29 Standard of excellence (5)
30 Territories (5)

## ACROSS

**1** Fatty or oily substance (6)
**4** Prison sentence for breakfast? (8)
**9** Sell goods abroad (6)
**10** Lift to reveal (8)
**12** Locomotive (5)
**13** Emphasise, stress importance (9)
**15** Deity (3)
**16** Loud or unpleasant sound (5)
**17** Bolted, sprinted (6)
**22** The thing, reflexively (6)
**24** Shout in approval (5)
**27** Put into service (3)
**28** Adornments, decorations (9)
**31** Jaunty jazz music (5)
**32** One's uniqueness (8)
**33** Ability to see (6)
**34** Drug tree for Hamlet's mother (8)
**35** Wheat or oats, say (6)

## DOWN

**1** Words of salutation (8)
**2** Stress, accentuation (8)
**3** Most powerful (9)
**5** Lubricated (5)
**6** Large, natural stream (5)
**7** Small, particular part (6)
**8** Merited through work (6)
**11** Small pool of rainwater (6)
**14** Break bread (3)
**18** Waste, garbage (6)
**19** Beyond normal limits (9)
**20** As practised by a GP (8)
**21** Not derived from Riga lion (8)
**23** Female pronoun (3)
**25** Tedious (6)
**26** Make attractive or lovable (6)
**29** Alma ..., old school (5)
**30** Observed (5)

**161**

## ACROSS

**8** Carbon material from burnt wood (8)
**9** Calamitous (6)
**10** Esoteric, obscure (6)
**11** Quickly and without warning (8)
**12** Option, selection (6)
**13** Detached from others (8)
**15** Curve that spans an opening (4)
**17** Twisting wind (7)
**19** Takes exception to the things? (7)
**22** Domain (4)
**24** She sells seashells on it (8)
**27** Designs, fashions (6)
**29** List of days (8)
**30** Physical substance (6)
**31** Brown, furry rodent (6)
**32** Every year (8)

## DOWN

**1** House of worship (6)
**2** Act of bringing into being (8)
**3** Part of the face (8)
**4** Work of established excellence (7)
**5** In which to make a film or programme (6)
**6** Light-proof box with lens (6)
**7** Most idiotic (8)
**14** Footwear (4)
**16** Bellow (4)
**18** Dear poet was on the machine (8)
**20** Lowest floor (8)
**21** I pay gent of this nationality (8)
**23** Withdraw to a place of peace and quiet (7)
**25** Record cover (6)
**26** Commands these priests and nuns? (6)
**28** Smoothly, uniformly (6)

## ACROSS

**8** Adventurer in unknown regions (8)
**9** Head of nursing (6)
**10** Short, sharp knock (3-3)
**11** Provides refuge (8)
**12** Valiant (6)
**13** Came to, with strangely naked awe (8)
**15** In a position to (4)
**17** Recipe (7)
**19** Type of Greek wine (7)
**22** Flight of fancy (4)
**24** Exquisitely fine (8)
**27** Seldom (6)
**29** Care a bit, oddly, about the micro-organisms (8)
**30** Spain and Portugal (6)
**31** Sham manoeuvres to distract (6)
**32** XVIII (8)

## DOWN

**1** Breathe out (6)
**2** Shoe with a high thick sole (8)
**3** Disapproving (8)
**4** Quartz glass (7)
**5** Tiny one-celled animal (6)
**6** Sculptured likeness (6)
**7** Grow, sprout (8)
**14** Are in the past (4)
**16** Lure, enticement (4)
**18** See op art in theatre (8)
**20** Net income (8)
**21** Scaly reptiles (8)
**23** Periods of 10 years (7)
**25** Concentrating, absorbed (6)
**26** Side to side (6)
**28** Hang about, with 25dn perhaps (6)

**ACROSS**

**8** Auld ... ..., the good old days (8)
**9** European city for New Year's Day concert (6)
**10** Seasoning and vegetable (6)
**11** Yearly (8)
**12** Questioning (6)
**13** Fidgety, uneasy (8)
**15** Posing no difficulty (4)
**17** Inclining, slanting (7)
**19** Fervid (7)
**22** Goals (4)
**24** Scatter, disseminate (8)
**27** Safe, protected (6)
**29** News journalist (8)
**30** Air, tune (6)
**31** Surface for projection of pictures (6)
**32** Picked out (8)

**DOWN**

**1** Auctioneers' mallets (6)
**2** Strange peaty gin drunk by this nationality? (8)
**3** H (8)
**4** Mends (7)
**5** Incidents (6)
**6** Sell to the consumer (6)
**7** Investigation of component parts (8)
**14** Leered at (4)
**16** 'Rock of ...' (hymn) (4)
**18** Proof, confirmation (8)
**20** Convocation (8)
**21** Ornamental chain (8)
**23** Most adjacent (7)
**25** For the time being, in short (3,3)
**26** Round (6)
**28** Steering mechanism (6)

## ACROSS

1 Articulate in a certain way (9)
9 Keg (6)
10 Citizen of Osaka, say (8)
11 Ordinary, usual (6)
12 Temporary suspension of business (6)
14 You, of old (4)
15 Correspondence of sounds of words (5)
16 Lifting machines and long-necked birds (6)
18 Perpetual (7)
21 Walked in shallow water (7)
24 Bad rev found in this type of word (6)
26 Dressed to these and you're well-turned-out (5)
30 Divisions of archaeological time (4)
31 Don Giovanni and Tosca (6)
32 Gift, flair (6)
33 Money left with the bank (8)
34 Say again (6)
35 Coming before (9)

## DOWN

2 Peregrinated (6)
3 More imminent (6)
4 Anxious, restless (6)
5 Brought into existence (7)
6 Act of kindness (6)
7 Lawbreaker (8)
8 Beside (9)
11 Nightcap (5)
13 Case for dealing cards (4)
17 The wine bottles have sad centre, oddly (9)
19 Evolves (8)
20 Wooden-soled 13 down (5)
22 Profound (4)
23 Having a narrow outlook (7)
25 To do with letting (6)
27 Relating to people of Scandinavia (6)
28 Appeared to be (6)
29 Brown dye (6)

**ACROSS**

**8** Precipitation (8)
**9** More than one (6)
**10** Nearly but not quite (6)
**11** Archetype (8)
**12** Show up (6)
**13** Witness (8)
**15** Unemployed (4)
**17** Flat highland (7)
**19** Midday meals (7)
**22** Put to death (4)
**24** Client (8)
**27** A score (6)
**29** Time of a particular event (8)
**30** Derided (6)
**31** Strict, harsh (6)
**32** State-wide (8)

**DOWN**

**1** Fast gait (6)
**2** Not guilty (8)
**3** They can be disease-bearers (8)
**4** Intoxicating liquor (7)
**5** Breaks apart (6)
**6** More active or engaged in work (6)
**7** Headlong, as biblical swine (8)
**14** Alexander ..., inventor of the telephone (4)
**16** Highest rank of British peer (4)
**18** Put a vessel in the water (8)
**20** Final or extreme (8)
**21** Compulsion (8)
**23** Smoothing (7)
**25** Outlined or tracked back (6)
**26** Cricket over with no runs (6)
**28** Surgical instrument used on the skull (6)

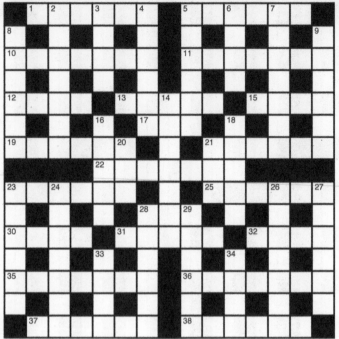

**ACROSS**

**1** Gained points (6)
**5** Young foreigner who works for a family (2,4)
**10** Days of rest (7)
**11** Announce, state (7)
**12** 'Friends, Romans, countrymen, lend me your ...' (Julius Caesar) (4)
**13** Apertures (5)
**15** Fish breath through it (4)
**17** Join by stitching (3)
**19** Revolver or six-shooter (6)
**21** Repeatedly change between two positions (6)
**22** Glib emu to be found in the country (7)
**23** End product (6)
**25** Indicated assent or recognition (6)
**28** Bashful, timid (3)
**30** Scottish dagger (4)
**31** Overturn or unsettle (5)
**32** Strange guns for the beasts (4)
**35** Plants with stinging hairs (7)
**36** Running amok as group (7)
**37** Deep openings in the earth's surface (6)
**38** Calm, staid (6)

**DOWN**

**2** Deliberately misleading fabrications (7)
**3** Quantity of paper (4)
**4** Dance venues, in short (6)
**5** Peter's brother in the New Testament (6)
**6** Written agreement between two states (4)
**7** List CIA letters at a slant (7)
**8** Slumbering (6)
**9** Companion or associate (6)
**14** Linear measurements (7)
**16** Peer of the realm (5)
**18** Citrus fruit (5)
**20** Rent out (3)
**21** Source of light and heat (3)
**23** Small, gnawing animal (6)
**24** Abrasion (7)
**26** Doctor of teeth (7)
**27** Prototype (6)
**28** Involuntary muscular contractions (6)
**29** Hankers, longs (6)
**33** European mountain range (4)
**34** Shallow part of stream to cross (4)

## ACROSS

**1** Allotted share (9)
**9** Renovate (6)
**10** Atom (8)
**11** Pillar (6)
**12** Close to (6)
**14** Storyline or piece of land (4)
**15** Sensitive fibre in the body (5)
**16** Involving the mind (6)
**18** Annual publication with weather forecasts etc. (7)
**21** Most affectionate, greetings perhaps (7)
**24** Scottish plaid (6)
**26** Test run, try-out (5)
**30** The two (4)
**31** Workers in metal (6)
**32** Showing signs of wear and tear (6)
**33** Mathematical statement that two are equal (8)
**34** Puts up, builds (6)
**35** Courier (9)

## DOWN

**2** Guide, commander (6)
**3** Procure (6)
**4** Shooter of arrows (6)
**5** Less costly (7)
**6** Far off (6)
**7** Narrow French loaf (8)
**8** Change into another language (9)
**11** Punctuation mark (5)
**13** Administrator of a college department (4)
**17** Delusions, pipe-dreams (9)
**19** ... Thatcher, Princess ... (8)
**20** Irritate, nettle (5)
**22** Wander about aimlessly (4)
**23** Let heat out of the fit person (7)
**25** Heads of orders of monks (6)
**27** Problems, concerns (6)
**28** Lend an ear (6)
**29** Tuesday before Lent (6)

**168**

### ACROSS

**8** Normal, usual (8)
**9** La Traviata and La Bohème (6)
**10** Modifying word (6)
**11** Stirred to action (8)
**12** Not moving (6)
**13** Tries one's hand at (8)
**15** Unlovely (4)
**17** Fence, say (7)
**19** Without a flaw (7)
**22** Decorates with frosting (4)
**24** Good-looking (8)
**27** Data in rows and columns (6)
**29** Softest, mildest (8)
**30** Furry growths of fungi (6)
**31** Measure for angles (6)
**32** Registering as a participant (8)

### DOWN

**1** Believe (6)
**2** Member of the board (8)
**3** Meal outdoors (8)
**4** Representative (7)
**5** Close-fitting foundation garment (6)
**6** Spiritualist (6)
**7** Imperial (8)
**14** Kind, sort (4)
**16** Stern, forbidding (4)
**18** Aroused (8)
**20** Rough calculation ties team up (8)
**21** Bury fear at this time of the year (8)
**23** Placed in the middle (7)
**25** Old fogey (6)
**26** Abided by (6)
**28** Culmination (6)

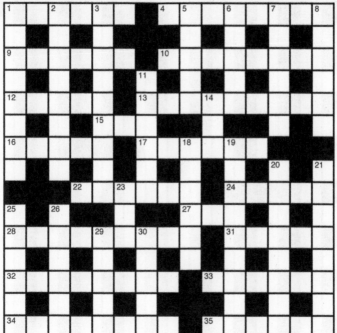

**169**

## ACROSS

**1** Change over (6)
**4** Melt, thaw (8)
**9** Baby (6)
**10** Refrained from (8)
**12** Marine substance, often forming reefs (5)
**13** Organised systems of faith (9)
**15** Utilise (3)
**16** Rate of movement (5)
**17** Leases them to artists (6)
**22** Cling, stick (6)
**24** At that place (5)
**27** Imitate the primate? (3)
**28** Basic or necessary (9)
**31** Relativity between two quantities (5)
**32** Transferring a train to another track (8)
**33** Positioned (6)
**34** ... Roosevelt (8)
**35** Pedalled (6)

## DOWN

**1** Piece of luggage (8)
**2** Passed on knowledge (8)
**3** Decided by reasoning (9)
**5** Best (5)
**6** Support for an injured arm (5)
**7** Soothing or antiseptic preparation (6)
**8** Firstborn (6)
**11** Slight wind (6)
**14** Frozen water (3)
**18** Takes without the owner's consent (6)
**19** Actually, really (9)
**20** Upright, perpendicular (8)
**21** Registered on paper or tape (8)
**23** Small, crude dwelling (3)
**25** Group of rich and fashionable folk (6)
**26** Pledge (6)
**29** Took account of (5)
**30** Close to the centre (5)

## ACROSS

**8** Come near to (8)
**9** Gained knowledge (6)
**10** Curved fruit (6)
**11** Usually (8)
**12** High-pitched and sharp (6)
**13** Most ridiculous (8)
**15** Looked at (4)
**17** Group of symbols expressing a rule (7)
**19** Ardent, sincere (7)
**22** Peruse (4)
**24** Mythical one-horned creatures (8)
**27** Become invisible (6)
**29** Gamp (8)
**30** Whimsical idea (6)
**31** Symptom of a cold (6)
**32** Parts of a whole (8)

## DOWN

**1** Scatter water about (6)
**2** Any life form (8)
**3** Equidistant and never intersecting lines (8)
**4** Since he, strangely, is this nationality (7)
**5** Two or more (6)
**6** It became a US territory in 1900 (6)
**7** Scrutiny of parts (8)
**14** Thought (4)
**16** Story and wool (4)
**18** Balm, salve (8)
**20** Moved forward (8)
**21** Last decade (8)
**23** Ran away from (7)
**25** Swerves, arches (6)
**26** Moved along on wheels (6)
**28** Cries out (6)

**171**

## ACROSS

**8** Provides sanctuary (8)
**9** Respiratory disorder (6)
**10** Debates or bickers (6)
**11** Masses of frozen water (8)
**12** Opt for (6)
**13** Expressing gratitude (8)
**15** As well as (4)
**17** A US mart on an Indonesian island? (7)
**19** Threads, fibres (7)
**22** Aspect, scene (4)
**24** Prince of the Catholic Church (8)
**27** Forcible contact between two things (6)
**29** French general and emperor (8)
**30** Young feline (6)
**31** Sat Lee down on the spiny herb (6)
**32** Most saccharine (8)

## DOWN

**1** Religious building (6)
**2** A cola mug for the eye disease (8)
**3** Suits, shirts, ties etc. (8)
**4** Casual tops (1-6)
**5** Photographic device (6)
**6** Sudden flash, of lightning say (6)
**7** Formed a mental picture (8)
**14** Flexible pipe for liquid (4)
**16** Molten rock (4)
**18** Continuing at full strength, no let-up (8)
**20** Gleams or glows intermittently (8)
**21** Craving (8)
**23** Malady, ailment (7)
**25** Half asleep (6)
**26** Does Den Lee sew with it? (6)
**28** Food made from milk (6)

## ACROSS

**8** Old mode of transport (8)
**9** Between red and blue (6)
**10** Empty (6)
**11** '... child is full of grace' (8)
**12** Respite (6)
**13** Of track and field sports (8)
**15** Unsightly (4)
**17** Mathematical rule to solve a problem (7)
**19** Residences of sovereigns (7)
**22** Particular thing (4)
**24** Laughter is said to be the best one (8)
**27** Fine layer on the surface, laid down over time (6)
**29** Worked hard and long (8)
**30** Diffident, uncertain (6)
**31** Austere, unadorned (6)
**32** Religious recluses (8)

## DOWN

**1** Harm, impair (6)
**2** Any living entity (8)
**3** Loyal and steadfast (8)
**4** Vital, pivotal (7)
**5** Oration (6)
**6** Viaduct, say (6)
**7** Period for recreation (8)
**14** Genre (4)
**16** Profit (4)
**18** Handled a deep rot (8)
**20** Bottles containing drugs for injection (8)
**21** Aesthetically pleasing (8)
**23** Children's toy bears (7)
**25** Smoothed (6)
**26** Jewish state (6)
**28** They take care of the sick (6)

## ACROSS

1 Moves upwards (6)
4 Sequestered (8)
9 Would car tic badly if it was this cold? (6)
10 Gifts (8)
12 Sixteen ounces (5)
13 Getting better (9)
15 Roadhouse (3)
16 9ac, for example (5)
17 Head of newspaper (6)
22 Elude, dodge (6)
24 Electronic communication (1-4)
27 Assistance, help (3)
28 Latent capacity, promise (9)
31 Frosting (5)
32 Volume of recipes (8)
33 Charge with a crime (6)
34 Dish out medicine (8)
35 Double-cross (6)

## DOWN

1 Successful contender (8)
2 Contained, encompassed (8)
3 Man-made structures (9)
5 Fight for a small fragment? (5)
6 Rope used to catch animals (5)
7 Is it played badly in tens? (6)
8 Signed off on the plan (6)
11 Movie-house (6)
14 Rodent (3)
18 Strange ladies have standards (6)
19 Compliance with orders (9)
20 Au fait (8)
21 To a small degree (8)
23 Child's bed (3)
25 Seasoned with aromatic ingredients (6)
26 She ... to Conquer (Goldsmith) (6)
29 Having high moral qualities (5)
30 Manacles (5)

## ACROSS

1 Circle of flowers (6)
5 Edible grains (6)
10 Less complicated or complex (7)
11 Takes a loan of (7)
12 Long, fleshy fish (4)
13 Tall structure (5)
15 You, of old (4)
17 Burgle (3)
19 Sadness, grief (6)
21 Lays away for future use (6)
22 Lower in stature (7)
23 Starchy vegetable (6)
25 Lost strength and became limp (6)
28 Early morning condensation (3)
30 Fruit of the blackthorn (4)
31 Duck with fine, soft down (5)
32 Bluish-white metallic element (4)
35 Raving, haranguing (7)
36 Lacking spirit or liveliness (7)
37 Blood poisoning (6)
38 Cried out (6)

## DOWN

2 Person who takes long walks in the country (7)
3 Fit (4)
4 Repugnance (6)
5 Spider's gossamer (6)
6 Scarce (4)
7 A different one (7)
8 Willow twigs (6)
9 Important questions or periodic publications (6)
14 Concerned, anxious, troubled (7)
16 Jobs and poles (5)
18 Long, narrow piece (5)
20 International health authority (3)
21 Make stitches (3)
23 Dough for pies (6)
24 Beat roundly (7)
26 Testimonial, expression of esteem (7)
27 Make up one's mind (6)
28 Songs of mourning (6)
29 John, founder of Methodism (6)
33 Sound of a snake (4)
34 Blue dye (4)

## ACROSS

1 Pronounced with full breathing, as the sound of H (9)
9 Cast one's mind back (6)
10 Evokes or calls forth (8)
11 Inside (6)
12 Backing group (6)
14 Regular (4)
15 Enrol, sign up (5)
16 Fully developed persons (6)
18 Accepted practices (7)
21 Decreased, cut down (7)
24 Most good-natured (6)
26 Cricket trophy (5)
30 Small, short-necked duck (4)
31 Holders, possessors (6)
32 Labourers below ground (6)
33 Wonderful, marvellous (8)
34 Offhand (6)
35 Places where people can be found (9)

## DOWN

2 Console, pacify (6)
3 Cause harm to (6)
4 Take into custody (6)
5 Oriental (7)
6 Posterior, derriere (6)
7 The religion that lit coach up (8)
8 Next to (9)
11 Interlace, strands of fabric perhaps (5)
13 'The Lord said ... Moses' (Bible) (4)
17 The study of the finances of the state (9)
19 Disease, ailment (8)
20 Pals, pairs (5)
22 Ronnie ..., Dubliner (4)
23 Greeted or honoured (7)
25 Flow of liquid (6)
27 Revulsion (6)
28 Escargots (6)
29 Reach a destination (6)

## ACROSS

**8** It's handed down from the past (8)
**9** Director of publication (6)
**10** Able to withstand attack (6)
**11** At the greatest distance (8)
**12** More adjacent (6)
**13** Ten march, unusually, on the business person (8)
**15** Overt (4)
**17** Soap for hair (7)
**19** Wandered off course (7)
**22** Fail to win (4)
**24** Sermoniser (8)
**27** Views, visions (6)
**29** Despite the fact that (8)
**30** Unlaced (6)
**31** ... de corps, team spirit (6)
**32** Woodwind instrument (8)

## DOWN

**1** Four-winged insect (6)
**2** Unit of weight (8)
**3** Would anorak go on the animal? (8)
**4** Fragrant toiletry (7)
**5** Panic (6)
**6** 12.5 per cent (6)
**7** Claptrap (8)
**14** Objectives (4)
**16** Long, round rod (4)
**18** Innocuous (8)
**20** Pool to be drawn upon when needed (8)
**21** Boxers or military planes (8)
**23** Grove of fruit trees (7)
**25** Loathes, detests (6)
**26** Inhabits as a ghost (6)
**28** Recurring melodies in a piece of music (6)

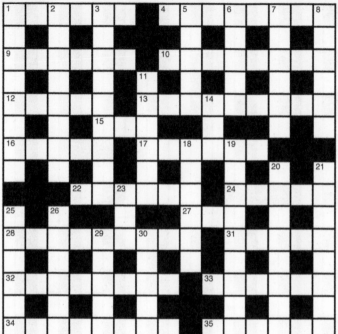

## ACROSS

**1** Crude (6)
**4** Staid Leo is kept apart from others (8)
**9** Protective covering (6)
**10** Precious stones (8)
**12** Two-masted sailing vessel (5)
**13** Electric discharge in the atmosphere (9)
**15** What person (3)
**16** Drama set to music (5)
**17** Furnish goods or services (6)
**22** City of Ukraine (6)
**24** Compassion, leniency (5)
**27** Try to do better than (3)
**28** King, queen or knave, in pack (5-4)
**31** Seasonally-flooded lowland (5)
**32** Lift to avert Leo, oddly (8)
**33** Densely-wooded area (6)
**34** Requested forcefully (8)
**35** Sentinel, look-out (6)

## DOWN

**2** Confessed (8)
**3** In the direction of Spain, say (9)
**5** Move from side to side (5)
**6** As far as something can go (5)
**7** Can tin be an acid? (6)
**8** Sketch (6)
**11** Shuts (6)
**14** Spring, skip (3)
**18** Moscow newspaper (6)
**19** Rock, mainly calcium (9)
**20** Highest in quality or quantity (8)
**21** Fellow-feeling in time of grief (8)
**23** It's now the EU (3)
**25** Long piece of writing (6)
**26** Building housing items of interest (6)
**29** Learn a skill (5)
**30** Isolated from others (5)

**ACROSS**

**8** Carbon used for drawing (8)
**9** Captured or trapped (6)
**10** Massages, dough perhaps (6)
**11** Full array of colours (8)
**12** Look up to (6)
**13** Floating pieces of ice (8)
**15** Curve over an opening (4)
**17** Road not turned in the windstorm (7)
**19** They're surrounded by water (7)
**22** Forty days of penance (4)
**24** Grow rapidly with increasing momentum (8)
**27** In any event (6)
**29** Continents, north and south (8)
**30** South Pacific island (6)
**31** Units of length (6)
**32** Clueless (8)

**DOWN**

**1** Whinged, snivelled (6)
**2** Act of bringing into being (8)
**3** Large cask holding 54 gallons of beer (8)
**4** Synthetic material (7)
**5** Plan, ruse (6)
**6** Understated, muted (6)
**7** Made a gesture of indifference (8)
**14** Part of lower jaw (4)
**16** Sound of a drum or a list of names (4)
**18** Emollient (8)
**20** Beginning (8)
**21** In any location (8)
**23** Narrow strip of rubber (7)
**25** Meriting respect or esteem (6)
**26** Right or way to enter (6)
**28** Be present at (6)

**179**

## ACROSS

1 Topmost point (6)
4 Difficulty, vicissitude (8)
9 Something seldom seen (6)
10 Last month (8)
12 On the inside (5)
13 Reckoned (9)
15 For each (3)
16 Church officer (5)
17 Most free from harm (6)
22 Division of a poem (6)
24 Course, path (5)
27 And not (3)
28 Man-made (9)
31 Keen-eyed bird (5)
32 Marine museum (8)
33 Word that qualifies another (6)
34 Strictest or grimmest (8)
35 Remove all trace with it (6)

## DOWN

1 Small fish, usually canned (8)
2 Mixture for soaking foods before cooking (8)
3 Translate into another language (9)
5 Proficient (5)
6 Reverie (5)
7 Normal practices in nuns' clothing? (6)
8 Cavalcade (6)
11 Human being (6)
14 Dwight D. Eisenhower, in short (3)
18 Can ref be from here? (6)
19 Capitulation (9)
20 Performers of tricks of manual dexterity (8)
21 Recall, recollect (8)
23 Unreachable tennis serve (3)
25 They come from countries such as India and Pakistan (6)
26 Go through, suffer (6)
29 Bird of the Rhone? (5)
30 Sellers of tickets at inflated prices (5)

**180**

## ACROSS

**8** Up to now (8)
**9** These shows can be a poser (6)
**10** Mountain range in Spanish-speaking countries (6)
**11** Most infuriated (8)
**12** Concurs (6)
**13** Eliminates errors (8)
**15** Molecule (4)
**17** Hard transparent coating (7)
**19** Pendent spears of frozen water (7)
**22** Prefix for before (4)
**24** Maiden of Odin in Norse mythology (8)
**27** Usual, standard (6)
**29** Slow to reveal emotion (8)
**30** Maker of suits (6)
**31** Strange caller to the underground room (6)
**32** State of great elation (8)

## DOWN

**1** In poor health (6)
**2** Baker's dozen (8)
**3** Little Rock is the state capital (8)
**4** Smoke the cob taco (7)
**5** Large eel (6)
**6** Light red (6)
**7** Strange test case for the tape (8)
**14** Leave out (4)
**16** Native to Bangkok, say (4)
**18** Roused from sleep (8)
**20** Monument to honour soldiers killed in war (8)
**21** Aisle (8)
**23** Sewing implements (7)
**25** Sounds of bells to announce funerals (6)
**26** Idolise, venerate (6)
**28** Handsome youth beloved of Aphrodite (6)

**181**

## ACROSS

**1** All but (6)
**4** Rival (8)
**9** Slit up the Spring flowers (6)
**10** Paper covering (8)
**12** Group of singers (5)
**13** Four-sided figure (9)
**15** Past, since (3)
**16** Happening, occurrence (5)
**17** Quick look (6)
**22** Set cap askew at the view (6)
**24** Racket (5)
**27** Fairy, pixie (3)
**28** They repair engines (9)
**31** Express in speech (5)
**32** Unit of weight (8)
**33** It entitles the bearer to entry (6)
**34** Left the forces without permission (8)
**35** Business that acts for another (6)

## DOWN

**1** The and a (8)
**2** Grown soft and pleasant with age (8)
**3** Detaches from another (9)
**5** Sudden, overpowering fright (5)
**6** Musical drama (5)
**7** Sufficient onto the day (6)
**8** Dissertations (6)
**11** Thick, heavy shoe (6)
**14** Silvery metal (3)
**18** Bear witness (6)
**19** Perplexing, puzzling (9)
**20** In error (8)
**21** Unbeknownst to anyone (8)
**23** Small object to fasten or attach (3)
**25** Had a cigarette (6)
**26** Instrument for weighing (6)
**29** Wrath, ire (5)
**30** Likeness, could be spitting (5)

## ACROSS

**1** More than one (6)
**5** Scold, censure (6)
**10** They move to music (7)
**11** Victory or great success (7)
**12** Fencing sword (4)
**13** Carving in relief (5)
**15** In addition (4)
**17** Moved very fast or managed (3)
**19** Browned by the sun (6)
**21** Small plot of ground (6)
**22** Reached a destination (7)
**23** Unorthodox doctrine (6)
**25** It's played badly in nest (6)
**28** Male humans (3)
**30** Touch with the tongue (4)
**31** Nymph said to have lured sailors to destruction on rocks (5)
**32** Bitter quarrel between two parties (4)
**35** Perform surgery or run a machine (7)
**36** Procedure regularly followed (7)
**37** Tan she got in Greece (6)
**38** Shelter, asylum (6)

## DOWN

**2** Mobile lamp (7)
**3** Water plant (4)
**4** East Indian sailor (6)
**5** It's fixed to something to hold it firm (6)
**6** Horizontal bar (4)
**7** Toppled, fell to the ground (7)
**8** Mention (6)
**9** 'Many are called but few are ...' (Bible) (6)
**14** Seafarer (7)
**16** Extravagant meal (5)
**18** Walked through water (5)
**20** Arid (3)
**21** Obtain (3)
**23** Sunken place (6)
**24** Wealthiest (7)
**26** Wanting (7)
**27** Complete soaked (6)
**28** They hoard money (6)
**29** '... my God to Thee' (hymn) (6)
**33** Domesticated, docile (4)
**34** Deep, wide chasm (4)

## ACROSS

**1** Invite to fight (9)
**9** Money received for work or investment (6)
**10** Person who finds the finance for a show (8)
**11** Detachment for security or reconnaissance (6)
**12** Small set-back space (6)
**14** Plant with fronds (4)
**15** Bundle, of grain stalks say (5)
**16** Toward the back of a boat (6)
**18** Lower in price (7)
**21** Outcomes, upshots (7)
**24** Unequivocally detestable (6)
**26** Correct in every detail (5)
**30** Wise men (4)
**31** Utter in unison (6)
**32** To some degree, not wholly (6)
**33** Everything that exists (8)
**34** Still in (3,3)
**35** Strange sandy weed found in the middle of the week (9)

## DOWN

**2** Equine animals (6)
**3** Women of refinement (6)
**4** Release from an obligation (6)
**5** Tallest living animal (7)
**6** Unnerves, deprives of courage (6)
**7** Ring it for access (8)
**8** Restock, refill (9)
**11** Talk long and foolishly (5)
**13** Retail establishment (4)
**17** Travel along with (9)
**19** Go and live in another country (8)
**20** Literary composition (5)
**22** Of this or that kind (4)
**23** Time for pleasure (7)
**25** Mark over a vowel in German (6)
**27** Lawsuit (6)
**28** Absorbent cloths (6)
**29** Once a soviet state (6)

**184**

## ACROSS

**8** Attractive (8)
**9** Medicine that induces vomiting (6)
**10** Extol (6)
**11** Sign over (8)
**12** Dissimilar (6)
**13** Soaked up (8)
**15** Fit to get to Elba? (4)
**17** The wind is strangely too darn wild (7)
**19** Enthusiastically (7)
**22** Old unit of length (4)
**24** Powerlessness, frailty (8)
**27** Short coat (6)
**29** Tiny organisms, can be good or bad (8)
**30** Yells, roars (6)
**31** Space for storing wine (6)
**32** The weather (8)

## DOWN

**1** Fruitless (6)
**2** Arithmetic calculation (8)
**3** Upper part of the face (8)
**4** Not taking sides (7)
**5** Copper, tin and iron (6)
**6** Ban public distribution (6)
**7** Of the stars or constellations (8)
**14** Fermented drink (4)
**16** Male children (4)
**18** Pet arose and handles the machine (8)
**20** Fixed, adapted or set right (8)
**21** Surrounded completely, caged (8)
**23** Mortified (7)
**25** Container for boiling water (6)
**26** Miscalculations (6)
**28** Group of houses (6)

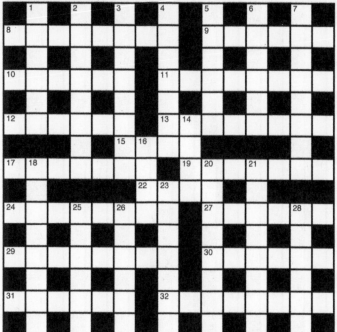

**185**

## ACROSS

**8** Black carbon material (8)
**9** Have in mind to do (6)
**10** Reptile with a bony shell (6)
**11** Nose openings (8)
**12** Unit of poetry (6)
**13** Each and all (8)
**15** Time and this wait for no man (4)
**17** Broke into sharp pieces (7)
**19** Calamity, disaster (7)
**22** Relieve pressure (4)
**24** He used to be known as a commercial traveller (8)
**27** Begins (6)
**29** One-storied dwelling (8)
**30** Totting up (6)
**31** Stopped or slowed a horse (6)
**32** Not long ago (8)

## DOWN

**1** Shove forward (6)
**2** Makes believe (8)
**3** Middling (8)
**4** Sloped or biased (7)
**5** Soft, thin paper (6)
**6** Describes violent weather (6)
**7** Sloped or disposed (8)
**14** Examines the animal doctors carefully? (4)
**16** Thought (4)
**18** Determines the dimensions (8)
**20** Investigate facts (8)
**21** Keeping watch over (8)
**23** Responses (7)
**25** Locomotive (6)
**26** Song, tune (6)
**28** Ravel, snarl up (6)

## ACROSS

**8** Helicopter, say (8)
**9** A feeling of ill will or hostility (6)
**10** Deliver from danger (6)
**11** Pants (8)
**12** A court held in this is not open to the public (6)
**13** Intimidated, amazed (8)
**15** Single and isolated (4)
**17** Set of algebraic symbols (7)
**19** Crisp, smooth, lustrous fabric (7)
**22** Oxide coating on iron (4)
**24** Reevaluate (8)
**27** Roar to the speaker (6)
**29** Italian who wrote of his sexual exploits (8)
**30** Deplore, lament (6)
**31** Dwarfed ornamental tree or shrub (6)
**32** Glowing, lambent (8)

## DOWN

**1** Picture-house (6)
**2** Frozen dessert (3,5)
**3** US game (8)
**4** Stopping place (7)
**5** Coax, sweet-talk (6)
**6** Hispanic afternoon nap (6)
**7** It gives energy and builds tissue (8)
**14** Animal doctors (4)
**16** Boating implements (4)
**18** Switchboard controller (8)
**20** Nuclear weapon (4,4)
**21** Piece broken off something else (8)
**23** By and large (7)
**25** Thinly scattered (6)
**26** Foreign and strange (6)
**28** Not transmitting or reflecting light (6)

## ACROSS

**8** Recuperation after illness (8)
**9** Rubber (6)
**10** Outdoor meal (6)
**11** Altos die, strangely, if left alone (8)
**12** Achieve (6)
**13** Way of regarding something (8)
**15** Very unattractive (4)
**17** Assemble in sequence (7)
**19** Sets down in writing or preserves in sound (7)
**22** Region (4)
**24** At any place (8)
**27** Area, territory (6)
**29** Ironed (8)
**30** Period of play in cricket (6)
**31** Pepper can make you do it (6)
**32** Range of a voice or musical instrument (8)

## DOWN

**1** Fight against (6)
**2** Local government building (4,4)
**3** Fruit of the Fagus tree (8)
**4** Archetypal (7)
**5** Vacation venue (6)
**6** Disengaged (6)
**7** Trusted in (8)
**14** Hoop for a wheel (4)
**16** Toothed wheel or with-it clothes (4)
**18** Decoration, adornment (8)
**20** Weird grannies get salaries (8)
**21** Establish or co-ordinate (8)
**23** Consumers of the written word (7)
**25** Lacking ease or grace, like a tree? (6)
**26** Resounded (6)
**28** No cues, strangely, for the weights (6)

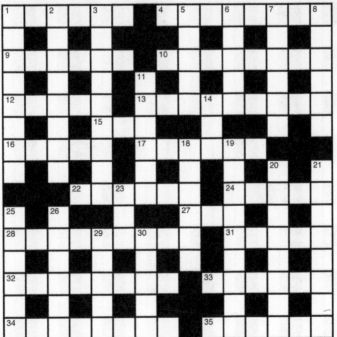

## ACROSS

**1** Long, pointed weapons (6)
**4** Having a material existence (8)
**9** Vitality (6)
**10** Metal loops for a rider (8)
**12** Optimal (5)
**13** Permissible (9)
**15** Everything (3)
**16** Go in (5)
**17** Close at hand (6)
**22** Group of elements working together (6)
**24** Court of the papal see (5)
**27** Liquid for printers (3)
**28** Permitted amount (9)
**31** Soft, creamy candy (5)
**32** Plentiful, ample (8)
**33** Covered passageway (6)
**34** Tottered (8)
**35** Facet (6)

## DOWN

**1** Typical example (8)
**2** Parts in a whole (8)
**3** Steadily, unvarying (9)
**5** Building for travellers (5)
**6** Stems left after grain is removed (5)
**7** Slightly fat (6)
**8** Hearken (6)
**11** Wrinkled tree-fruit with a hard shell (6)
**14** Belonging to us (3)
**18** Military land forces (6)
**19** Loud noises from explosion of fuel in the exhaust (9)
**20** College alumnus (8)
**21** Window for the patriot? (8)
**23** Ocean (3)
**25** Type of rock is a blast, oddly (6)
**26** Not quite a sentence (6)
**29** Triangular, thick piece (5)
**30** The time being (5)

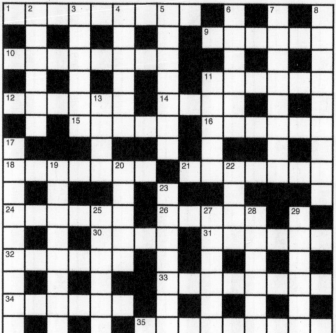

## ACROSS

**1** Dimension from front to back (9)
**9** Spicy sausage (6)
**10** Small, flat, sweet cakes (8)
**11** Expel from a country (6)
**12** Pick (6)
**14** Gain by effort (4)
**15** Elder (5)
**16** Be there (6)
**18** Major road (7)
**21** Gratify (7)
**24** Capacity for rational thought (6)
**26** Nursemaid (5)
**30** Crease (4)
**31** Grown-ups (6)
**32** Soft as down (6)
**33** Having a mottled effect (8)
**34** Sharp rejoinder (6)
**35** Small pieces broken off (9)

## DOWN

**2** Dimension from top to bottom (6)
**3** Crazy bird (6)
**4** Attached with pointed metal piece (6)
**5** Relatives in hospital? (7)
**6** Express grief (6)
**7** Knives fixed to the ends of rifles (8)
**8** Have a dirty bash on these anniversaries? (9)
**11** Theatrical work (5)
**13** Killed intentionally (4)
**17** For that reason (9)
**19** Tip (8)
**20** Pester, needle (5)
**22** Be inclined (4)
**23** Final consumer (3,4)
**25** Bids, tenders (6)
**27** Identifying (6)
**28** Young, upwardly mobile, professional person of the 1980s (6)
**29** City thoroughfare (6)

## ACROSS

**8** Tiro, novice (8)
**9** Head-covering for Muslim women (6)
**10** Round figure (6)
**11** Imaginary sea-creatures (8)
**12** Harmless or kind (6)
**13** The Quiet ... (Graham Greene) (8)
**15** About 0.4 hectares (4)
**17** North American bison (7)
**19** Payments made as marks of appreciation (7)
**22** Notion, thought (4)
**24** Three-sided figure (8)
**27** Sample of cloth (6)
**29** Five-toed pachyderm (8)
**30** Walk like a duck (6)
**31** Request forcefully (6)
**32** Spatter about (8)

## DOWN

**1** Make fun of (6)
**2** Misbehaviour (8)
**3** Hell-like (8)
**4** Functions and relations of words in sentences (7)
**5** Sparse (6)
**6** On one, one might see 29ac (6)
**7** Area covered with trees and shrubs (8)
**14** Small pond (4)
**16** Wind in a series of loops (4)
**18** Unfurled (8)
**20** Towards the Orient (8)
**21** Forsakes, leaves behind (8)
**23** Tooth doctor (7)
**25** Seem to be (6)
**26** Keeps watch over (6)
**28** Sedately, with self-possession (6)

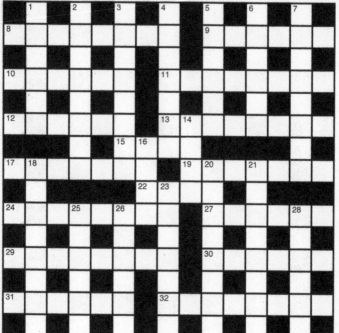

## ACROSS

**8** Fine or subtle (8)
**9** Fire-breathing, mythical creature (6)
**10** Not faint or feeble (6)
**11** Missed a step and nearly fell (8)
**12** Extreme fear (6)
**13** Reasonable (8)
**15** Allowing entry and exit (4)
**17** Oho, Spam, strangely, is used for the hair (7)
**19** Casual tops (1-6)
**22** Stake, job or mail (4)
**24** Does Amos grin at the life form? (8)
**27** Anxious, restless (6)
**29** Lacking seriousness (8)
**30** Consuming food (6)
**31** Group of houses (6)
**32** Had a right to be in the deli tent (8)

## DOWN

**1** 'Do not go ... into that good night' (Thomas) (6)
**2** 1,000 grams (8)
**3** Large leaping mammal (8)
**4** Time away from work (7)
**5** Adapt, alter (6)
**6** Woody, tropical grass (6)
**7** Formal agreement (8)
**14** Busy insects (4)
**16** Dads or sweet drinks (4)
**18** Inoffensive (8)
**20** Learners (8)
**21** Who a person is (8)
**23** Left out (7)
**25** Entreaty (6)
**26** Reflections (6)
**28** Vocalist (6)

## ACROSS

1 Formula (6)
4 Rostrum, podium (8)
9 Four-sided, regular polygon (6)
10 Of the land of the Pharaohs (8)
12 Inn for motorists (5)
13 Joining, fastening (9)
15 ... Angeles (3)
16 Big (5)
17 This is a chum's tree, strangely (6)
22 Evaluate (6)
24 Joining of two or more together (5)
27 Belonging to a female (3)
28 Person who makes and carries out decisions (9)
31 Relating to the rise and fall of the sea (5)
32 Is the continental a Peru one? (8)
33 Rooms on board (6)
34 Uninhabited (8)
35 Grown-up people (6)

## DOWN

1 Take after (8)
2 Opposes the surfaces in shops? (8)
3 Lines of latitude (9)
5 Illumination (5)
6 Subject matter, theme (5)
7 Genesis (6)
8 Be in charge of people or projects (6)
11 Annoy continually (6)
14 Exclamation of discovery (3)
18 Pounded to small pieces (6)
19 Area surrounded by walls or buildings (9)
20 It has vanes that generate power (8)
21 Dissection of parts (8)
23 Took a seat (3)
25 Myth (6)
26 Hairy growths (6)
29 Part of a shoe (5)
30 Effigy, icon (5)

**193**

## ACROSS

1 Features and arrangement of a place (9)
9 News article (6)
10 Watchful (8)
11 Measure for temperature (6)
12 Buccaneer, sea robber (6)
14 Threadlike growth (4)
15 Narrow raised band (5)
16 Pasture (6)
18 Think or mirror (7)
21 Rosy set of odd shellfish (7)
24 Blank space around text (6)
26 Offspring or edition (5)
30 Hard by (4)
31 Most aged (6)
32 Suspension of a session for a rest (6)
33 XIV (8)
34 Also-rans (6)
35 System of communication over wires (9)

## DOWN

2 Wrest (6)
3 Stringed instrument (6)
4 Astonished, stunned (6)
5 Emerged from eggs (7)
6 Stern, harsh (6)
7 Or griped about the breakfast dish (8)
8 Or else (9)
11 Indistinctly (5)
13 'Every ... we say goodbye, I cry a little' (Cole Porter) (4)
17 Chiefly, principally (9)
19 Prophesy (8)
20 Fruits of the pine (5)
22 The immaterial part of a person (4)
23 Fire fag at this animal (7)
25 Put in (6)
27 Protected (6)
28 Newspaper head (6)
29 Dormant (6)

## ACROSS

**1** Branch of biology, studies the structure of tissue (9)
**9** Come to light (6)
**10** Machine controller (8)
**11** Bosom (6)
**12** Plates on a snake's skin (6)
**14** Length by breadth (4)
**15** Language of ancient Rome (5)
**16** Forever (6)
**18** Esteem (7)
**21** Person trained to compete in sports (7)
**24** Dens we discover in the northern country (6)
**26** Hangs around lazily (5)
**30** Upholstered seat (4)
**31** Football team (6)
**32** Discern (6)
**33** Medical institution (8)
**34** Received in return from service (6)
**35** Engaged in conversation (9)

## DOWN

**2** Crash (6)
**3** Excitement, buzz (6)
**4** Cutting-edge (6)
**5** Circular band of flowers (7)
**6** Winds pal, sir, up in continuous loops (6)
**7** Distinct, discrete (8)
**8** Demonstrated against (9)
**11** Animal (5)
**13** Repose (4)
**17** Made a gift to (9)
**19** Places of refuge (8)
**20** Narrow paddle boat (5)
**22** Hades (4)
**23** Came into conflict (7)
**25** Shun, avoid (6)
**27** Children of a ... God (play) (6)
**28** Sets in sequence (6)
**29** Show a connection (6)

**ACROSS**

**8** In the right way (8)
**9** Compares (6)
**10** Group of elements comprising a whole (6)
**11** Immersed (8)
**12** Unobserved (6)
**13** Creative (8)
**15** Besides (4)
**17** Classification of racing car (7)
**19** Science that studies living organisms (7)
**22** Throw lightly and casually (4)
**24** Find out, detect (8)
**27** Travel paths (6)
**29** Physical aggression (8)
**30** See, pal is not awake (6)
**31** Heavenly guardians (6)
**32** Ingredient parts (8)

**DOWN**

**1** Colouring stick (6)
**2** Against the current (8)
**3** Felonious (8)
**4** Wear them while 30ac (7)
**5** Small room or cabinet for storage (6)
**6** Lower garments (6)
**7** Going in (8)
**14** Takes without consent (4)
**16** Overdue (4)
**18** Beliefs (8)
**20** Lead Otis so that he's away from others (8)
**21** Stamped with a name (8)
**23** Issued commands (7)
**25** Less frantic, more relaxed (6)
**26** Disappear (6)
**28** Pact, accord (6)

## ACROSS

**8** Do all babes play the game? (8)
**9** Carmen and The Marriage of Figaro (6)
**10** Make known (6)
**11** At the end, final (8)
**12** Small ball of coloured glass, a toy (6)
**13** Gather in one place (8)
**15** Closed (4)
**17** Handle, use (7)
**19** As a rule (7)
**22** Lease (4)
**24** Sends on, dispatches (8)
**27** Broadcast again (6)
**29** Microscopic organisms (8)
**30** Whimsical idea (6)
**31** Two or more (6)
**32** Dynamic (8)

## DOWN

**1** A maple, strangely, for the name (6)
**2** Tenth month in the Roman calendar (8)
**3** With the least delay (8)
**4** Flat highland (7)
**5** Actors tread them (6)
**6** Channel of communication (6)
**7** These lines are all pearl (8)
**14** Daze, stupefy (4)
**16** Group of cattle or sheep (4)
**18** In all likelihood (8)
**20** More curious or unfamiliar (8)
**21** Hunger (8)
**23** Fled (7)
**25** Overly diluted, thin (6)
**26** Very seldom (6)
**28** Nuclear (6)

## ACROSS

**1** Refrain (6)
**4** Large mammal (8)
**9** Pastmaster (6)
**10** Person who works with their hands (8)
**12** Sudden expulsion of air from the lungs (5)
**13** Empower, permit (9)
**15** Male cat (3)
**16** Space between two lines that intersect (5)
**17** Important person, with large, bald head? (6)
**22** Toward the tail of a vessel (6)
**24** Become fit through exercise (5)
**27** Foot digit (3)
**28** Worldwide (9)
**31** Bring up (5)
**32** Lived in (8)
**33** Promise (6)
**34** Each and all (8)
**35** Scene, panorama (6)

## DOWN

**1** Conjuror, illusionist (8)
**2** Means of communication (8)
**3** The guards turn out to be relatives (9)
**5** Lowest or smallest (5)
**6** Snap, in short (5)
**7** Scared (6)
**8** Lathe operator and English painter (6)
**11** Walk about leisurely (6)
**14** In what way? (3)
**18** Mildly, lightly or kindly (6)
**19** Holds the attention (9)
**20** Distance north or south of the equator (8)
**21** Integral, inbuilt (8)
**23** Thick liquid distilled from coal (3)
**25** Sudden outburst, uproar (6)
**26** Curved, closed line (6)
**29** Hollow or vacant (5)
**30** Hank of wool (5)

## ACROSS

**8** Divulge (8)
**9** On ship or plane (6)
**10** Light on a height for navigation or warning (6)
**11** Illuminating (8)
**12** Roman Catholic devotion over nine days (6)
**13** Gathering, collection (8)
**15** Period of fasting (4)
**17** Fixed form of words (7)
**19** Add as part of something else (7)
**22** Certain (4)
**24** Crabwise (8)
**27** The unpredictable element of life (6)
**29** Wind generator (8)
**30** City for the non-old, oddly (6)
**31** Large gun (6)
**32** Illness, malady (8)

## DOWN

**1** Old Roman orator (6)
**2** Dish made from milkfat (3,5)
**3** Southern English county (8)
**4** Type of harp, using wind (7)
**5** Lines of mountains (6)
**6** Lowest part (6)
**7** Creased, crumpled (8)
**14** Agitate, arouse (4)
**16** Undemanding (4)
**18** It's not a copy (8)
**20** Ornamental chain (8)
**21** Acquiring skill or knowledge (8)
**23** Serving no purpose (7)
**25** Finishing (6)
**26** Foreigners or extraterrestrials (6)
**28** Plump for (6)

## ACROSS

**8** Exercised authority over (8)
**9** Joyful, uplifted (6)
**10** It may be flying or on the table (6)
**11** Investigation of component parts (8)
**12** European state (6)
**13** Chart of days of the year (8)
**15** Nearly new (4)
**17** Competition (7)
**19** Bored a hole or trained by repetition (7)
**22** Rest (4)
**24** Flowers (8)
**27** Dowdy and dated (6)
**29** South American country (8)
**30** Reverberates (6)
**31** Latest (6)
**32** Reached over (8)

## DOWN

**1** Is it a fruit or vegetable? (6)
**2** One who buys and sells (8)
**3** Immense (8)
**4** Go ahead (7)
**5** Evoke (6)
**6** Deep gorge or ravine (6)
**7** Fragile, fine (8)
**14** Tots (4)
**16** Stalk, shank (4)
**18** Spectator (8)
**20** Mirrors or thinks about (8)
**21** Expressing mirth (8)
**23** Abashed (7)
**25** Tool to be found in hovels? (6)
**26** Paths of celestial bodies (6)
**28** Annoyed or resentful (6)

**200**

## ACROSS

**8** House on a Spanish estate (8)
**9** In foreign parts (6)
**10** More tranquil (6)
**11** From birth to death (8)
**12** Savage (6)
**13** Movable parts of aircraft wings (8)
**15** Retained part of a ticket (4)
**17** In reality, actual (2,5)
**19** Neck of land between two seas (7)
**22** Occident (4)
**24** Wheat product used in pasta (8)
**27** Most uncommon (6)
**29** Surprised (8)
**30** Drink of the gods (6)
**31** Think up, create (6)
**32** Not entered (8)

## DOWN

**1** Mails a sausage (6)
**2** After-dinner liqueur (3,5)
**3** Most irate (8)
**4** Group arranged as if in a painting (7)
**5** Legal (6)
**6** Fissure in the earth's crust (6)
**7** Capital of Nepal (8)
**14** Wading bird of warm regions (4)
**16** Urban area (4)
**18** Throwing out (8)
**20** Throttle (8)
**21** Ready money (4,4)
**23** It vibrates to sound (7)
**25** I be Ron, strangely, with this surname (6)
**26** Small arms off larger bodies of water (6)
**28** Frightened (6)

**ACROSS**

**1** Sound made by a hen after laying an egg (6)
**4** They protect against airborne poisons (8)
**9** Reason for doing something (6)
**10** Accost, come face to face with (8)
**12** The gas is there, oddly (5)
**13** Exterminate, extinguish (9)
**15** Take in marriage (3)
**16** Major division of a long poem (5)
**17** Advise, acquaint with (6)
**22** Lacking traditional musical structure (6)
**24** Slides sideways (5)
**27** Prune, cut the top off (3)
**28** Restore to previous position (2-7)
**31** Cleanse the body (5)
**32** Observing the rules of the game (4,4)
**33** Test for suitability (3,3)
**34** Under an obligation (8)
**35** Side way, little travelled (6)

**DOWN**

**1** Begin (8)
**2** Getting hold of or becoming infected (8)
**3** Twirl over for the leafy moss (9)
**5** Distinctive odour (5)
**6** Civilian clothing for a military person (5)
**7** Catchword (6)
**8** Couch (6)
**11** Relating to the middle value (6)
**14** Two of a kind (3)
**18** Cut down, trees say (6)
**19** Bars Perry from having the fruit (9)
**20** Highly skilled performer (8)
**21** Acceded (8)
**23** Plump for (3)
**25** Structure made in one place and placed elsewhere, in short (6)
**26** Conclude, end (6)
**29** Part of the calyx of a flower (5)
**30** Old saw (5)

**202**

## ACROSS

**8** Physical, not abstract (8)
**9** Something done (6)
**10** Reach adulthood (6)
**11** Scrutinised (8)
**12** Island in the West Indies (6)
**13** Biting, as a wasp (8)
**15** Quarry, target (4)
**17** Set free (7)
**19** One can paint a thousand words, it's said (7)
**22** Equally balanced (4)
**24** Height above the ground (8)
**27** Prohibit, veto (6)
**29** Fragments of transparent quartz (8)
**30** Snuggle, cuddle (6)
**31** Expose, unmask (6)
**32** Defeat by skilful manoeuvring (8)

## DOWN

**1** El ..., place of fabulous wealth (6)
**2** Correct (8)
**3** Grows (8)
**4** Invert (7)
**5** ... Five-O, (1970s' TV show) (6)
**6** Twine (6)
**7** Controller (8)
**14** Species (4)
**16** Hollow grass (4)
**18** Increased, augmented (8)
**20** Without limit (8)
**21** Tedious, dull (8)
**23** Account from one point of view (7)
**25** Published, brought out (6)
**26** Not in a position to (6)
**28** They're lazy and inactive (6)

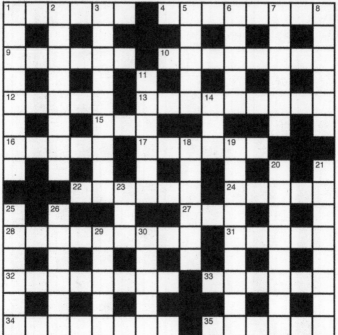

**203**

## ACROSS

1 Woe, wretchedness (6)
4 Document proving citizenship (8)
9 Oral communication (6)
10 Won victory over (8)
12 Country and porcelain (5)
13 Heedful, regardful (9)
15 Pile on a fabric (3)
16 Imitating, copying (5)
17 Line that intersects a curve at two or more points (6)
22 Lea (6)
24 Moan (5)
27 Residue of fire (3)
28 Accumulator, gatherer (9)
31 Perceive the flavour (5)
32 Allocated (8)
33 Piece of cheap, showy jewellery (6)
34 Sudden, unexpected event (8)
35 Viewpoint (6)

## DOWN

1 Composer or performer (8)
2 Particular, exact (8)
3 Parallelogram with four right angles (9)
5 Person who does business on behalf of another (5)
6 Rear of a ship (5)
7 Set of clothes (6)
8 More orderly (6)
11 Slipped back (6)
14 Epoch, period (3)
18 Person lacking in courage (6)
19 Drinks at bedtime (9)
20 Capable of happening (8)
21 Concern or curiosity (8)
23 Part of a circle (3)
25 Atlantic and Pacific (6)
26 More intimate (6)
29 Enthusiastic, avid (5)
30 Swarms, abounds (5)

## ACROSS

**1** Recollects (9)
**9** Ask for firmly (6)
**10** Corner to opposite corner (8)
**11** Association of teams for competition (6)
**12** Type of cloth or thread (6)
**14** Rip the eye moistener? (4)
**15** Stratified rock (5)
**16** Feel remorse (6)
**18** System of production, distribution and consumption (7)
**21** Areas (7)
**24** Most pleasing (6)
**26** Hobo (5)
**30** You, of old (4)
**31** Capacity for rational thought (6)
**32** Fruits of the vine (6)
**33** Time between two events (8)
**34** Brain-teaser (6)
**35** Process of acquiring knowledge (9)

## DOWN

**2** Person who determines the final text (6)
**3** Numbers for rowing crews (6)
**4** Tropical fruit (6)
**5** Connected (7)
**6** Stringent (6)
**7** Pouched mammal (8)
**8** Announce (9)
**11** Sizeable (5)
**13** State and river of the US (4)
**17** Adolescents (9)
**19** Woods of fruit trees (8)
**20** Legends to present truths (5)
**22** Animal hunted for food or sport (4)
**23** Learnt by reading (7)
**25** Takes without the owner's consent (6)
**27** Region around the North Pole (6)
**28** Brightly-coloured, tropical bird (6)
**29** Home of the Grimaldis (6)

## ACROSS

**8** Tangible possession (8)
**9** Employees' organisations (6)
**10** Group of inter-related working parts (6)
**11** Relaxed, no ceremony (8)
**12** Unnoticed (6)
**13** Stopped (8)
**15** Bale out if you can (4)
**17** Set form of words or method (7)
**19** Speak to (7)
**22** Alone in Oslo (4)
**24** Recollect (8)
**27** Did Mum sue this building? (6)
**29** Separating into parts (8)
**30** Angels of mercy (6)
**31** Pay no attention to (6)
**32** Poppycock (8)

## DOWN

**1** Drawing stick (6)
**2** Put mares against the current (8)
**3** Mini Carl is unlawful (8)
**4** Quintessential (7)
**5** Endure pain (6)
**6** Threadlike structures (6)
**7** Intruders, conquerors (8)
**14** Actual (4)
**16** Foundation, bottom (4)
**18** Gaps, opportunities (8)
**20** Primary, outstanding (8)
**21** Booked, a seat say (8)
**23** Beginnings (7)
**25** Newspaper head (6)
**26** Cooked in hot water (6)
**28** Anxious, restless (6)

## ACROSS

**8** Chance event (8)
**9** Man or beast (6)
**10** Good ones make good neighbours, they say (6)
**11** Seat to relax in (8)
**12** Area, territory (6)
**13** Willing to give unstintingly (8)
**15** Advanced in years (4)
**17** Animal and city of the US (7)
**19** Outbuildings for automobiles (7)
**22** Chamber for baking (4)
**24** Slope of a small mountain (8)
**27** Panted (6)
**29** Competitions (8)
**30** Asian country (6)
**31** Showed pleasure (6)
**32** Hearer (8)

## DOWN

**1** Strategy (6)
**2** Devilment (8)
**3** Relating to spring, summer etc. (8)
**4** Unusual (7)
**5** Fish of knowledge (6)
**6** Strangely, there I can be one or the other (6)
**7** Free play (8)
**14** Verge (4)
**16** Well-behaved, kind, or virtuous (4)
**18** Regimentals (8)
**20** Most outraged (8)
**21** Engrossed (8)
**23** Water craft and containers (7)
**25** Loose off (3,3)
**26** Indoors (6)
**28** Football team (6)

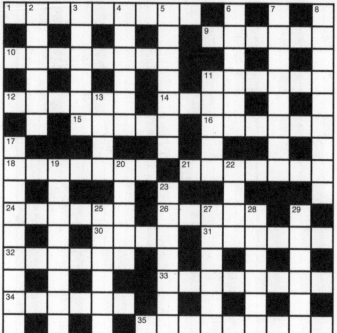

**ACROSS**

1 Pass from sight (9)
9 Strict, austere (6)
10 Particular, definite (8)
11 The strange pathos of a potassium compound (6)
12 Soft warm fabric (6)
14 Fastened (4)
15 Range of hills (5)
16 Suppose (6)
18 Most contiguous (7)
21 Makes up one's mind (7)
24 Religious cult practised in Haiti, involves witchcraft (6)
26 Well-rounded, stout (5)
30 Temporary army quarters (4)
31 Broadcasts again (6)
32 Monkey and blood component (6)
33 Scantily (8)
34 On water (6)
35 Exciting undertaking (9)

**DOWN**

2 Pierce with a sharp stake (6)
3 Expert with bow and arrow (6)
4 Blew in short gusts (6)
5 Levelled a charge against (7)
6 Reduce in rank (6)
7 Observed, mentioned (8)
8 Motorise (9)
11 Small pouch for money (5)
13 Refer to (4)
17 Global, all-inclusive (9)
19 Admittedly (8)
20 Give a toss for covered collonades in ancient Greece (5)
22 Arrived (4)
23 Adverse, antipathetic (7)
25 Relating to the eye (6)
27 Suave and sophisticated (6)
28 Drinking call, good health to you (6)
29 Learnt about the horn (6)

## ACROSS

1 Breaking and overturning earth (9)
9 Area, territory (6)
10 Binding agreement (8)
11 Ravel, snarl up (6)
12 Unremitting (6)
14 Moderately cold (4)
15 Artistic, nonverbal communication (5)
16 Earth or Saturn (6)
18 Large, orange fruit (7)
21 Person of letters (7)
24 Far distant (6)
26 Aspects, panoramas (5)
30 Dislike intensely (4)
31 Short humorous scene (6)
32 Triads, triplets (6)
33 Roused from sleep (8)
34 Guarantee, promise (6)
35 It's said to be the mother of invention (9)

## DOWN

2 Eyed (6)
3 Unfastened, unlaced (6)
4 Paradise (6)
5 Perceives, sees (7)
6 Recollect (6)
7 Crossways (8)
8 They create useful objects (9)
11 Subject matter (5)
13 Position in a hierarchy (4)
17 Of the soul (9)
19 Learn by heart (8)
20 Abstractions, conceits (5)
22 Bird of prey (4)
23 Mean, middling (7)
25 Principle, not practice (6)
27 Abscond (6)
28 Conduits for waste matter (6)
29 Receive willingly (6)

**209**

ACROSS

## ACROSS

**8** Biting insect (8)
**9** Babe-in-arms (6)
**10** Aid (6)
**11** Increase, procreate (8)
**12** Suffer from hunger (6)
**13** Natural depressions (8)
**15** Propelled oneself in water (4)
**17** Language spoken in his glen, strangely (7)
**19** Heartfelt (7)
**22** Places of rest for travellers (4)
**24** Swift, deer-like animal (8)
**27** Manoeuvre (6)
**29** Baby's dummy (8)
**30** Spicy or savoury condiment (6)
**31** Hydrophobia (6)
**32** Travel bag (8)

## DOWN

**1** Close-fitting, foundation garment (6)
**2** Rodent with bushy tail (8)
**3** Suffering, worry (8)
**4** Rum loaf in the recipe (7)
**5** Cushion for sleep (6)
**6** Is CIA far from the continent? (6)
**7** Considers to be a part (8)
**14** Sign of something about to happen (4)
**16** Strike with lash or rod (4)
**18** Not causing death (8)
**20** Small celestial body (8)
**21** Ornamental chain (8)
**23** Closest to being the most penny-pinching? (7)
**25** Exact, draw out (6)
**26** Ineffectual or indolent (6)
**28** Be firm (6)

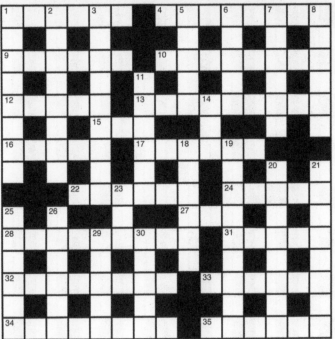

**ACROSS**

1 Low, woody bushes (6)
4 Hunting dog (8)
9 Sends payment (6)
10 Substitutes, supplants (8)
12 Variation within limits (5)
13 Give more details (9)
15 Waste piece of cloth (3)
16 Starched, rigid (5)
17 Brings up (6)
22 Me (6)
24 Extremely cold region (5)
27 Tune (3)
28 Gardaí, gendarmes (9)
31 Ways out (5)
32 It constitutes 78 percent of earth's
   atmosphere (8)
33 Shrewd, sharp (6)
34 State of suffering (8)
35 Movement upward (6)

**DOWN**

1 Astonish (8)
2 Sentimental or amorous (8)
3 Winged insect and swimming stroke (9)
5 Rigoletto, say (5)
6 Greeting (5)
7 Not dressed (6)
8 Concave plates (6)
11 Stage in a scale (6)
14 Public transport vehicle (3)
18 Small baby (6)
19 States (9)
20 Elevation above sea level (8)
21 Outlook, vista (8)
23 Female pronoun (3)
25 Uncovered (6)
26 Strange staple for items of crockery (6)
29 Singing group (5)
30 Encounters (5)

**211**

ACROSS

**ACROSS**

1 Artificial, man-made compound (9)
9 Periodical, summarises the news (6)
10 Ballot (8)
11 Correcting musical pitch (6)
12 Tree plantation (6)
14 Defeat thoroughly (4)
15 Discernment, refinement (5)
16 Plant with stinging hairs (6)
18 Upshots (7)
21 Gain with effort (7)
24 These few are the elite (6)
26 Bird of prey (5)
30 Notion (4)
31 Acquired information (6)
32 Rips, splinters (6)
33 Thought up, created (8)
34 More extended (6)
35 Chief executive of a republic (9)

**DOWN**

2 Colour of cowardice (6)
3 Slip to show payment of entrance fee (6)
4 Lives (6)
5 Disregarded (7)
6 Thin, weaken (6)
7 Denigrate, disparage (8)
8 Walked unsteadily (9)
11 School garment (5)
13 Canvas on board (4)
17 Exactly (9)
19 Ought not to (8)
20 Inclines to take care of? (5)
22 Hollow, cavity (4)
23 Having more weight (7)
25 ... or, one or the other (6)
27 Handwear (6)
28 Warranted (6)
29 Concealed (6)

**212**

## ACROSS

**8** Come close (8)
**9** Not capable (6)
**10** Noxious vapour (6)
**11** Government of the people by the people (8)
**12** Brute (6)
**13** Of a state (8)
**15** Ova (4)
**17** It's traditionally used on the canals of Venice (7)
**19** 'When ... hang by the wall / And Dick the shepherd blows his nail' (Shakespeare) (7)
**22** Repast (4)
**24** Black ... (Evelyn Waugh) (8)
**27** Strong vegetables (6)
**29** Be at variance (8)
**30** Vital organs (6)
**31** Explosive expulsion of air (6)
**32** Propensity (8)

## DOWN

**1** Alternative, choice (6)
**2** Took for granted (8)
**3** Going in the same direction, always the same distance apart (8)
**4** Apportioning out (7)
**5** Yield, end product (6)
**6** Woody grass (6)
**7** Final or extreme (8)
**14** Continent (4)
**16** Form of play or sport (4)
**18** Points of view (8)
**20** Apparel (8)
**21** Prevailing weather environments (8)
**23** Consequences or possessions (7)
**25** Place of prayer (6)
**26** Middle-Eastern state (6)
**28** Advance warning (6)

## ACROSS

**1** Noon (6)
**4** Fastened by sewing (8)
**9** Instructions for cooking (6)
**10** Airport building (8)
**12** Subcontinent (5)
**13** Antipodean continent (9)
**15** Bend in reverence or submission (3)
**16** From that time (5)
**17** Permits (6)
**22** Casual garment (1-5)
**24** Synthetic fabric (5)
**27** Bring to a close (3)
**28** Other-worldly (9)
**31** African country, site of an ancient civilisation (5)
**32** Flight depots (8)
**33** End, wind up (6)
**34** Terrible event (8)
**35** Assented, acquiesced (6)

## DOWN

**1** Most tipsy (8)
**2** Making a choice (8)
**3** Blast heap of letters (9)
**5** Steer into the plants (5)
**6** Less wild (5)
**7** Part to be grasped (6)
**8** Monetary unit (6)
**11** The 50th state (6)
**14** A pair (3)
**18** Latterly (6)
**19** Feeling curiosity or doubt (9)
**20** Period for recreation (8)
**21** Told on, shopped (8)
**23** Strike (3)
**25** Land mass in water (6)
**26** Tributary of the Euphrates River (6)
**29** Shackles (5)
**30** Undo a knot (5)

## ACROSS

1 Uncommonly (9)
9 Exact payment (6)
10 Slam Sean badly for his selling (8)
11 Person who serves at tables (6)
12 Remains on the surface of liquid (6)
14 Around which something rotates (4)
15 Clear, colourless, odourless, tasteless liquid (5)
16 Rely (6)
18 Masticating (7)
21 Pentecost (7)
24 People sharing the same culture (6)
26 Lubricated (5)
30 Rip, rend (4)
31 Of the soil (6)
32 Divisions of time (6)
33 Put in proper order (8)
34 Fruit and colour (6)
35 Had ownership of (9)

## DOWN

2 Almost (6)
3 Swing from one extreme to the other (6)
4 As good as (6)
5 Line for fastening ship's rigging (7)
6 Small group of words (6)
7 Siblings (8)
8 Demeaning (9)
11 Extent from side to side (5)
13 Cab (4)
17 Branch of knowledge concerned with wealth resources (9)
19 Lengthened (8)
20 Church service held at the 9th hour (5)
22 Thought, conception (4)
23 Destructive windstorm (7)
25 He rots in different ones (6)
27 Acquires knowledge or skills (6)
28 Beverages (6)
29 Food made from milk (6)

**215**

## ACROSS

**8** Ruminant of cold areas (8)
**9** Greek nymph and ornamental shrub (6)
**10** Established lines of travel (6)
**11** Sensational, theatrical (8)
**12** Deed (6)
**13** Apportioned (8)
**15** Flat, thin slab to cover surface (4)
**17** Largest (7)
**19** Space for 11 across art (7)
**22** Simple, uncomplicated (4)
**24** Rough and ruff, say (8)
**27** Leave (6)
**29** Molecule (8)
**30** Fruit and colour (6)
**31** Oppose (6)
**32** Highly valued possession (8)

## DOWN

**1** Extremely courageous (6)
**2** Working with wool and needles (8)
**3** Farm labourers of old (8)
**4** Proceeding in small stages (7)
**5** Standards of perfection (6)
**6** Bounded forward (6)
**7** Does this professional have an Erin gene? (8)
**14** Scenery etc. of 11 across productions (4)
**16** Detail, element (4)
**18** Alone, set apart (8)
**20** H (8)
**21** The sound of approval (8)
**23** Views (7)
**25** A brown soup (6)
**26** Pleasure craft (6)
**28** Consider, view (6)

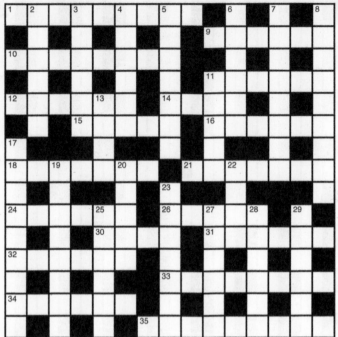

**ACROSS**

1 Pipe dreams, illusions (9)
9 A motto for the fruit or veg? (6)
10 Local death of body tissue (8)
11 Narrow strip of material for decoration (6)
12 British river (6)
14 Revise text or film (4)
15 Flat, circular plates (5)
16 Writing tool (6)
18 Loaded one on top of another (7)
21 Disrobe (7)
24 Alcove (6)
26 Desired, with optimism (5)
30 Public service vehicle (4)
31 Laid bare (6)
32 Any row in this country? (6)
33 Questioned or inspected (8)
34 Kinsmen (6)
35 Identify as previously known (9)

**DOWN**

2 Stunned (6)
3 Attached a label (6)
4 Beer mugs (6)
5 Highest Himalayan mountain (7)
6 Mannerly, courteous (6)
7 Food cooked outside (8)
8 Innumerable (9)
11 Mature, develop (5)
13 Area for skating (4)
17 Space traveller (9)
19 Correctness, precision (8)
20 Make an attempt (5)
22 Profound (4)
23 See chin of the nationality (7)
25 Monies risked on a gamble (6)
27 The vegetable is too apt, oddly (6)
28 Deigns to make a pattern? (6)
29 Adverts, alludes (6)

## ACROSS

**8** Furthermore (8)
**9** Instrument for obliterating (6)
**10** Younger or lower in rank (6)
**11** The area inside (8)
**12** Next to (6)
**13** Giving leave to (8)
**15** Having the power or resources (4)
**17** Destructive windstorm (7)
**19** Female deity (7)
**22** Discontinue (4)
**24** Make smaller (8)
**27** Hit repeatedly with fists (6)
**29** Trailers with living quarters (8)
**30** Sir, set up the sibling (6)
**31** Serious, unremitting (6)
**32** Got hold of (8)

## DOWN

**1** Magnitude of sound (6)
**2** Institution to express belief in a god (8)
**3** Business expense (8)
**4** Number in a sequence (7)
**5** Of the mind (6)
**6** Not wide (6)
**7** Main female characters (8)
**14** Plastic building bricks (4)
**16** Gaffer, manager (4)
**18** Performed surgery (8)
**20** Across from (8)
**21** Of home and family (8)
**23** Strain (7)
**25** Peruser of text (6)
**26** Astonished (6)
**28** Football team (6)

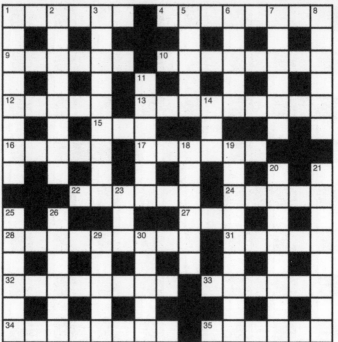

**ACROSS**

**1** Arid region (6)
**4** Tiny piece (8)
**9** Easy, uncomplicated (6)
**10** Whole formed by separate elements (8)
**12** Route of a planet (5)
**13** Exertions to develop endurance or skill (9)
**15** Poorly (3)
**16** Visible element of a recording (5)
**17** Arch of the foot (6)
**22** Handy, functional (6)
**24** Lining of the stomach of a cow as food (5)
**27** The self (3)
**28** Lively, spirited (9)
**31** Very slow, in music (5)
**32** Represent in words (8)
**33** Sole, solitary (6)
**34** Catastrophe (8)
**35** They act for others (6)

**DOWN**

**1** Liquefy, melt (8)
**2** Are You ...? (Nuala O'Faolain) (8)
**3** People connected by blood or marriage (9)
**5** Place of residence (5)
**6** Subject matter (5)
**7** Route of a river (6)
**8** Firstborn (6)
**11** Faith (6)
**14** Long-tailed rodent (3)
**18** Pick and choose (6)
**19** Praising (9)
**20** Ten ring O for a gas (8)
**21** Gets over an illness (8)
**23** Optical organ (3)
**25** Repaired (6)
**26** Periodic population count (6)
**29** Youthful females (5)
**30** Data arranged in rows and columns (5)

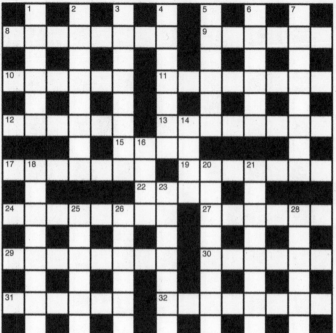

**219**

## ACROSS

**8** Sticky substance obtained from boiled animal tissue (8)
**9** Catch in a snare (6)
**10** This person pays too much attention to formal rules (6)
**11** Window above a door (8)
**12** Walked fast with long steps (6)
**13** Internal organs (8)
**15** Fill to satisfaction (4)
**17** Eastern method of self-defence without weapons (7)
**19** A look like this is sidelong or suspicious (7)
**22** Legal wrong (4)
**24** Words of gratitude (5,3)
**27** Piece of jewellery thought to be a protection against evil (6)
**29** Does Carol use this piece of fairground equipment? (8)
**30** Loathe, hate (6)
**31** Strangely, Ali had this flower (6)
**32** Revere (8)

## DOWN

**1** Flaw or imperfection (6)
**2** Slender tubes of pasta (8)
**3** Anxiety, trouble (8)
**4** Pamphlet or booklet (7)
**5** Ate pun of the hard fruit (6)
**6** Territory of Athens in ancient Greece (6)
**7** Universal religion (8)
**14** Proximate (4)
**16** Car, in short (4)
**18** Disturbance or turmoil (8)
**20** Social or financial status (8)
**21** Extramarital sex (8)
**23** Survive longer than (7)
**25** Ribbon strip of pasta (6)
**26** He's unquestioningly obedient (6)
**28** Artificial and inferior (6)

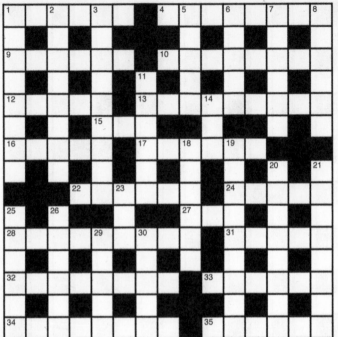

**220**

## ACROSS

1 Repudiate or disinherit (6)
4 Mrs ..., who confused words with others that sounded similar (8)
9 Insect with limbs raised as if in prayer (6)
10 Dependable (8)
12 Magistrate (5)
13 Without question (9)
15 Looking pale and sickly (3)
16 Reddish brown dye used on hair (5)
17 Talk unintelligibly (6)
22 Forward, brash (6)
24 Utilisation (5)
27 Elderly (3)
28 He acts between producer and consumer (9)
31 Hut built of snow (5)
32 Ideas (8)
33 Picture-house (6)
34 Advocate of the principles of monarchy (8)
35 Proteins produced by cells (6)

## DOWN

1 Large bottle in a wicker basket (8)
2 Ridge created by the wind in deserts and beaches (4,4)
3 Used on walls to cover up a misdemeanour? (9)
5 Change to improve (5)
6 Goodbye, farewell (5)
7 Refund (6)
8 Pod use is fake (6)
11 Equatorial forest (6)
14 Spherical shape (3)
18 Farther (6)
19 Learning, scholarship (9)
20 Light teasing repartee (8)
21 Leo named the soft drink (8)
23 Female sheep (3)
25 Caveat ..., let the buyer beware (6)
26 Extreme silliness (6)
29 Lawful (5)
30 Science dealing with quantity and shapes, in short (5)

## ACROSS

1 Evaporate (6)
5 Hallowed place associated with a sacred person (6)
10 Pamphlet (7)
11 Show of daring or brilliance (7)
12 Informal talk (4)
13 Venomous snake (5)
15 Long and difficult trip (4)
17 Young woman coming out in society, in short (3)
19 Unwrinkled (6)
21 Large seabird (6)
22 Aer Lingus or Ryanair, say (7)
23 An obvious truth (6)
25 Quality that that has the power to provoke pity or sadness (6)
28 Cash on delivery, in short, for the fish (3)
30 Travelled on the back of an animal (4)
31 Imbiber (5)
32 Spoken examination (4)
35 Anxious, uneasy (7)
36 Come to be aware (7)
37 Candy, doubly good in France? (6)
38 Likeness of a person in sculpture (6)

## DOWN

2 Pear-shaped tropical fruit (7)
3 Inactive or workshy (4)
4 Car modified to increase speed (3,3)
5 Residential district on the outskirts of a city (6)
6 Wander about aimlessly (4)
7 Uncharged atomic particle (7)
8 Old counting device (6)
9 Woven container (6)
14 Baggage carrier in a hotel (7)
16 Secret store of valuables (5)
18 Hymn of praise (5)
20 Objective male pronoun (3)
21 Measure of the economy, in short (3)
23 Albanian capital (6)
24 Experience or live through (7)
26 Fatty fish (7)
27 Tray, could be silver (6)
28 Relation, could be kissing? (6)
29 Edict (6)
33 Explosive device (4)
34 Young cow or bull (4)

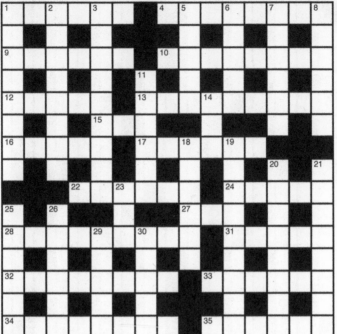

**222**

## ACROSS

1 Not far away (6)
4 Fireproof material, dangerous to health (8)
9 ... longue, chair for reclining (6)
10 Italian Renaissance man, first name (8)
12 Play set to music (5)
13 Useful device, gadget (9)
15 Small drink or small bite (3)
16 Homer's epic poem on the siege of Troy (5)
17 Exaggerated sense of one's own importance (6)
22 Tattered along the edges (6)
24 A narrow gorge with a stream running through it (5)
27 Historical period (3)
28 Prediction as to how something will turn out (9)
31 Denizen of the eternal city (5)
32 About to occur (8)
33 Soft warm garment (6)
34 Fiddlesticks (8)
35 In the middle of (6)

## DOWN

1 Localised death of cells (8)
2 The world of college or university (8)
3 Non-participating spectator (9)
5 Ovine animals (5)
6 Lassitude (5)
7 Autocrat or despot (6)
8 Earlier (6)
11 Linens for the dining table (6)
14 Hawaiian garland of flowers (3)
18 Most peculiar (6)
19 Dance of the ... Fairy (9)
20 Covered a dish with spirit and set it alight (8)
21 Narrowest or leanest (8)
23 Gone, past, since (3)
25 Right to buy at an agreed price by a stated date (6)
26 Unexceptional, ordinary (6)
29 The time being (5)
30 Air-filled cavity in the skull (5)

## ACROSS

1 National flag of the UK (5,4)
9 From that place (6)
10 Believable (8)
11 Carrier of infection or course of a missile (6)
12 N. American Indian tribe (6)
14 Give off, heat say (4)
15 Sum, aggregate (5)
16 Cheap and vulgar tastelessness (6)
18 Continuing forever (7)
21 Large, heavy knife (7)
24 Mistreat, misapply (6)
26 Translucent gemstones (5)
30 Republic in southeastern Asia (4)
31 Satisfied thirst (6)
32 Decayed area in a tooth (6)
33 Grandiloquence, oratory (8)
34 Signify, mean (6)
35 Maladies, sicknesses (9)

## DOWN

2 Ordinary (6)
3 Out of fashion, headgear perhaps (3-3)
4 Miscellaneous collection of things sold together (3,3)
5 Twisted yarns for embroidery (7)
6 Old Jewish community in East European town (6)
7 Bring up a topic or prepare the way for (8)
8 Recovered, resurrected (9)
11 Panorama (5)
13 Become a member (4)
17 Agent that destroys disease-carrying microorganisms (9)
19 Making certain (8)
20 Zones (5)
22 Prisoner's quarters (4)
23 Opening of the nose (7)
25 Detective who follows a trail (6)
27 Toward the rear of a vessel (6)
28 Shoes with wooden soles (6)
29 Make fun of (6)

**224**

## ACROSS

**8** Sheer, utter (8)
**9** Referring to tiny particles (6)
**10** Academic award (6)
**11** Tended (8)
**12** Artist's workroom (6)
**13** Tilt a can at the ocean (8)
**15** Repugnant (4)
**17** Go backwards (7)
**19** Clear and detailed (7)
**22** Archaic you (4)
**24** Buy (8)
**27** Treat with excessive indulgence (6)
**29** Full array of colours (8)
**30** Narrative song of popular origin (6)
**31** Very brave (6)
**32** Weeds with prickly-edged leaves (8)

## DOWN

**1** Thing, article (6)
**2** Oatmeal dish (8)
**3** Many (8)
**4** Of the healing sciences (7)
**5** Unit of pressure, French philosopher and programming language (6)
**6** Movement or proposal (6)
**7** Previous decade (8)
**14** Classification (4)
**16** Acquires (4)
**18** Fitted out with whatever's necessary (8)
**20** State in which power rests with elected representatives (8)
**21** Unabridged, whole (8)
**23** Protective head coverings (7)
**25** It lays eggs in the nests of other birds (6)
**26** Second largest continent (6)
**28** Ecstatic (6)

## ACROSS

**1** Ascends, mounts (6)
**4** Went at a fast gait (8)
**9** Native American (6)
**10** One-off (8)
**12** Swimming birds with scores of nothing? (5)
**13** Exactly alike (9)
**15** Boat to pull larger one (3)
**16** In addition (5)
**17** Not accessible to view (6)
**22** Avoids the lower garment? (6)
**24** Expanse of sea (5)
**27** Tavern (3)
**28** Arduous, backbreaking (9)
**31** Take place (5)
**32** Native of republic in West Africa (8)
**33** Of gods (6)
**34** Assembled (8)
**35** Look (6)

## DOWN

**1** Youngsters (8)
**2** Point to (8)
**3** Jack and the ... (9)
**5** 'I will ... and go now' (Yeats) (5)
**6** Of little weight (5)
**7** Contract of insurance (6)
**8** 'Through a glass ...' (Bible) (6)
**11** Superior or taller (6)
**14** Bob the head (3)
**18** Blueprint (6)
**19** Study of the finances of the state (9)
**20** Become conscious of (8)
**21** Most furious (8)
**23** Unwell (3)
**25** Drink of milk or cream, eggs and alcohol (6)
**26** Solid lump of a precious metal (6)
**29** Of considerable size (5)
**30** Mental or physical representation (5)

**226**

## ACROSS

**8** Kindling (8)
**9** Tie, secure (6)
**10** Furrow, rut (6)
**11** Does Iran fall in the cloudburst? (8)
**12** Pay tribute to, commend (6)
**13** Most diminutive (8)
**15** Moreover (4)
**17** Whirling wind (7)
**19** Extreme mental distress (7)
**22** Number for a club (4)
**24** Twice 22ac (8)
**27** Informal, dress say (6)
**29** All undomesticated creatures (8)
**30** Departs from the sheets (6)
**31** Most secure (6)
**32** Native of Palermo, say (8)

## DOWN

**1** Reflective glass (6)
**2** Lowering of rank (8)
**3** Frontal bone (8)
**4** Location of a dwelling (7)
**5** Land of Malawi and Mozambique (6)
**6** Handy (6)
**7** Comes to be aware (8)
**14** Low sound of pain (4)
**16** Sole (4)
**18** The first in oil rage, strangely (8)
**20** Adornment for the throat (8)
**21** Volatile, precarious (8)
**23** Extreme or deeply felt (7)
**25** Concealed from view (6)
**26** Is, lives (6)
**28** Spaces for sports events (6)

**227**

## ACROSS

**8** Fish tank (8)
**9** Implement to cause harm (6)
**10** Bunny (6)
**11** Made information available (8)
**12** Salvage (6)
**13** Weedkiller or pesticide, for instance (8)
**15** Remain (4)
**17** Below, under (7)
**19** Low-lying wetlands with grassy vegetation (7)
**22** Bad tuna for the relative (4)
**24** Musical performances (8)
**27** Push forward suddenly (6)
**29** Gamp (8)
**30** Long-tailed primate (6)
**31** Mood or something funny (6)
**32** Leeway, scope (8)

## DOWN

**1** Figure with four equal sides (6)
**2** Meal cooked outdoors (8)
**3** Least clean (8)
**4** IRA came to the continent (7)
**5** A dozen (6)
**6** US territory since 1900 (6)
**7** Temperate (8)
**14** Religious song (4)
**16** The other one from this (4)
**18** Tremendous, gigantic (8)
**20** Tries (8)
**21** Force, might, potency (8)
**23** Generally (7)
**25** Cardboard box (6)
**26** Kings, queens, presidents etc. (6)
**28** Pays out (6)

## ACROSS

**1** Involving money (9)
**9** 'The Lord giveth and He ... away' (6)
**10** Magnificent, splendid (8)
**11** For the time being, in short (3,3)
**12** Motor (6)
**14** Uncommon (4)
**15** Closely crowded together (5)
**16** The fruits are important source of oil (6)
**18** Neatly arranged or well-behaved (7)
**21** Steady, even (7)
**24** Sharp, piercing cry (6)
**26** Device signalling danger (5)
**30** Round trip (4)
**31** Taking to the air (6)
**32** Estimate (6)
**33** Came to consciousness (8)
**34** Amount available to borrow (6)
**35** Greatly frightened (9)

## DOWN

**2** Mutton or Clare, say (6)
**3** Apprehensive (6)
**4** Selected, picked (6)
**5** Promised, guaranteed (7)
**6** Leaf of honour (6)
**7** Time of celebration (8)
**8** Science that deals with the properties of substances (9)
**11** Question or examine thoroughly (5)
**13** Nigh (4)
**17** Erect (9)
**19** Regulated activities or showed the way (8)
**20** Pale yellow fruit (5)
**22** Young female (4)
**23** Waste, refuse (7)
**25** Of tiny particles (6)
**27** Illicit romance (6)
**28** Emphatically me (6)
**29** Involuntary nasal explosion (6)

**ACROSS**

**8** Feud, fight (8)
**9** It holds a ship (6)
**10** Skin disorder (6)
**11** Determined the dimensions (8)
**12** Opening in a volcano (6)
**13** Arrange by categories (8)
**15** Reflection of sound (4)
**17** Member of the armed forces (7)
**19** Grains used as food (7)
**22** Inquires (4)
**24** Illustrate in words (8)
**27** Lacking grace in movement (6)
**29** Obtained, gained (8)
**30** Students (6)
**31** Nations ruled by one authority (6)
**32** Balderdash, tommyrot (8)

**DOWN**

**1** Association football (6)
**2** Caused to happen (8)
**3** Is agreed, oddly, to differ (8)
**4** Does Mac host this organ? (7)
**5** Tropical yellowish fruit (6)
**6** Happens (6)
**7** Potent, forceful (8)
**14** ..., stock and barrel (4)
**16** Shellfish with pincers (4)
**18** Defeat, conquer (8)
**20** Breaking free (8)
**21** Having the tools to do the job (8)
**23** Dispatching, transmitting (7)
**25** Sauce made from fruit puree (6)
**26** Sir, ale is available in this country (6)
**28** Scatter water about (6)

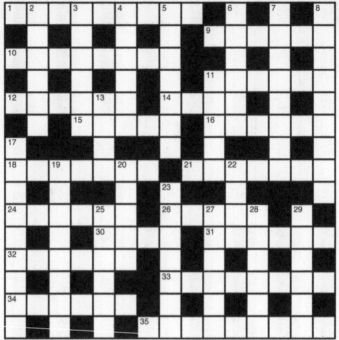

**ACROSS**

1 Radio or television show (9)
9 Spill the beans (6)
10 The time something happens (8)
11 Band of colour (6)
12 Parallel layers (6)
14 Dull, persistent pain (4)
15 Witty remark about the willow? (5)
16 Area, territory (6)
18 Heavy outer garment (7)
21 Most deficient in beauty (7)
24 Yearly (6)
26 Rough or unkind (5)
30 Spanish house (4)
31 CIA Tom is unusually tiny (6)
32 Exceptional cleverness (6)
33 Propelling with a short, light oar (8)
34 Freedom from danger (6)
35 Underlying structure (9)

**DOWN**

2 Repeat, recount (6)
3 Small, yellowish, tropical fruits (6)
4 Beast (6)
5 The Boomtown Rats didn't like them (7)
6 Sofa (6)
7 Certain, sure (8)
8 Every second one (9)
11 Gesture of the shoulders (5)
13 Mexican rolled pancake (4)
17 Most curious (9)
19 Pocket tool (8)
20 Book of maps (5)
22 Slope, slant, lean (4)
23 More keen or more bitter (7)
25 Keenness of perception (6)
27 No fixed pattern (6)
28 Cavity, space (6)
29 Victor (6)

**ACROSS**

**1** Group of members large enough to transact business (6)
**5** Usual, standard (6)
**10** Two rhyming lines of verse (7)
**11** Put into, bank account say (7)
**12** At high volume (4)
**13** Adult females (5)
**15** Large woody plant (4)
**17** Informal father (3)
**19** Not often (6)
**21** Assail, assault (6)
**22** Trash (7)
**23** Choosing by ballot (6)
**25** Custodian, steward (6)
**28** Primary colour (3)
**30** Window ledge (4)
**31** Offensively inquisitive (5)
**32** Predatory canine animal (4)
**35** Camera I got from the US (7)
**36** Gear son up for fruit (7)
**37** Not the ones already mentioned (6)
**38** Oldest (6)

**DOWN**

**2** Abnormal (7)
**3** Small stream (4)
**4** Way of doing (6)
**5** Indicated assent (6)
**6** Mature and ready to be eaten (4)
**7** Find US tiara in this country (7)
**8** Weighing instrument (6)
**9** Sudden flash, of lightning say (6)
**14** Children's game played with little balls (7)
**16** Bony outgrowths on the heads of some animals (5)
**18** Formerly used as an anaesthetic (5)
**20** Drinking vessel (3)
**21** Inquire (3)
**23** Relating to sight (6)
**24** Highest (7)
**26** Farm tools to break the soil (7)
**27** Say no (6)
**28** Mountain ashes (6)
**29** Reduce in rank (6)
**33** Ten US cents (4)
**34** Imperial unit of length (4)

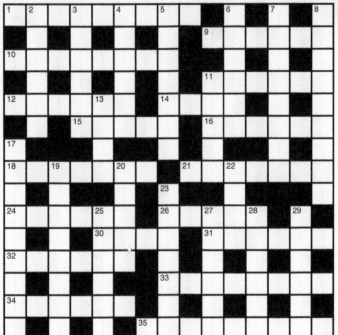

## ACROSS

**1** It says something about the subject in a sentence (9)
**9** Evening meal (6)
**10** It entitles travel abroad (8)
**11** Formal, ceremonial (6)
**12** Rough, uncouth (6)
**14** Gave temporarily (4)
**15** Entire amount (5)
**16** Snoozing (6)
**18** Comes into view (7)
**21** Smooth mixture to cover walls (7)
**24** Breaks open suddenly (6)
**26** Momentary brightness (5)
**30** Submerged ridge of rock near the surface (4)
**31** Bellowed (6)
**32** Political gathering to select a candidate, US-style (6)
**33** Small one-storied houses (8)
**34** First in age (6)
**35** Customary ways of operation (9)

## DOWN

**2** Capacity for rational thought (6)
**3** Gobi, say (6)
**4** Wardrobe in the US (6)
**5** Fully, completely (7)
**6** Fliers and ships' guides (6)
**7** Money paid for use of money (8)
**8** Carry to another place (9)
**11** Mollusc with spiral shell (5)
**13** Couch (4)
**17** Cookouts (9)
**19** Coax, inveigle (8)
**20** '... are red, violets are blue' (5)
**22** Too (4)
**23** Commissioned member of armed forces (7)
**25** An obvious truth (6)
**27** Polar region (6)
**28** US state (6)
**29** Unyielding, harsh (6)

**233**

## ACROSS

**8** Piece of luggage (8)
**9** Explanation or justification (6)
**10** Type of shrub or tree (6)
**11** Run-of-the-mill (8)
**12** Fatigue resulting from air travel (3,3)
**13** Outlook on a matter (8)
**15** Repulsive (4)
**17** Restriction (7)
**19** Hen cars on the big farms (7)
**22** Eons (4)
**24** Depict verbally (8)
**27** Sentinel, look-out (6)
**29** Metric weight (8)
**30** Mostly (6)
**31** Of dogs (6)
**32** XIX (8)

## DOWN

**1** Tart filled with savoury ingredients (6)
**2** Someone who insists on something (8)
**3** Tirade, diatribe (8)
**4** Of or near the thighbone (7)
**5** Time to pay (6)
**6** It attracts iron (6)
**7** GPO rider has it for breakfast (8)
**14** Rubber covering (4)
**16** Seize, snatch (4)
**18** This nationality held wrongly in camera (8)
**20** Accepting as true (8)
**21** Jail inmates (8)
**23** Mary, gen up on the country (7)
**25** No chip on this composer's shoulder (6)
**26** Serial country? (6)
**28** Respite, alleviation (6)

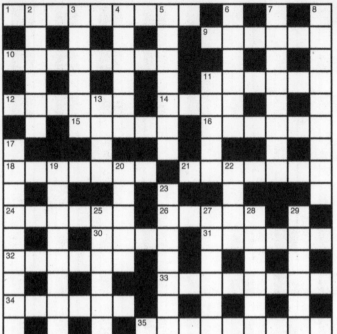

**234**

## ACROSS

**1** Assuming to be true, suspecting (9)
**9** Go or come after (6)
**10** Member of the board (8)
**11** Silky coat of the Angora goat (6)
**12** Cherry-red (6)
**14** Makes with difficulty, a living say (4)
**15** Cut the fleece of sheep (5)
**16** Go or come back (6)
**18** Is Nils sad with all that water around? (7)
**21** Academic awards (7)
**24** Remove the trigger from (6)
**26** Subject matter (5)
**30** Rest (4)
**31** Asiatic wild ass (6)
**32** Aim to (6)
**33** Roused from sleep (8)
**34** Outer reaches (6)
**35** Adorned, bedecked (9)

## DOWN

**2** Joined as one (6)
**3** Synopsis, summary (6)
**4** Hindu tradition of a widow dying on her husband's funeral pyre (6)
**5** Room for a baby (7)
**6** Humorous (6)
**7** Enjoyment, delight (8)
**8** Mindfulness, consciousness (9)
**11** Combine, coalesce (5)
**13** Front of the leg (4)
**17** They're powered by moving air (9)
**19** One's existence (8)
**20** Fearful expectation (5)
**22** Smile with teeth showing (4)
**23** State again (7)
**25** Upper House (6)
**27** Is this vegetable too pat? (6)
**28** Court held in this is not open to the public (6)
**29** Remove text (6)

**235**

### ACROSS

**1** Medical institutions (9)
**9** Extend in one or more directions (6)
**10** Prominent aspects of something (8)
**11** Rigid, strict (6)
**12** Refers to the period before Easter (6)
**14** Printers' mediums (4)
**15** Pacific, say (5)
**16** Appearance (6)
**18** Thin straits connecting two bodies of water (7)
**21** Pots for boiling (7)
**24** Long, heavy wave (6)
**26** Imperial land measures (5)
**30** Large container for rubbish (4)
**31** Me ripe for the group of states? (6)
**32** Candy, comfits (6)
**33** Spot-on (8)
**34** Puts up, builds (6)
**35** Antecedents (9)

### DOWN

**2** Threw wide (6)
**3** Staple vegetable (6)
**4** Seat of power (6)
**5** Enumerating (7)
**6** More than is needed (6)
**7** Wild hyacinth (8)
**8** Promote (9)
**11** Large, edible rays (5)
**13** Reverberate (4)
**17** Wholly absorbed, in thought perhaps (9)
**19** Alleviated, eased (8)
**20** Has a job (5)
**22** Those people (4)
**23** Is Pat Cain in charge of the ship? (7)
**25** One's property after death (6)
**27** Bring to safety (6)
**28** Animating force in living things (6)
**29** Author (6)

**236**

## ACROSS

**8** Asset (8)
**9** On ship, train or plane (6)
**10** Runs off to get married (6)
**11** Salaries etc. (8)
**12** Group of musical notes (6)
**13** Likely cost (8)
**15** Ship's complement (4)
**17** Hard grey rock (7)
**19** Statement of transactions or verbal report (7)
**22** Appellation (4)
**24** Endeavours (8)
**27** Adjudge (6)
**29** Highly valued possession (8)
**30** Deserves (6)
**31** Guard (6)
**32** Leaning (8)

## DOWN

**1** Riches, assets (6)
**2** Carp (8)
**3** Vista (8)
**4** Arbitrator (7)
**5** Orange incentive? (6)
**6** Dais, rostrum (6)
**7** Startle (8)
**14** Moved through water (4)
**16** Lease (4)
**18** Went back (8)
**20** Formalities on a special occasion (8)
**21** Came to pass (8)
**23** Facets, views (7)
**25** Glass-like coating on metal or pottery (6)
**26** Imperial measures and currency (6)
**28** Study of the physical properties of light (6)

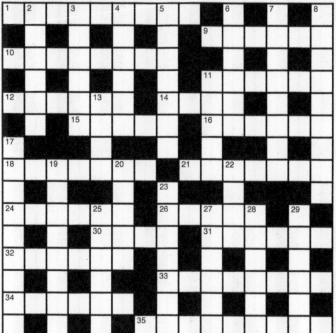

**237**

## ACROSS

**1** They pay for goods and services (9)
**9** Powdery substance of lime and clay (6)
**10** Gleamed or glowed intermittently (8)
**11** Onerous or difficult load (6)
**12** Gentle wind (6)
**14** Carbonised vegetable matter (4)
**15** Long region of high pressure (5)
**16** Verse (6)
**18** Large, densely-wooded area (7)
**21** Derived pleasure from (7)
**24** Pass away (6)
**26** Vagrant, drifter (5)
**30** Continent (4)
**31** Long, pointed weapons (6)
**32** Seat of a ruler (6)
**33** Alone, set apart (8)
**34** Considered or looked at (6)
**35** Depth of feeling or energy (9)

## DOWN

**2** Toward a higher place (6)
**3** ... is the Night (F Scott Fitzgerald) (6)
**4** Changed from solid to liquid (6)
**5** Decreased, cut down (7)
**6** Outcome (6)
**7** Inclination, propensity (8)
**8** Benchmarks (9)
**11** Area drained by a river (5)
**13** Locking devices with toothed edges (4)
**17** Efficacious (9)
**19** Gave an account (8)
**20** Pronoun for people or things (5)
**22** Sudden upward movement (4)
**23** Broadcasting company (7)
**25** Kitchen appliances and large, grassy tracts (6)
**27** On land from sea (6)
**28** Parts of flowers (6)
**29** Pressing, compelling (6)

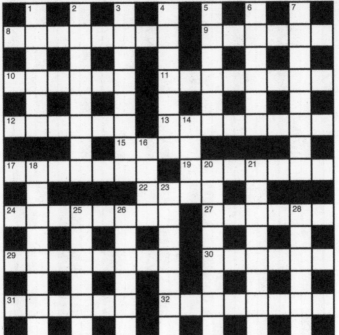

## ACROSS

**8** Extinct animal (8)
**9** Motive or explanation (6)
**10** Change for the better (6)
**11** Annoyance, irritant (8)
**12** Smack (6)
**13** Communications (8)
**15** Stately, aquatic bird (4)
**17** The language of shin gel (7)
**19** Puts clothes on (7)
**22** Further (4)
**24** Rough idea (8)
**27** Power of recall (6)
**29** Parts of a tree or of a large organisation (8)
**30** Small bite (6)
**31** More than one (6)
**32** Caribou (8)

## DOWN

**1** Broadest (6)
**2** Concerning countries under the control of and settled by another (8)
**3** Elms rash is non-toxic (8)
**4** Darn, Mag is an older relative (7)
**5** Oranges and apples (6)
**6** Yellow 5dn (6)
**7** It's made of sand and cement (8)
**14** Concludes (4)
**16** Interrogatory word (4)
**18** Lint Ross has in his nose (8)
**20** Mushy, sentimental (8)
**21** One individual (8)
**23** Free time (7)
**25** Take no notice of (6)
**26** For a short time (6)
**28** Moved along on wheels (6)

**239**

## ACROSS

8 Metric weight (8)
9 Bawdy, vulgar (6)
10 Serviette (6)
11 Scrutinised (8)
12 Vehicle for a coffin (6)
13 Distinguish, name (8)
15 Heavenly light (4)
17 Hermit (7)
19 Routinely (7)
22 Organised force (4)
24 Tiny portion (8)
27 Only, and nothing more (6)
29 Apertures (8)
30 Established customs (6)
31 Breakfast food (6)
32 XIX (8)

## DOWN

1 Optical illusion (6)
2 Young domestic cock (8)
3 Female member of royal family (8)
4 Memory loss (7)
5 Act, conduct oneself (6)
6 Creative person (6)
7 Happy and optimistic (8)
14 Percussion instrument (4)
16 Small, short-necked duck (4)
18 Illustrations, instances (8)
20 Grand orchestral composition (8)
21 Wild cobras at the circus (8)
23 Motives, explanations (7)
25 Let nun into the passage (6)
26 Stick of wax with a wick (6)
28 Written message (6)

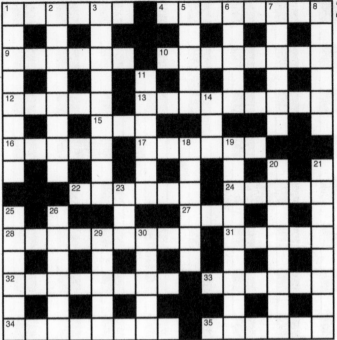

## ACROSS

**1** Abrupt (6)
**4** Abided, by rules say (8)
**9** Have an impact on (6)
**10** Attendance check (4,4)
**12** Creep (5)
**13** Oddly, queerly (9)
**15** Tree for the fire? (3)
**16** Incident (5)
**17** Hanging piece of frozen water (6)
**22** Communicates by letter (6)
**24** Climb, stairs say (5)
**27** Anger (3)
**28** Feigned, faked (9)
**31** Sail-rope on the bed? (5)
**32** Took into custody (8)
**33** Small wealthy state (6)
**34** Innocuous, innocent (8)
**35** Touch, sight etc. (6)

## DOWN

**1** Grabbed or kidnapped (8)
**2** Conquered (8)
**3** Moving staircase (9)
**5** Smell, aroma (5)
**6** Steel tower supporting high-tension wires (5)
**7** Icons (6)
**8** Holdups, postponements (6)
**11** Peculiar thirst for the top (1-5)
**14** It forms an arch (3)
**18** Internal (6)
**19** Milestone for a rock (9)
**20** Digits (8)
**21** Bases, posts (8)
**23** Alehouse (3)
**25** Scatter water about (6)
**26** Horror (6)
**29** Artist's stand (5)
**30** One-piece garment (5)

## ACROSS

**8** Eat it at Mom's hour (8)
**9** Itineraries (6)
**10** Fluid (6)
**11** Ruminates (8)
**12** Card game (6)
**13** Formal ritual (8)
**15** Go West for this dish (4)
**17** First light (7)
**19** Posing the least difficulty (7)
**22** In which to lay eggs (4)
**24** Essays (8)
**27** Fitted snugly into (6)
**29** 'Let a smile be your ...' (song) (8)
**30** Curled, wound (6)
**31** Tempests (6)
**32** Parts of the weather (8)

## DOWN

**1** More active in work (6)
**2** At the top of the arm (8)
**3** Virtue, righteousness (8)
**4** Hug (7)
**5** Like better (6)
**6** Gallery for old objects (6)
**7** Formally arranged gatherings (8)
**14** Female sheep (4)
**16** Portable shelter (4)
**18** Final or extreme (8)
**20** Set upon (8)
**21** Tilted (8)
**23** Gets away from (7)
**25** Lapses (6)
**26** Buff up (6)
**28** Incidents, happenings (6)

**242**

ACROSS

**ACROSS**

**8** Punishments to atone for sin (8)
**9** Song in praise of a nation (6)
**10** Gesticulate (6)
**11** All that is (8)
**12** Tasty kernel (6)
**13** Fine powder of precious metal (4,4)
**15** Kitchen appliance (4)
**17** Rest time (7)
**19** Engage in boisterous, drunken merry-making (7)
**22** Outbuilding for storage (4)
**24** Think deeply (8)
**27** Mellifluous (6)
**29** Intangible asset of a business's reputation (8)
**30** Room for storage (6)
**31** Movie theatre (6)
**32** Orations (8)

**DOWN**

**1** Repeat aloud from memory (6)
**2** Profits or incomes (8)
**3** Creator of three-dimensional works of art (8)
**4** Allay (7)
**5** He was thrown to the lions (6)
**6** Turn up at (6)
**7** Carries on, perseveres (8)
**14** At some time in the past (4)
**16** Sleeveless garment (4)
**18** Relating to the management of wealth (8)
**20** Dependent on something habit-forming (8)
**21** Film of viscous liquid floating on top of water (3,5)
**23** Diabolical, infernal (7)
**25** Without question (6)
**26** Man or beast (6)
**28** Rubbed out (6)

## ACROSS

1 Member of royal family (6)
4 Full array of colours (8)
9 All non-artificial phenomena (6)
10 Emphatic, assertive (8)
12 John Millington ..., playwright (5)
13 Removed one's clothes (9)
15 Forty winks (3)
16 Choose by vote (5)
17 Strut, swagger (6)
22 Arrangement of parts functioning together (6)
24 Punctilious (5)
27 No ... or buts (3)
28 Pay it and concentrate (9)
31 Crinkled fabric and thin pancake (5)
32 Remembrances of things past (8)
33 Except on condition that (6)
34 Shrink (8)
35 Thwarted, defeated (6)

## DOWN

1 Imposed a penalty (8)
2 Planned, meant to (8)
3 Craft of a woodworker (9)
5 Self-respect, feeling of self-worth (5)
6 Secret store, hoard (5)
7 Say no to waste (6)
8 Air, song (6)
11 Figure operated by strings (6)
14 Sprint (3)
18 Directing one's efforts (6)
19 Gradual increase in volume (9)
20 Cheerio, so long (8)
21 Emphasised (8)
23 Be seated (3)
25 Worked with land or animals (6)
26 Nuclear (6)
29 Boldness and fibre (5)
30 Notions, thoughts (5)

## ACROSS

**8** Shook from fear or cold (8)
**9** Creature (6)
**10** Cloth, material (6)
**11** Audible acclaim (8)
**12** Basement (6)
**13** Performances of music (8)
**15** Individual article (4)
**17** Dried leaves for smoking (7)
**19** Hanging ice (7)
**22** Rank the quality of (4)
**24** Barking up the wrong tree (8)
**27** Contact, bang (6)
**29** Calamity (8)
**30** Short lengths (6)
**31** Cloth for the nose, in short (6)
**32** Least dark (8)

## DOWN

**1** Agrees that this is an oily substance (6)
**2** Gamp (8)
**3** Form of energy (8)
**4** Proceed forwards (7)
**5** Make moist (6)
**6** Buccaneer, sea robber (6)
**7** Container for magnetic tape (8)
**14** Fail to mention (4)
**16** Ripped, ruptured (4)
**18** Prototype (8)
**20** Overhead linings of rooms (8)
**21** Volume (8)
**23** With wrath or ire (7)
**25** Parallel rails (6)
**26** Young feline (6)
**28** Say it for the camera (6)

## ACROSS

**1** Arrangement of the earth to the gay gopher (9)
**9** It houses historical objects (6)
**10** Unswerving (8)
**11** Frictionless (6)
**12** Easy undertaking, piece of cake (6)
**14** It springs eternal (4)
**15** Stay temporarily, with bed and board (5)
**16** Heavenly paths (6)
**18** Spiritual leaders (7)
**21** Closings, conclusions (7)
**24** Place of safety (6)
**26** Public transport vehicles (5)
**30** Puerto ... (4)
**31** Gain (6)
**32** Soft offer? (6)
**33** Prone (8)
**34** Information about a future event (6)
**35** Making music through pursed lips (9)

## DOWN

**2** Full, intact (6)
**3** Loose fragments of rock (6)
**4** Contended or debated (6)
**5** Wooden cages for small animals (7)
**6** Warm season (6)
**7** A lowering in rank (8)
**8** Highlight (9)
**11** Piece of cutlery (5)
**13** Exhibition spaces for wild animals (4)
**17** Performing surgery (9)
**19** Without limit (8)
**20** Of them (5)
**22** The males have antlers (4)
**23** Do away with (7)
**25** Country, sounds fat and oily (6)
**27** Empty areas (6)
**28** Relating to people living in groups (6)
**29** Town and woodland bird (6)

## ACROSS

**8** Final or extreme (8)
**9** Torn (6)
**10** Be owned by (6)
**11** Attentiveness (8)
**12** Closer (6)
**13** Coolant I place there (8)
**15** Kiln or tandoor, say (4)
**17** Hair cleaner (7)
**19** Giving temporarily (7)
**22** Children's playthings (4)
**24** Move from one place to another (8)
**27** Soft, thin paper (6)
**29** Garb (8)
**30** Blank space around text (6)
**31** Leave the ship and go there (6)
**32** Observing (8)

## DOWN

**1** State without proof (6)
**2** Metric weight (8)
**3** Leaping animal (8)
**4** Conveyance for transport (7)
**5** Northern ocean (6)
**6** Animating force (6)
**7** Small item of cutlery (8)
**14** Merely (4)
**16** Ballot (4)
**18** Inoffensive (8)
**20** Guess, reckon (8)
**21** Area, region (8)
**23** Sources (7)
**25** Country, state (6)
**26** Was unsuccessful (6)
**28** Workers' organisations (6)

## ACROSS

1 Guessed (9)
9 Give rise to (6)
10 Rectifies (8)
11 Give heed (6)
12 Tension (6)
14 Way out (4)
15 Misplaces (5)
16 Court game (6)
18 Bring back to former glory (7)
21 Withdrawn from active participation (7)
24 If a car could go to the continent (6)
26 Scottish landowner (5)
30 Mental image (4)
31 Provoke to sew? (6)
32 Behemoths, titans (6)
33 Former, preceding (8)
34 Desired (6)
35 Gave formally (9)

## DOWN

2 Fires a missile (6)
3 Al's ire is taken out on the state (6)
4 Right to enter (6)
5 Simplest (7)
6 Provoke, set off (6)
7 Clasp, clip or hook say (8)
8 Close to (9)
11 Metric unit (5)
13 For one performer (4)
17 Putting in order (9)
19 Uttered a loud, high-pitched cry (8)
20 Understands written language (5)
22 Wheel covering (4)
23 Hanging piece inside a bell (7)
25 Metropolises (6)
27 Places in a grave (6)
28 Plan, sketch (6)
29 Refer indirectly (6)

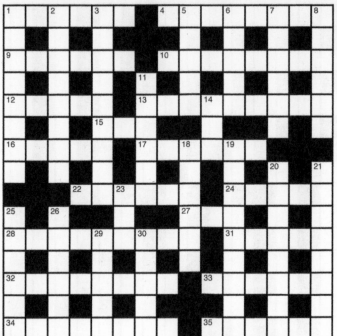

## ACROSS

**1** Uncontrolled, jerky motion (6)
**4** Affectionate strokes (8)
**9** Breathe out (6)
**10** Building for offices of urban government (4,4)
**12** Rents out these birds (5)
**13** Print in sloping letters (9)
**15** Hairpiece (3)
**16** Scorch on the surface (5)
**17** Trill, yodel (6)
**22** Of minute matter (6)
**24** Glowing part of fire (5)
**27** Sense organ (3)
**28** One who goes with you (9)
**31** Commence (5)
**32** Hollow cylinder for the laboratory (4,4)
**33** Dais, rostrum (6)
**34** Certified or supported (8)
**35** Gauge (6)

## DOWN

**1** Long, detailed essay (8)
**2** Built-in, integral (8)
**3** Chilled perspiration (4,5)
**5** Hello or goodbye in Hawaii (5)
**6** Boredom, tedium (5)
**7** Infamous Russian leader (6)
**8** Serving tray (6)
**11** Native American dwelling (6)
**14** Throw in a high arc (3)
**18** Of the immediate past (6)
**19** Life preservers (9)
**20** Confidently optimistic and cheerful (8)
**21** Authors' pseudonyms (8)
**23** Be in possession of (3)
**25** Implement for cutting long grass (6)
**26** Entertained (6)
**29** Essential oil from flower (5)
**30** Fill, with colour or feeling (5)

**249**

## ACROSS

**1** Do too much (6)
**5** Country, canal and hat (6)
**10** Kiev is the capital (7)
**11** Describe in words or make a picture (7)
**12** Australian flightless birds (4)
**13** Reddish-brown dye (5)
**15** Aquatic vertebrate (4)
**17** Measure of thermal insulation (3)
**19** Remove cargo (6)
**21** Combination into one (6)
**22** Stress, strain (7)
**23** Pestilence, scourge (6)
**25** Loud showman and dog (6)
**28** Disorderly crowd (3)
**30** Near in time or place (4)
**31** Venomous snake (5)
**32** Contributions to the poor (4)
**35** Mrs de Winter (novel by D. du Maurier) (7)
**36** Blockade, railing (7)
**37** Roofed structure in the garden (6)
**38** Stunned, slow to react (6)

## DOWN

**2** Being almost the same (7)
**3** Horizontal bar (4)
**4** Egg dish (6)
**5** Metal or plastic tubing, or trimming on garment (6)
**6** Rule, standard, pattern (4)
**7** Gin or vodka with dry vermouth (7)
**8** Furniture with drawers (6)
**9** Mark between parts of a compound word (6)
**14** Round-the-clock, unceasing (7)
**16** One item of information (5)
**18** Of the moon (5)
**20** Scottish river (3)
**21** Pocket for a watch (3)
**23** Small food storeroom (6)
**24** Branch of mathematics (7)
**26** Putting to death (7)
**27** Holiday destination (6)
**28** Musical emperor of Japan (6)
**29** It feeds on blood at night (6)
**33** Continuous dull pain (4)
**34** Group of three (4)

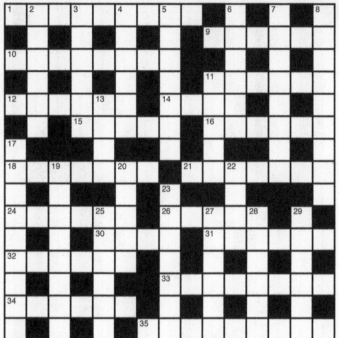

**250**

## ACROSS

**1** British painter and police officer (9)
**9** Bathing suit for the atoll? (6)
**10** Write carelessly (8)
**11** Recommendation for a course of action (6)
**12** Muscle in the arm (6)
**14** Lazily, without due attention (4)
**15** Malicious burning of property (5)
**16** Spookier (6)
**18** Garbage collector (7)
**21** State capital of Georgia (7)
**24** If not (6)
**26** Thin, crisp biscuit or bread (5)
**30** Molten rock from volcanoes (4)
**31** Type of paint (6)
**32** Allowable margin, latitude (6)
**33** Fortified troop station (8)
**34** Receptacle for plug (6)
**35** Brotherly (9)

## DOWN

**2** Beautiful exotic flower (6)
**3** Shrub from Persia? (6)
**4** Superior of a group of nuns (6)
**5** Looking suggestively (7)
**6** Stain by knotting fabric to produce a pattern (3-3)
**7** Member of a country (8)
**8** Fantastic but vain hope (4,5)
**11** Awake and watchful (5)
**13** Formal dance at the end of school year (4)
**17** Having no smell (9)
**19** Ability to meet financial obligations (8)
**20** Analyse to find the properties (5)
**22** Right to retain property until a debt is paid (4)
**23** Proud, pompous gait (7)
**25** Dribble from the mouth (6)
**27** Animal to hunt rats and rabbits (6)
**28** Straight sword with narrow blade (6)
**29** Felt hat with creased crown (6)

## ACROSS

**8** They're traditionally burned at Christmas (4-4)
**9** Dreadful, very sad (6)
**10** Esteem (6)
**11** Tiny diet, strangely, for individuality (8)
**12** Ask to call (6)
**13** Presenting for acceptance (8)
**15** Plus (4)
**17** Violent whirling wind (7)
**19** Come into possession of (7)
**22** Military land force (4)
**24** Treatment and prevention of disease (8)
**27** Also-rans (6)
**29** Material, concrete (8)
**30** Routine, ordinary (6)
**31** Arbitrary (6)
**32** Lift (8)

## DOWN

**1** Happening without warning (6)
**2** Catholicism, say (8)
**3** Is it on the face of the deaf hero? (8)
**4** The Inuit (7)
**5** The thing, reflexively (6)
**6** Server at table (6)
**7** One who hears (8)
**14** Mass of small bubbles (4)
**16** Temporary provision of money (4)
**18** An operating cost (8)
**20** Type of round container (8)
**21** Against the current (8)
**23** Answered (7)
**25** Interior (6)
**26** Remuneration (6)
**28** Motive or explanation (6)

## ACROSS

**1** Fruit or vegetable? (6)
**4** Ventures (8)
**9** Overseas (6)
**10** Buyer, client (8)
**12** Taut or strained (5)
**13** Sets of letters (9)
**15** Written account of a voyage (3)
**16** Pastoral (5)
**17** Me Gran is a Teuton (6)
**22** Bought and sold (6)
**24** Flavourful relish (5)
**27** Obtained (3)
**28** Mark with festivities (9)
**31** Loose flowing garments (5)
**32** Made visible (8)
**33** Taking wing (6)
**34** 'Hello ..., my old friend' (Simon & Garfunkel) (8)
**35** River of India (6)

## DOWN

**1** Farm vehicles (8)
**2** Seafarers (8)
**3** Voyager, say (9)
**5** Dull heavy sound (5)
**6** Non-speaking actor (5)
**7** Treat with over-indulgence (6)
**8** Accentuate (6)
**11** Having a sharp, uneven edge (6)
**14** Meat of the hog (3)
**18** Long, narrow ranges of hills (6)
**19** Oz (9)
**20** Rolling over and over, as a gymnast might (8)
**21** Communications (8)
**23** Tune, melody (3)
**25** Frightened (6)
**26** Trefoil plant (6)
**29** It's in the skull (5)
**30** Regions (5)

**253**

**ACROSS**

8 Furthermore (8)
9 Mistakes in printed matter (6)
10 Liquid in gas form (6)
11 Small amount of liquid (8)
12 Spot (6)
13 Impacted on (8)
15 Race around the measurement (4)
17 Twisting wind (7)
19 Answer or react (7)
22 Respiratory organ (4)
24 Smallholders in olden times (8)
27 Once every 52 weeks (6)
29 The organisms found in bait race (8)
30 Beliefs, dogmas (6)
31 Stern, pitiless (6)
32 Gaining knowledge (8)

**DOWN**

1 Spud (6)
2 Religious worship or great love (8)
3 Aloft, above (8)
4 System and structure of language (7)
5 Abatement, of pain say (6)
6 Icy region (6)
7 Large fish, valued for its roe (8)
14 Plant with fronds (4)
16 Young male horse (4)
18 Controls machinery (8)
20 Of the land of the Nile (8)
21 Intending or preparing (8)
23 Commonly (7)
25 Long seat with a back (6)
26 Looked after the sick (6)
28 Potential, dormant (6)

**ACROSS**

**8** Hold a view (8)
**9** Many-layered vegetables (6)
**10** Travelling a route regularly (6)
**11** Facial hair (8)
**12** Come into view (6)
**13** Stealing cattle (8)
**15** Allowing entry and exit (4)
**17** Direct or determine (7)
**19** Oh what a ... web we weave, when first
we practise to deceive (7)
**22** 'It came ... the midnight clear' (carol) (4)
**24** Property or practices passed down (8)
**27** Not present (6)
**29** Officer presiding at meetings (8)
**30** Roared (6)
**31** Eight pints (6)
**32** Percussion instrument (8)

**DOWN**

**1** Very fast pace (6)
**2** Oblique, not straight (8)
**3** It has very powerful hind legs (8)
**4** Unknowing (7)
**5** Three-dimensional shapes (6)
**6** Five US cents (6)
**7** Way in (8)
**14** 'Render ... Caesar the things which are
Caesar's' (Bible) (4)
**16** Wad of tobacco and electrical accessory
(4)
**18** Aloft, above (8)
**20** Investigation of component parts (8)
**21** Petrol in the US (8)
**23** Popular edible seed pods (7)
**25** Hanging ice (6)
**26** Equipping with weapons (6)
**28** Bait, provoke (6)

## ACROSS

**8** Openly, in front of all (8)
**9** Stringed instrument (6)
**10** Remember (6)
**11** One's individuality (8)
**12** Collision, blow (6)
**13** Gathering of spectators or listeners (8)
**15** Large-eyed birds (4)
**17** Seize, catch (7)
**19** Before now (7)
**22** Take one's ease (4)
**24** Minors (8)
**27** Thick digits (6)
**29** Available only at certain times of the year (8)
**30** Notice of a traffic offence (6)
**31** Undergo a change (6)
**32** Quickly and without warning (8)

## DOWN

**1** Depository for ancient objects (6)
**2** Nice, satisfying (8)
**3** Does this artist lop crust off? (8)
**4** Characteristic (7)
**5** Assented (6)
**6** Miniature (6)
**7** Tiny piece (8)
**14** Utilises (4)
**16** Are, in the past (4)
**18** The least they are is fit (8)
**20** Posture or stance on a topic (8)
**21** Put a vessel in the water (8)
**23** Everlasting (7)
**25** Passage from the Bible read aloud (6)
**26** Leased (6)
**28** Four-winged insect (6)

## ACROSS

**8** Full, intact (8)
**9** Not having been perused (6)
**10** Unprincipled (6)
**11** Plant for purifying, oil say (8)
**12** Invest with priestly authority (6)
**13** They feed on wood (8)
**15** Placid, calm (4)
**17** Native of Kabul, say (7)
**19** Using or containing too many words (7)
**22** Quartz with bands of colour (4)
**24** Remove the seat from a horse (8)
**27** Chronological records (6)
**29** Reference book, published annually (8)
**30** Pick-me-ups (6)
**31** Go without food (6)
**32** Point at which combustion occurs (8)

## DOWN

**1** Window in a sloping roof (6)
**2** Move towards (8)
**3** Sheets, pillowcases etc. (3,5)
**4** Release bodily fluid (7)
**5** Feel pain (6)
**6** Oil-rich sultanate (6)
**7** Equity, justice (8)
**14** The green-eyed monster (4)
**16** Precursor of the violin (4)
**18** They're part of the cooling system of engines (8)
**20** Making great demand on skill (8)
**21** Piece of paper money (4,4)
**23** It's worn under the collar (7)
**25** Goddess of the dawn (6)
**26** Herder (6)
**28** Reader at certain universities (6)

## ACROSS

**1** Turning point, dividing line (9)
**9** Surface of the earth (6)
**10** Spoke evil of (8)
**11** Enjoy the taste (6)
**12** Pleasure obtained by inflicting pain on others (6)
**14** Salespeople, in short (4)
**15** Majestic (5)
**16** In the throes of separate ones (6)
**18** Menaces (7)
**21** A bit weird (7)
**24** Financial takings (6)
**26** Fertile tract in a desert (5)
**30** Former association of communist republics (4)
**31** Hold in high regard (6)
**32** Except on condition that (6)
**33** Knolls, mounds (8)
**34** Smoothly (6)
**35** Take into custody (9)

## DOWN

**2** Man, say (6)
**3** Cure-all potion (6)
**4** Body-shaking dance (6)
**5** Advanced in years (7)
**6** Bust (6)
**7** Continental (8)
**8** Spoken communications to audiences (9)
**11** Physical activity (5)
**13** Upholstered seat (4)
**17** Positions, stances (9)
**19** Remembered (8)
**20** Long lock of hair (5)
**22** Sudden, short attack (4)
**23** Adoration (7)
**25** Body tissue that expands (6)
**27** Member of ship's crew (6)
**28** Calm and even (6)
**29** Fractured, damaged (6)

## ACROSS

**1** Account describing events (8)
**9** Unoccupied (6)
**10** Army unit (8)
**11** Edible tuber (6)
**12** Passageways (6)
**14** Exclusive, only (4)
**15** One of a race of brutes in Gulliver's Travels (5)
**16** Putting a question to (6)
**18** Lived (7)
**21** Small babies (7)
**24** Entree (6)
**26** Madness (5)
**30** Hackney car (4)
**31** Travelling about or going astray (6)
**32** A concept not yet verified (6)
**33** Spectators or listeners (8)
**34** Fight back (6)
**35** Unnecessarily pessimistic (9)

## DOWN

**2** Pronounce not guilty (6)
**3** Actually (6)
**4** Beat the seeds out of grain (6)
**5** Meat from a deer (7)
**6** Small, light boats (6)
**7** Diana can be a native of this country (8)
**8** Most powerful (9)
**11** Simple, unadorned (5)
**13** Orient (4)
**17** Act of leaving (9)
**19** Augment (8)
**20** Make an effort to write one? (5)
**22** Just, meet (4)
**23** Ma, tie it up and copy it (7)
**25** Strain (6)
**27** Instrument for injection (6)
**28** Take into custody (6)
**29** Makes into law (6)

**259**

## ACROSS

1 Oracular, predicting events (9)
9 Great flood (6)
10 Spring-flowering shrub (8)
11 Let sac be a chess piece (6)
12 Meeting of spiritualists (6)
14 Vessel for travelling on water (4)
15 Relating to the rise and fall of the sea (5)
16 Thief (6)
18 Break down into constituent parts (7)
21 Most delicate or most lenient (7)
24 Not uniform or smooth (6)
26 Pertain or cite (5)
30 Inactive or lazy (4)
31 Pass, as time (6)
32 Mature animals (6)
33 Sentimental tale designed to arouse
  sympathy (3,5)
34 Rubbish, detritus (6)
35 Escapade, exploit (9)

## DOWN

2 Death is a grim one (6)
3 Powerful (6)
4 Worn away, ground down (6)
5 Dishonourable (7)
6 Smoothly, in music (6)
7 Appropriate, meet (8)
8 Pass into or through (9)
11 Goods aboard (5)
13 Metropolis (4)
17 As a matter of course (9)
19 Passable, alright (8)
20 Causes to go (5)
22 Combustible material (4)
23 Put on clothes (7)
25 ... / or (6)
27 Lacking strength or vigour (6)
28 Knock at the door (3-3)
29 Moneylender who charges excessive
  rates interest (6)

## ACROSS

**8** Disappeared animal makes a peculiar raid on us (8)
**9** Earlier than (6)
**10** Win victory over (6)
**11** Illustrations, draft plans (8)
**12** Eastern market place (6)
**13** Abstract or general ideas (8)
**15** One thing on a list (4)
**17** Raised level area (7)
**19** Flattening (7)
**22** Brief written record (4)
**24** Audible amusement (8)
**27** Topmost point (6)
**29** Making with yarn (8)
**30** From side to side (6)
**31** Heavenly beings (6)
**32** Item of jewellery (8)

## DOWN

**1** Picture-house (6)
**2** Signed agreement to perform some action (8)
**3** I ate crab that contained micro-organisms (8)
**4** Bring forth, yield or manufacture (7)
**5** Come into possession of (6)
**6** Place of work (6)
**7** Cause to be afraid (8)
**14** Leave out (4)
**16** Song (4)
**18** Acquiring a skill (8)
**20** Diligent search for knowledge (8)
**21** Figures (8)
**23** Roots, derivations (7)
**25** Collect together in one place (6)
**26** Strong desire for drink (6)
**28** Invertebrate creature (6)

## ACROSS

**1** All in the mind (9)
**9** Dense woodland (6)
**10** Royal, regal (8)
**11** Invent (6)
**12** Book for rough notes (6)
**14** Edible seeds (4)
**15** View, sight (5)
**16** Evaluation, assessment (6)
**18** Detonate (7)
**21** Old pennies and policemen (7)
**24** Antidepressant drug (6)
**26** Beginning or early stages (5)
**30** Spherical plaything (4)
**31** Citrus fruit (6)
**32** Noise of a gun firing (6)
**33** Young male attendant on board (5,3)
**34** Summarises briefly (6)
**35** Litter for the sick (9)

## DOWN

**2** Field of grass (6)
**3** Invitees (6)
**4** All living things (6)
**5** Directions for dishes (7)
**6** Line of action (6)
**7** Calming drug (8)
**8** In other respects (9)
**11** Payload (5)
**13** Reflection of sound waves (4)
**17** Not permanent or lasting (9)
**19** Search for mineral deposits (8)
**20** Old gold coin (5)
**22** Person of equal standing (4)
**23** Beg or court (7)
**25** Short, sharp or sudden (6)
**27** Grave or gloomy (6)
**28** Can tin be an acid? (6)
**29** Disregard (6)

## ACROSS

1 Physical material (9)
9 European principality (6)
10 Imaginary place of great wealth (2,6)
11 Recesses or suitable positions (6)
12 Stern, harsh (6)
14 Hard, edible fat (4)
15 Edge where two roof slopes meet (5)
16 Affluence, riches (6)
18 Horizontal branches that produce new plants (7)
21 Representative (7)
24 Widely known (6)
26 Exterior (5)
30 Beside (4)
31 Exposed, revealed (6)
32 Odours, aromas (6)
33 Lines of text at the tops of articles (8)
34 Dramas set to music (6)
35 Assigned to a position (9)

## DOWN

2 Less pleasing to the sight (6)
3 Short downpour (6)
4 Astounded (6)
5 Selects (7)
6 Respectful, courteous (6)
7 Roman religion (8)
8 Social unit living together (9)
11 Freshly, very recently (5)
13 Food grain (4)
17 Senior member of college faculty (9)
19 Enumerated (8)
20 '... are red, violets are blue' (5)
22 Peek (4)
23 Religious devotion (7)
25 Remove cargo (6)
27 Fruit or vegetable? (6)
28 Area, territory (6)
29 Old measure for length (6)

## ACROSS

**8** In the open air (8)
**9** Wise old sayings (6)
**10** Former president of US and vacuum cleaner (6)
**11** Dainty (8)
**12** Unequivocally detestable (6)
**13** A big hand (8)
**15** Scottish isle (4)
**17** Russian ballet company (7)
**19** Least demanding (7)
**22** High in stature (4)
**24** Quarantined (8)
**27** Threw carelessly (6)
**29** More attractive (8)
**30** Tested the flavour (6)
**31** Secured against leakage (6)
**32** Quickly and without warning (8)

## DOWN

**1** Oval-shaped edible seed (6)
**2** Former, preceding (8)
**3** Strong black coffee (8)
**4** On which vehicles travel (7)
**5** Horse's pace (6)
**6** Dashboard (6)
**7** They treat teeth (8)
**14** Remove the rind (4)
**16** Plaything flown in the wind (4)
**18** Onlooker (8)
**20** Elevation above sea level (8)
**21** Took a firm stand (8)
**23** Abode (7)
**25** Recently (6)
**26** Each of three equal parts (6)
**28** In a balanced way (6)

## ACROSS

1 Apprehension, alarm (6)
4 Changed over (8)
9 Cleared areas of land (6)
10 Approximately 2.2lbs (8)
12 Care for the sick (5)
13 Being present at (9)
15 Wise old saying (3)
16 Armoured military vehicles (5)
17 Not at a specified place (6)
22 Think highly of (6)
24 Open sore (5)
27 Fall behind or cover to prevent heat loss (3)
28 Halted car at the important church (9)
31 Unkind or cruel (5)
32 Most primitive (8)
33 Duck, related to mallard and teal (6)
34 Most sugary (8)
35 Addressed God (6)

## DOWN

1 Positive (8)
2 Guiding or showing the way (8)
3 Talked to (9)
5 Between ribs and hips (5)
6 Sharp-pointed tip on a stem (5)
7 Lion-hearted (6)
8 Impairment, harm (6)
11 Southernmost state of the US (6)
14 Female sheep (3)
18 Magical incantations (6)
19 More badly behaved (9)
20 Hardly at all (8)
21 Left without father or mother (8)
23 Angry or insane (3)
25 Groups of eight performers (6)
26 Suffer from hunger (6)
29 Have being (5)
30 Relaxes or sleeps (5)

## ACROSS

1 Thus, hence (9)
9 Sudden feeling of excitement (6)
10 System for improving memory (8)
11 Swallowing food (6)
12 Steps, walks (6)
14 Auricles (4)
15 Fills to satisfaction (5)
16 Vacation spot (6)
18 External (7)
21 Commends, hails (7)
24 Break out (6)
26 Among, amid (5)
30 Notion, thought (4)
31 Courses, paths (6)
32 Except, save (6)
33 Renege in the builder of bridges, say (8)
34 Unit of instruction (6)
35 Change to another language (9)

## DOWN

2 Craving food (6)
3 Cuban dances (6)
4 Most delicate or topmost (6)
5 Most affluent (7)
6 Group of words without a verb (6)
7 Callers (8)
8 Most tenuous or meagre (9)
11 Bloomer (5)
13 Bits of information (4)
17 It's better to travel this way than to arrive, perhaps (9)
19 Lacking skill in handling delicate situations (8)
20 Tall grasses of wet areas (5)
22 Furthermore (4)
23 Not professional (7)
25 Hand-gun (6)
27 Mythical monster (6)
28 Underground passage (6)
29 Dislike thoroughly (6)

**ACROSS**

8 Blameless (8)
9 Not capable (6)
10 Threadlike structures (6)
11 US lift (8)
12 Artist's workroom (6)
13 Of the body (8)
15 Relative speed (4)
17 The grass is always thus on the other side of the hill (7)
19 Toothed wheel (7)
22 Pairs (4)
24 Grow, multiply (8)
27 Risk-free (6)
29 Most amusing (8)
30 Superintend (6)
31 Meet and greet (6)
32 Person related by blood or marriage (8)

**DOWN**

1 'Tis sin, oddly, to demand (6)
2 Boiled oatmeal and prison sentence (8)
3 Beach, strand (8)
4 Endeavour, try (7)
5 Strictly, solely (6)
6 The capital is Honolulu (6)
7 Distribute according to a plan (8)
14 Exceptionally courageous person (4)
16 Poetry, music, painting etc. (4)
18 Give up, abdicate (8)
20 Congregate (8)
21 No Cos cut up to get these fruits (8)
23 Occidental (7)
25 Fortuitous (6)
26 Deflects, heads off (6)
28 Area, neighbourhood (6)

**ACROSS**

8 M (8)
9 Place of perfect happiness (6)
10 Occur (6)
11 Allayed, alleviated (8)
12 Dishonesty, misrepresentation (6)
13 Declares to be guilty (8)
15 One unit (4)
17 Leaves for smoking (7)
19 Aran and Blasket (7)
22 Piece of paper money (4)
24 One who pays attention (8)
27 Verses with same-sounding ends of lines (6)
29 Lines spoken by fictional characters (8)
30 On land from sea (6)
31 Warning in a legal document (6)
32 Does this writing rile arty sort? (8)

**DOWN**

1 Wheel of a pulley (6)
2 Writ ordering attendance in court (8)
3 Attracting iron (8)
4 Move forward (7)
5 Selected, picked (6)
6 African country (6)
7 Said or did again (8)
14 Exclude (4)
16 Quality of sound, voice say (4)
18 The first (8)
20 Domestic staff (8)
21 In any position (8)
23 Hospital attendant is tidy (7)
25 Speaker (6)
26 Times after sunset (6)
28 Mistakes (6)

## ACROSS

**1** Rank in the martial arts (5,4)
**9** Withstand (6)
**10** Aesthetic (8)
**11** Lend an ear (6)
**12** Bring back to life (6)
**14** Sycamore or ash, say (4)
**15** Get a feeling (5)
**16** Out of ... (film) (6)
**18** Think well of (7)
**21** Associated, linked (7)
**24** One hundred cents (6)
**26** Slender missile (5)
**30** Lump caused by a blow (4)
**31** Not capable (6)
**32** Dance venues, in short (6)
**33** Commercial enterprise (8)
**34** Belonging to them (6)
**35** Wine carafes (9)

## DOWN

**2** Pantry (6)
**3** Crucial stage or turning point (6)
**4** It's fixed to something to hold it firm (6)
**5** Situated (7)
**6** Creed (6)
**7** Locality, area (8)
**8** Norms (9)
**11** Make an exit (5)
**13** Vote that blocks a decision (4)
**17** Contestant (9)
**19** Made shiny and smooth (8)
**20** Infectious agent (5)
**22** King of the jungle (4)
**23** Able, competent (7)
**25** On ship, train or plane (6)
**27** Country of the tsars (6)
**28** Wrinkled nut (6)
**29** More humid (6)

**ACROSS**

8 Named or styled as (2-6)
9 Sick feeling (6)
10 Heart-breaking (6)
11 Opportunity to evade difficulty (8)
12 Superior (6)
13 Giant Ron is ill-informed (8)
15 One time (4)
17 Form a mental picture (7)
19 Most proximate (7)
22 Takes a seat (4)
24 People receiving medical care (8)
27 Pitched tent (6)
29 Butterfly bush (8)
30 Small horses (6)
31 Writing implement (6)
32 Dirtiest, drabbest (8)

**DOWN**

1 Rough (6)
2 Expressing great amusement (8)
3 Minute particle (8)
4 Peaceful and delightful (7)
5 Issue an injunction (6)
6 Originator (6)
7 Overhead surfaces (8)
14 Chap, fellow (4)
16 Lay eggs here (4)
18 Determines the dimensions (8)
20 Bolting (8)
21 Soulful or amorous (8)
23 They're surrounded by water (7)
25 Accuse of a crime (6)
26 Sewing implement (6)
28 Nonetheless (4,2)

## ACROSS

**1** Sleazy, squalid (6)
**4** Ocean (8)
**9** Clauses added to legal documents (6)
**10** Desire for food (8)
**12** Piece of playground equipment (5)
**13** Places, sites (9)
**15** Function (3)
**16** Artist's stand (5)
**17** Become visible (6)
**22** Mediterranean country (6)
**24** Woodwind instrument (5)
**27** Foot digit (3)
**28** Person who moves from place to place (9)
**31** Roll of tobacco for smoking (5)
**32** Next day (8)
**33** Colour between red and blue (6)
**34** Terrible event (8)
**35** Nevertheless (6)

## DOWN

**1** Tense (8)
**2** Having the healthiest reddish colour (8)
**3** Not uniform (9)
**5** Subject matter (5)
**6** Awake and watchful (5)
**7** Dress and suit maker (6)
**8** Food from milk curds (6)
**11** Polite word (6)
**14** Chopping tool (3)
**18** Pleasing to look at (6)
**19** Fondness, tenderness (9)
**20** One-storied house (8)
**21** Clandestinely (8)
**23** Hear with it (3)
**25** Talented (6)
**26** Useful gadgets (6)
**29** Continental coins (5)
**30** Make amends for (5)

## ACROSS

**8** Fine or subtle (8)
**9** Hook for a ship (6)
**10** Not faint or feeble (6)
**11** Point of connection in electric circuit (8)
**12** More adjacent (6)
**13** Legendary lost island (8)
**15** And nothing more (4)
**17** Hair cleaner (7)
**19** Men and women (7)
**22** Use it to roast (4)
**24** Arms store or periodical (8)
**27** Ambits of the planets (6)
**29** Members of a state (8)
**30** Premeditated killing (6)
**31** Middle-Eastern state (6)
**32** Sets in motion, a ship say (8)

## DOWN

**1** Stinging plant (6)
**2** 1,000 grams (8)
**3** Large leaping mammal (8)
**4** In the middle (7)
**5** Vat, firkin (6)
**6** Something done (6)
**7** Situation of an alto icon (8)
**14** Printed characters (4)
**16** Middle of the day (4)
**18** Most burdensome (8)
**20** Vast (8)
**21** Deduct (8)
**23** Ships or containers for liquid (7)
**25** Man or beast (6)
**26** Standards to aim for (6)
**28** Topics, subjects (6)

## ACROSS

**8** Class or division of similar subjects (8)
**9** Fabric woven from plant fibres (6)
**10** For selling and repairing motors (6)
**11** KLM and Qantas (8)
**12** Badge showing military rank (6)
**13** Ascribed (8)
**15** To boot (4)
**17** Destructive windstorm (7)
**19** Climbing devices (7)
**22** Espy (4)
**24** Person appointed to liquidate assets (8)
**27** Heavy, metal tool (6)
**29** Ducks to ride on two wheels? (8)
**30** Requiring less effort (6)
**31** Group of countries under a single authority (6)
**32** Periods before nightfall (8)

## DOWN

**1** Not engaged (6)
**2** Diplomatic minister and his staff (8)
**3** Frontal bone (8)
**4** Night attire (7)
**5** From which great oak trees grow (6)
**6** How long is a piece of it? (6)
**7** Ancestor (8)
**14** Unaccompanied (4)
**16** Mislay (4)
**18** Vanquish, defeat (8)
**20** Lets heat up for the sports people (8)
**21** Of one's country (8)
**23** Exerted force on (7)
**25** Foreign and exciting (6)
**26** Changed direction abruptly (6)
**28** Vigour, vitality (6)

**ACROSS**

8 Disappears (8)
9 Edible bulbs (6)
10 Peculiar cleric in a shape (6)
11 Upriver (8)
12 Assuagement (6)
13 Accumulated, brought together (8)
15 Put into service (4)
17 North American bison (7)
19 This hour is just before dawn (7)
22 Smaller quantity (4)
24 Bony structure (8)
27 Made with needle and thread (6)
29 Throw the slob lawn (8)
30 They conduct heat and electricity (6)
31 Protective covering for a record (6)
32 Interchangeable words (8)

**DOWN**

1 Nautical (6)
2 Shenanigans (8)
3 Jolly, light-hearted (8)
4 Alleviate (7)
5 Sorted out the English county (6)
6 Menacing (6)
7 They enter by force to conquer (8)
14 Tacks on (4)
16 Alone (4)
18 In an unsympathetic way (8)
20 Taking as fact (8)
21 Working with wool and needles (8)
23 Language spoken in his glen (7)
25 Attorney (6)
26 London river (6)
28 Row, list (6)

## ACROSS

1 Mythological ferryman for Hades (6)
4 Unique, outstanding (8)
9 Observe (6)
10 Instruments for measuring angular distances (8)
12 1.77 pints (5)
13 Instrument for viewing distant objects (9)
15 Jurisdiction of a bishop (3)
16 Military trainee (5)
17 Frightens (6)
22 Reasons, grounds (6)
24 Beethoven's 'choral' symphony (5)
27 Humour or mental capacity (3)
28 Power to affect persons or events (9)
31 Golf clubs (5)
32 Particular, explicit (8)
33 Creature (6)
34 Stopped (8)
35 Mature animals (6)

## DOWN

1 Strife, clash of ideas (8)
2 Elevation above sea level (8)
3 Group of musicians (9)
5 Perfect (5)
6 Movable barriers (5)
7 City for the odd non-old (6)
8 Took a breather (6)
11 Takes without the owner's consent (6)
14 To do so is human (3)
18 Reply (6)
19 Made reference to (9)
20 Unofficial or casual (8)
21 Sounds of air forced through small openings (8)
23 Employ (3)
25 Touched with the lips (6)
26 Volunteers, puts forward (6)
29 Single items (5)
30 Hubbub (5)

**ACROSS**

**8** Painstakingly careful (8)
**9** 'Many young men of ... said goodbye' (John B Keane) (6)
**10** Capital city of Tasmania (6)
**11** As a rule (8)
**12** Higher in status or age (6)
**13** Component parts (8)
**15** Proficient (4)
**17** Mathematical expression for solving problems (7)
**19** Brief view (7)
**22** Footwear (4)
**24** Dwindle (8)
**27** Jollity, merriment (6)
**29** Width across the centre of a circle (8)
**30** Aim, purpose (6)
**31** Unstick (6)
**32** Nasal cavities (8)

**DOWN**

**1** Pick (6)
**2** Any life form (8)
**3** Relating to the arts and customs (8)
**4** Stretch of water joining two seas (7)
**5** Deprive of food (6)
**6** Recount, tell (6)
**7** The tales the fit folk tell (8)
**14** Child's construction set (4)
**16** Freshwater fish and lowest voice (4)
**18** Complying with commands (8)
**20** Having the longest lower limbs (8)
**21** Our mites are wet (8)
**23** Sea fish (7)
**25** Disturb the smoothness of (6)
**26** Horn of a deer (6)
**28** Ravel, snarl up (6)

## ACROSS

**8** The sky covered by dark clouds (8)
**9** Writer (6)
**10** Hackneyed phrase (6)
**11** Went away (8)
**12** Spanish title for a married woman (6)
**13** Commonplace and ordinary (8)
**15** Misplace (4)
**17** Large ape (7)
**19** Spears of frozen water (7)
**22** Air, melody (4)
**24** The witching hour (8)
**27** Stand firm (6)
**29** Also (8)
**30** Principles (6)
**31** Swan Lake or The Nutcracker (6)
**32** Least dark or least heavy (8)

## DOWN

**1** Gradually acquire new characteristics (6)
**2** Green vegetable (8)
**3** Game in which batman scores (8)
**4** Applies the mind to learning (7)
**5** Representative part (6)
**6** Stout, tough (6)
**7** Remade to be medium (8)
**14** Blood-carrying vessel (4)
**16** Swearword or solemn word (4)
**18** From which copies are made (8)
**20** Upper limits (8)
**21** Sealed case for a tape (8)
**23** Absolutely, completely (7)
**25** Movable bar in a compass (6)
**26** Responsible for a reprehensible act (6)
**28** Scatter water about (6)

## ACROSS

**8** A bank that deals with commercial interests (8)
**9** Is unable to (6)
**10** Signboard above a shop (6)
**11** Position, site (8)
**12** Food grain (6)
**13** '... child is full of grace' (8)
**15** At any time (4)
**17** Baby's milk substitute (7)
**19** Brief look (7)
**22** Something imagined in the mind (4)
**24** Thin, pliable sheet of living tissue (8)
**27** Except, save (6)
**29** Adversity, travail (8)
**30** Coiffure (6)
**31** Divulge (6)
**32** Interchangeable words (8)

## DOWN

**1** Scold, censure (6)
**2** Popular dessert (3,5)
**3** Always equidistant, never intersecting (8)
**4** Sports contender (7)
**5** Frozen drop of water (6)
**6** Joined as one (6)
**7** Sale and sail, say (8)
**14** Exhort, press (4)
**16** Having an exaggerated sense of self-importance (4)
**18** Managed a machine (8)
**20** Chuckling, chortling (8)
**21** Strips between panes of a window (8)
**23** Most profound (7)
**25** Emblems, labels (6)
**26** For a short time (6)
**28** Mussed up the herbaceous plants (6)

**ACROSS**

8 The smallest particle (8)
9 Ted or I could bring out a newspaper (6)
10 Control, direct (6)
11 M (8)
12 Island in the West Indies (6)
13 Intelligent (8)
15 Second-hand (4)
17 Colossal (7)
19 Hitting a golf ball off a tee (7)
22 Otherwise (4)
24 Buy (8)
27 Scatter water about (6)
29 Agitating or rousing (8)
30 Reddish-yellow (6)
31 Filmhouse (6)
32 Health facility (8)

**DOWN**

1 Small state (6)
2 This state strangely awed Lear (8)
3 Lots, myriad (8)
4 Put back in place (7)
5 Account (6)
6 Utter and ridiculous failure (6)
7 Water jet (8)
14 Attaches (4)
16 Perceives (4)
18 Projecting land mass (8)
20 Answer, reply (8)
21 Relating to eruption in earth's surface (8)
23 Prolonged (7)
25 Floor-covering (6)
26 Creature (6)
28 Gesture of communication (6)

## ACROSS

**8** Biting fly (8)
**9** Prepared wood (6)
**10** Tangible thing (6)
**11** Annoying person or thing (8)
**12** Took by force (6)
**13** Spot, tag (8)
**15** Capable (4)
**17** Farewell (7)
**19** Terribly (7)
**22** Flank, verge (4)
**24** Contemplates (8)
**27** Sudden sharp pain in 22ac (6)
**29** Very small organisms (8)
**30** Lacking ease or grace, like a tree? (6)
**31** Rule, control (6)
**32** Blackness (8)

## DOWN

**1** Twin, dual (6)
**2** Compressed, forced into a tight space (8)
**3** Anniversary of nativity (8)
**4** Local administrative body (7)
**5** Hit sharply (6)
**6** Forcible contact (6)
**7** Undisturbed by strife (8)
**14** No longer living (4)
**16** Most outstanding (4)
**18** Handler of a machine (8)
**20** ... Ho (film) (8)
**21** Mythical one-horned creatures (8)
**23** There's water all around them (7)
**25** The second of two (6)
**26** Showing concern (6)
**28** Food made from milk (6)

## ACROSS

**8** Large smooth rocks (8)
**9** Pit for extracting stone (6)
**10** Muscle in the arm (6)
**11** Distinctive forms of dress (8)
**12** Short jacket and Spanish dance (6)
**13** Reaped (8)
**15** Overt (4)
**17** Exceptionally courageous woman (7)
**19** Missed a step, stumbled (7)
**22** In addition (4)
**24** Does it suit Rome to be damp? (8)
**27** Divisions of time (6)
**29** Clasps in the arms (8)
**30** Figure in inn, yet, strangely (6)
**31** Imperial colour (6)
**32** If all ran in the showers (8)

## DOWN

**1** Small block with dots for table game (6)
**2** One's other self (5,3)
**3** Item of cutlery (8)
**4** Mollify (7)
**5** Short spurt of liquid (6)
**6** Inveigle by gentle urging (6)
**7** First public performance of a play or movie (8)
**14** Highly organised insects (4)
**16** Conference is one variety of the fruit (4)
**18** Extraordinarily large (8)
**20** Soulful or amorous (8)
**21** Does Finn keep the small tool? (8)
**23** Time to relax (7)
**25** Long contrasting band (6)
**26** Male relatives (6)
**28** Establishments for travellers (6)

## ACROSS

1 Exactness, sharpness (9)
9 Empty (6)
10 Take to it if the ship is sinking (8)
11 Caribbean islands (6)
12 Strict (6)
14 Small ball with hole through the middle (4)
15 Move to music (5)
16 Long-established US aircraft company (6)
18 Most well-off (7)
21 Freed from impurities by processing (7)
24 Spanish dictator (6)
26 Burdens, cargoes (5)
30 Hindu system of exercises for body and mind (4)
31 Revenue from outlay (6)
32 Delivered a blow (6)
33 Prolonged (8)
34 Implement for deleting (6)
35 Bought (9)

## DOWN

2 Stopped or slowed a horse (6)
3 Masticated (6)
4 Taken without the owner's consent (6)
5 Tenth month (7)
6 Assembly of troops (6)
7 Italian cheese, often grated (8)
8 Yardsticks (9)
11 Secret store, hoard (5)
13 Dissolute fellow and garden tool (4)
17 Manual workers with great skill (9)
19 Find the director in a charm (8)
20 Ghost, spectre (5)
22 Gradually lose colour (4)
23 Flat, raised land (7)
25 Rode a bicycle (6)
27 North Pole area (6)
28 Unit of a poem (6)
29 Light wind (6)

## ACROSS

**1** Ethereal, intangible (9)
**9** Charge with a crime (6)
**10** Felon (8)
**11** Plunging part of a machine (6)
**12** Godlike (6)
**14** Thin strip of wood or metal (4)
**15** Body fibre that transmits impulses (5)
**16** Old coin, twenty-one shillings (6)
**18** Ship-shape (7)
**21** Thought highly of (7)
**24** Uttered through the medium of speech (6)
**26** Sit on eggs (5)
**30** Collection of items of information (4)
**31** Motive or explanation (6)
**32** Mend (6)
**33** Odds-on (8)
**34** Artillery gun (6)
**35** Manner of marching with legs straight and high (5,4)

## DOWN

**2** Give leave to (6)
**3** Stay behind (6)
**4** Painful to touch or easy to chew (6)
**5** Books of maps (7)
**6** In place (2-4)
**7** Sneer lit up the hearer (8)
**8** Norms, touchstones (9)
**11** Called a name over a PA system (5)
**13** Close by (4)
**17** Build, fabricate (9)
**19** Letting fall (8)
**20** Of the moon (5)
**22** Ceremonial staff and a spice (4)
**23** Oh, so Pam uses it on her hair? (7)
**25** Director of publication (6)
**27** Bodies of soldiers (6)
**28** Annoy persistently (6)
**29** Sheepdog (6)

**ACROSS**

**8** Thousands of millions (8)
**9** Second-largest continent (6)
**10** Spear of frozen water (6)
**11** Not needed (8)
**12** Neighbouring (6)
**13** Willing to give unstintingly (8)
**15** Elderly (4)
**17** Rotating windstorm (7)
**19** Outbuildings for automobiles (7)
**22** Always (4)
**24** Ovation (8)
**27** Point to aim at (6)
**29** Naive or not guilty (8)
**30** Anxiety (6)
**31** See Zen at the first sign of a cold (6)
**32** Precipitation (8)

**DOWN**

**1** Group with a common bond (6)
**2** Selection by ballot (8)
**3** Above the eyebrows (8)
**4** Allay, alleviate (7)
**5** Formerly Formosa (6)
**6** Danish monetary units (6)
**7** Timetable, plan (8)
**14** Margin (4)
**16** Departs (4)
**18** Adversary (8)
**20** Beautiful (8)
**21** Flying vehicle (8)
**23** Risk or take a chance on (7)
**25** Undo, make less tight (6)
**26** Bumpy (6)
**28** Without difficulty (6)

**284**

## ACROSS

**8** Cover for paper (8)
**9** Foreign and colourful (6)
**10** Fabric for sail, tent and picture (6)
**11** Gradual improvement or development (8)
**12** Latin epic by Virgil (6)
**13** Numbers (8)
**15** Goals, objectives (4)
**17** Take by force (7)
**19** Some time before (7)
**22** Appends (4)
**24** Force applied to a surface (8)
**27** Stiffening carbohydrate (6)
**29** Strong liquor in the basin? (8)
**30** Mix in with crowd (6)
**31** Work hard to achieve (6)
**32** Collection of rules governing a Christian church (5,3)

## DOWN

**1** Breathe in (6)
**2** Weightiest (8)
**3** Think about (8)
**4** Answer or react (7)
**5** Improve (6)
**6** Abhorrence (6)
**7** Diffuse, melt (8)
**14** Utilised (4)
**16** Contiguous (4)
**18** Boar acts up in the circus (8)
**20** Taking for granted (8)
**21** Finding out (8)
**23** Protective military manoeuvres (7)
**25** Animating force (6)
**26** Undoes a knot (6)
**28** Room underneath (6)

## ACROSS

1 Vanish (9)
9 Act of kindness (6)
10 Mishap (8)
11 Alfresco dining (6)
12 Living creatures (6)
14 Small pond (4)
15 Slumber (5)
16 Highest models of excellence (6)
18 Because of that (7)
21 Huge, vast (7)
24 User of a bow in her car? (6)
26 Cage for rabbits (5)
30 Mental impression (4)
31 Vigorously healthy (6)
32 Spectres, wraiths (6)
33 With little or no delay (8)
34 Subdivisions of a play (6)
35 Exercising authority over (9)

## DOWN

2 They're short in niches (6)
3 Extraterrestrials (6)
4 Satisfy, gratify (6)
5 Try (7)
6 Diverse, assorted (6)
7 Water-spray (8)
8 Dealt with, moved things along (9)
11 Three-sided object that separates light
into colours (5)
13 Adhesive (4)
17 Most odd (9)
19 Surrounded completely, caged (8)
20 Feathered fliers (5)
22 Disabling liquid sprayed in the face (4)
23 Would Mao shop for this cleaner? (7)
25 One or the other (6)
27 Seat of a monarch (6)
28 Occur (6)
29 Totalitarian Russian leader (6)

**286**

## ACROSS

**8** Horsedrawn vehicle (8)
**9** Short digits (6)
**10** Without an occupant (6)
**11** Farm vehicles (8)
**12** Easing of pain (6)
**13** They're trained to compete in sports (8)
**15** Offensive to the eye (4)
**17** Weird foul arm of the set method (7)
**19** Long strips, for the hair perhaps (7)
**22** Require (4)
**24** Marriage ceremonies (8)
**27** Large African antelopes (6)
**29** Single-cell organisms, can be good or bad (8)
**30** Disks as substitute for coins (6)
**31** Advance information (6)
**32** Authorised to use lent diet badly (8)

## DOWN

**1** Harm, impair (6)
**2** Is Morgan a life form? (8)
**3** Reliable, unwavering (8)
**4** Not supporting either side (7)
**5** Append, affix (6)
**6** Reptile with a bony shell (6)
**7** Bare need in the Scottish city (8)
**14** Inflatable rubber ring (4)
**16** Association of criminals (4)
**18** Controller, of telephone say (8)
**20** One's uniqueness (8)
**21** Ben talks about the bedclothes (8)
**23** Breaks loose (7)
**25** Small, particular part (6)
**26** Harbours, a belief say (6)
**28** Moved to music (6)

## ACROSS

**1** Proprietorship, possession (9)
**9** Join the ends of, rope say (6)
**10** Naughtiness (8)
**11** Breakfast food (6)
**12** Gun, for instance (6)
**14** Not far away (4)
**15** Closely constrained, constricted (5)
**16** Credence (6)
**18** Meet a need (7)
**21** Grades (7)
**24** Peruser (6)
**26** Encounters (5)
**30** Unit of land (4)
**31** Symbol for a sound (6)
**32** The physical world (6)
**33** Statements of money owed for goods or services (8)
**34** Tiny amount of food (6)
**35** Handrail on a staircase (9)

## DOWN

**2** Author (6)
**3** Not including (6)
**4** Gliding over snow (6)
**5** Very young children (7)
**6** Ball, orb (6)
**7** In addition, also (8)
**8** Stinging sea creature (9)
**11** Telegram, wire (5)
**13** Lubricates (4)
**17** Study of celestial bodies (9)
**19** They betray causes and countries (8)
**20** Powerful effect or influence (5)
**22** Movable barrier in a fence or wall (4)
**23** Ace Mira on the continent (7)
**25** Deserved (6)
**27** Football team (6)
**28** Dirty marks (6)
**29** Rub out, excise (6)

## ACROSS

**8** Middling (8)
**9** Jail (6)
**10** Awkward, inept (6)
**11** It's grey to me, this branch of maths (8)
**12** Principality (6)
**13** Married men (8)
**15** Stirling ..., Kate ... (4)
**17** XVI (7)
**19** Facing the rising sun (7)
**22** Cipher (4)
**24** Arctic animal (8)
**27** Religious address (6)
**29** Physical potency (8)
**30** Nirvana, paradise (6)
**31** Make·a difference to (6)
**32** Lucid (8)

## DOWN

**1** Pulpy fruit eaten as a vegetable (6)
**2** One who buys and sells (8)
**3** Describes one's net pay (4-4)
**4** Distances from end to end (7)
**5** Protective garments (6)
**6** Movie-house (6)
**7** Enclosed passageway (8)
**14** Not new (4)
**16** Long ago (4)
**18** Recognise, name (8)
**20** One who professes great sensitivity to art (8)
**21** Bullfighter (8)
**23** Group of fruit trees (7)
**25** Required (6)
**26** 12½ per cent (6)
**28** These shows are a poser, oddly (6)

## ACROSS

**1** Get rid of, take away (6)
**4** Gathering together in large numbers (8)
**9** Vehicle on runners, for snow and ice (6)
**10** Humorous or satirical drawings (8)
**12** Apropos, concerning (5)
**13** Meddle, poke into (9)
**15** Part of a circle (3)
**16** Ascend, escalate (5)
**17** Pot and drum (6)
**22** Pacesetter (6)
**24** Made mention of (5)
**27** Young goat (3)
**28** At a very early stage of development (9)
**31** Hearing, say (5)
**32** Person who uses science to solve practical problems (8)
**33** Deliberately misleading fabrication (6)
**34** Nonplus (8)
**35** Not often (6)

## DOWN

**1** Exploration of facts (8)
**2** Device to aid the memory (8)
**3** Edible seed, root, stem, leaf or bulb (9)
**5** Show a response (5)
**6** Colourless, odourless and tasteless liquid (5)
**7** Smoothed with heat (6)
**8** Ring for sealing a pipe joint (6)
**11** Passed the tongue over (6)
**14** Newt (3)
**18** Is the bird a complete failure? (6)
**19** Expanse of scenery (9)
**20** Touchstone, benchmark (8)
**21** Textual matter added on (8)
**23** Tending (3)
**25** Rates of movement (6)
**26** Digit (6)
**29** Located inside (5)
**30** Concepts (5)

**ACROSS**

**8** Extinct reptile (8)
**9** Rubber (6)
**10** Spanish capital (6)
**11** Scare (8)
**12** Woody, tropical grass (6)
**13** Passed on knowledge (8)
**15** Small rodents (4)
**17** They fight conflagrations (7)
**19** Nearest (7)
**22** Capture, secure (4)
**24** Natural and unavoidable catastrophe (3,2,3)
**27** Shapes a soft substance (6)
**29** Shaped like a ring (8)
**30** Ministered to (6)
**31** Human beings (6)
**32** Quickly and without warning (8)

**DOWN**

**1** Albanian capital (6)
**2** Ghastly, frightful (8)
**3** Attractive (8)
**4** Deal illegally in vehicles? (7)
**5** Respite, balm (6)
**6** To a degree (6)
**7** Umpires (8)
**14** A hard one shows some nerve (4)
**16** Teachers' trade union (4)
**18** Slanted (8)
**20** Flavoured soft drink (8)
**21** Rodent with bushy tail (8)
**23** Where one lives (7)
**25** Take up residence (6)
**26** Gilded, pale yellow (6)
**28** Profoundly (6)

**291**

## ACROSS

**8** Order to appear in court (8)
**9** London river (6)
**10** Bird of prey (6)
**11** Average, mediocre (8)
**12** This nationality rang me up (6)
**13** Letting fall (8)
**15** You, of old (4)
**17** Native of Beijing, say (7)
**19** Closest to (7)
**22** Consumes food (4)
**24** Upper-case letters (8)
**27** Kidney-shaped nut (6)
**29** Strong-arm tactics (8)
**30** Promptly, without delay (6)
**31** Business that serves other businesses (6)
**32** Inclination, propensity (8)

## DOWN

**1** Showing compassion (6)
**2** Sample (8)
**3** Long, tapering flags (8)
**4** Artificial (3-4)
**5** Artist's workroom (6)
**6** Lap log at this pace (6)
**7** Imports, senses (8)
**14** Lease (4)
**16** Back of the foot (4)
**18** Court sessions in which testimony is taken (8)
**20** Breaking free (8)
**21** Returned to its original condition (8)
**23** Agrees, complies (7)
**25** Towards the interior of a country (6)
**26** Irritates, bothers (6)
**28** Lure, tempt (6)

**292**

## ACROSS

**8** Mender of machines (8)
**9** Mars or Uranus (6)
**10** Undergo (6)
**11** Tutored, schooled (8)
**12** Place for the practice of art (6)
**13** Revealed in private (8)
**15** Ode (4)
**17** Abbreviate (7)
**19** Enormous (7)
**22** Attractive or cunning (4)
**24** Alarm (8)
**27** Hold, keep back (6)
**29** Discord, split (8)
**30** Fastener for millinery (6)
**31** Shut (6)
**32** Rambled, roamed (8)

## DOWN

**1** Substance used in cheese-making (6)
**2** Ball and socket joint (8)
**3** Paper container (8)
**4** Branch of study of the physical world (7)
**5** Call into question (6)
**6** State capital is Honolulu (6)
**7** Young hares (8)
**14** Leave undone (4)
**16** On one occasion (4)
**18** Horrendous, gruesome (8)
**20** Trader (8)
**21** Had a right (8)
**23** Obscure, nameless (7)
**25** Young salmon (6)
**26** Three equal parts (6)
**28** In the same place, used in referencing (6)

## ACROSS

**1** Shielded from danger (9)
**9** A court held in it is private (6)
**10** Would rat go pip for the odd propagandist? (8)
**11** Add flavour at a time of year (6)
**12** Expose (6)
**14** Small shelter, for doves say (4)
**15** Perfume (5)
**16** Bower, pergola (6)
**18** Happy, satisfied (7)
**21** Adult (5-2)
**24** Burrowing rodent (6)
**26** Group of singers, in church perhaps (5)
**30** Plastic building bricks (4)
**31** Imaginary perfect state (6)
**32** Exultant (6)
**33** Reserved and uncommunicative (8)
**34** Principles of belief (6)
**35** Introduced (9)

## DOWN

**2** Describes worn or torn clothes (6)
**3** Sir and Lord, say (6)
**4** Round shape (6)
**5** Anticipates (7)
**6** Go at top speed through a working life? (6)
**7** Is it used to open oats at the table? (8)
**8** Pardon, Sir, are they small quantities of water, strangely? (9)
**11** Rising step (5)
**13** Deeds (4)
**17** Pasta made from tight peas (9)
**19** Elucidates (8)
**20** Made a mistake (5)
**22** Fail to do (4)
**23** Child's two-wheeled vehicle (7)
**25** Chooses by vote (6)
**27** Light weights (6)
**28** Decayed, stinking (6)
**29** Ferocious, savage (6)

## ACROSS

**8** With no worries (8)
**9** Slim or tenuous (6)
**10** Acid of oranges and lemons (6)
**11** Small short-bodied dogs (8)
**12** Shipworm (6)
**13** Enumerated (8)
**15** Lower limbs (4)
**17** Opening of the nose (7)
**19** Apparent or obvious (7)
**22** Edge, facet (4)
**24** Dreadful occurrence (8)
**27** The smaller of two (6)
**29** Native of Palermo, say (8)
**30** Amend, alter (6)
**31** Away from the sea (6)
**32** Observing (8)

## DOWN

**1** Maritime (6)
**2** Most light-hearted (8)
**3** Green vegetable (8)
**4** Wagering (7)
**5** Place of retreat in India (6)
**6** Godlike (6)
**7** Unlucky for some (8)
**14** Pre-owned (4)
**16** Instead (4)
**18** Standpoints (8)
**20** Distance travelled per unit of time (8)
**21** Space between two places (8)
**23** Pressing and smoothing (7)
**25** Creature (6)
**26** Sets of threes (6)
**28** Machine that converts energy into motion (6)

**295**

## ACROSS

1 Three-sided shapes (9)
9 In abundance (6)
10 Universal (8)
11 Official emissary (6)
12 Musically smooth (6)
14 Crop with nutritious oil-rich seeds (4)
15 Cooking stove or location for target practice (5)
16 Hearsay (6)
18 Sloping typeface (7)
21 Material for covering roads (7)
24 Ocean (6)
26 Bellows, hollers (5)
30 Hemispherical roof (4)
31 Parts of flowers (6)
32 Apostles and jury (6)
33 Accomplished (8)
34 Disqualify oneself, as a judge might (6)
35 Jason's companions in the search for the Golden Fleece (9)

## DOWN

2 Death is the grim one (6)
3 Rectangular block of hewn stone (6)
4 Eight pints (6)
5 Defences of objectionable behaviour (7)
6 French cake (6)
7 Popular drink (4,4)
8 Commemorate or eulogise (9)
11 Ancient Greek harps (5)
13 Public service vehicle (4)
17 Tiny replica (9)
19 Spectators or listeners (8)
20 Narrow light boat (5)
22 Unadulterated (4)
23 The Almighty (7)
25 Counsel (6)
27 Greek sun-god (6)
28 Verse of a poem (6)
29 Even if, although (6)

## ACROSS

**8** Soundlessly (8)
**9** Groups of singers (6)
**10** Unit of instruction (6)
**11** Fish tank (8)
**12** Does Ma wail in the African state? (6)
**13** Engrossed (8)
**15** Olfactory organ (4)
**17** Concerning other nations (7)
**19** Least difficult (7)
**22** Motor vehicles (4)
**24** Frightened or surprised suddenly (8)
**27** Council in a Communist country (6)
**29** Inhabitant of a small settlement (8)
**30** Way of doing something (6)
**31** It hardens when water is added (6)
**32** Magnificent, glorious (8)

## DOWN

**1** Picture-house (6)
**2** Coax, inveigle (8)
**3** Strikingly beautiful or attractive (8)
**4** Nightwear (7)
**5** Comes to mind (6)
**6** Repugnance, revulsion (6)
**7** Pants (8)
**14** It's made with hops (4)
**16** At one time in the past (4)
**18** Acquired (8)
**20** Gather together (8)
**21** Requesting the pleasure of (8)
**23** Where a building is located (7)
**25** Palliation (6)
**26** Ignites or illumines (6)
**28** Strikingly strange (6)

## ACROSS

**1** Target (9)
**9** Posing less difficulty (6)
**10** Russian urns with a spigot at the base (8)
**11** Orange root vegetable (6)
**12** Recount (6)
**14** Russian monarch (4)
**15** Ship's merchandise (5)
**16** Emblems, of membership say (6)
**18** State of things as they actually exist (7)
**21** Evidence from the accused (7)
**24** Half man and half fish (6)
**26** Mountain range in South America (5)
**30** Hairy coat of a mammal (4)
**31** Rational motive (6)
**32** Not long ago (6)
**33** Uncovered (8)
**34** Written communication (6)
**35** Of surpassing excellence (9)

## DOWN

**2** Flat-bottomed jar (6)
**3** Strange and fascinating (6)
**4** Dealer, monger (6)
**5** Caller, guest (7)
**6** African desert (6)
**7** Got inner gas (8)
**8** Uttered words of dissent (9)
**11** Conductor for transmitting electric power (5)
**13** Car for hire (4)
**17** Chiefly, in the first place (9)
**19** Tip Oscar for the fruits (8)
**20** Article of faith (5)
**22** Take flight (4)
**23** Someone who provides food and service (7)
**25** Temporary suspension of breath, in sleep say (6)
**27** Worthless talk (6)
**28** Overland journey by hunters (6)
**29** Dignified and sombre in manner (6)

**ACROSS**

**8** Describes a marriage when a previous one is still valid (8)
**9** Stank (6)
**10** A severe shortage of food (6)
**11** A staunch sort of plant? (8)
**12** Expel from a community or group (6)
**13** A vote to select (8)
**15** In addition (4)
**17** US city, famously burned during the civil war (7)
**19** Animating forces or hard liquors (7)
**22** Officer below the captain on a commercial ship (4)
**24** Portray in words (8)
**27** Deliberate discourteous act (6)
**29** Stick of black carbon material used for drawing (8)
**30** Go to UNESCO for the weights (6)
**31** Make violently angry (6)
**32** Large boa of South America (8)

**DOWN**

**1** Noisy insect (6)
**2** Important Roman Catholic church (8)
**3** To a moderate extent (8)
**4** Breaks free (7)
**5** Shop-lined passageway (6)
**6** Group of seven (6)
**7** Scale for the force of the wind (8)
**14** Mislaid or irretrievable (4)
**16** Young sheep (4)
**18** Growing structures for biting (8)
**20** Computer for one (8)
**21** Lennox, Sugar Ray and Mary (8)
**23** Type of harp, strings sound when wind passes over them (7)
**25** Starchy grains (6)
**26** Pressed and smoothed (6)
**28** Cruel, wicked and inhuman persons (6)

## ACROSS

**8** It's considered unlucky by some (8)
**9** Plump bird with cooing voice (6)
**10** Prickly bushes (6)
**11** Most fortunate (8)
**12** Conflict and discord (6)
**13** Cooking by vapour (8)
**15** Persistence of sound when the source has stopped (4)
**17** Directions for doing or making something (7)
**19** Calendar month (7)
**22** Exchange goods etc. for money (4)
**24** Laid low, out of action (8)
**27** Room for business (6)
**29** Composition for orchestra and a soloist (8)
**30** Almost not (6)
**31** False (6)
**32** Words that can be interchanged (8)

## DOWN

**1** Physiological need to drink (6)
**2** Mao grins strangely at the being (8)
**3** Short film about current events (8)
**4** The ... Patient (film) (7)
**5** North American Indian tribe (6)
**6** Self-centredness (6)
**7** Meaningless words (8)
**14** Implement, instrument (4)
**16** Form of a word in a sentence (4)
**18** Being in the process of departing (8)
**20** Apparel (8)
**21** Money contributed at a religious service (8)
**23** Give support or approval to (7)
**25** Becomes liable for (6)
**26** Inner part of a seed or grain (6)
**28** Linear array of numbers (6)

## ACROSS

**8** Attracting iron or steel (8)
**9** Type of monkey and blood component (6)
**10** Engraved or cut by chipping away (6)
**11** Without reservation or stipulation (8)
**12** Incapable of sustaining life (6)
**13** Opening, hole (8)
**15** Weedy grass, often occurs in grain fields (4)
**17** The belief that there is no God (7)
**19** British soldier or Butlin's worker (7)
**22** Flower in the eye? (4)
**24** ... da Vinci (8)
**27** Treeless plain in the Arctic regions (6)
**29** Exerts a force, draws (8)
**30** Copper and iron, say (6)
**31** Soft caps with no brim (6)
**32** Continued for (8)

## DOWN

**1** Elongated fruit (6)
**2** All that exists (8)
**3** Pupils or undergraduates (8)
**4** Academic person (7)
**5** Twist, squirm (6)
**6** Widow, surviving partner (6)
**7** Feeling of great elation (8)
**14** Type of disembodied spirit or graceful young girl (4)
**16** 'See ... the winter's snow' (carol) (4)
**18** Gate and Abbey (8)
**20** Conjecture (8)
**21** Steady and unceasing (8)
**23** Cooked by dry heat in an oven (7)
**25** Matrons, midwives etc. (6)
**26** Niche, nook (6)
**28** Easement, alleviation (6)

# The Solutions

**1**

```
F  A  B     D        S  B        F
C  O  M  P  L  E  T  E     U  N  R  E  A  D
R     P     D        P  F  O        I
A  M  O  R  A  L     R  E  F  I  N  E  R  Y
A     O     I        A  E  C        N
A  T  T  A  I  N     V  E  R  B  O  T  E  N
C        E  V  E  N              S
A  F  G  H  A  N  I     V  E  R  B  O  S  E
O              O  N  Y  X        A
P  R  E  A  M  B  L  E     A  N  N  A  L  S
C     U     L     C        C  K        E
Y  E  A  R  B  O  O  K     T  O  N  I  C  S
F     O     T     T        I  O        T
F  E  R  R  I  C     I  G  N  I  T  I  O  N
D     A     H        E     G     E     R
```

**2**

```
N  E  I  G  H  B  O  U  R     G     N     D
   N     E     L     N     U  N  L  A  C  E
T  O  N  E  D  E  A  F     E     I     S
   U     G     E     O     M  I  L  L  E  T
A  G  R  E  E  D     L  A  O  S     F     I
   H     E  A  S  E  D     T  S  H  I  R  T
F     R        S        T        U
O  S  M  O  S  I  S     S  O  O  N  E  S  T
R     I     N     P        B        E
E  N  L  I  S  T     O  R  B  I  T     M
T     I     K  E  E  L     E  T  H  N  I  C
A  N  T  H  E  R     E        D     E  M
S     A     W     C  U  S  P  I  D  O  R
T  U  N  N  E  L     A     I     R  S
E     T     R     S  T  A  T  E  S  M  A  N
```

**3**

```
   A  D  A  G  I  O     R  I  C  H  E  S
A     I     A     B     E     H     X  S
M  I  S  U  S  E  S     M  O  I  S  T  E  N
O     T     P     E     E     C     R  E
U  T  A  H     A  S  I  D  E     F  E  T  E
N     N     G     S  T  Y     A     M  Z
T  I  T  T  E  R     C     S  C  H  E  M  E
            L  I  G  H  T  E  R
F  I  L  L  I  P     I     T  I  C  K  E  R
U     E     D     B  E  T     D     N  E
R  A  C  E     F  O  R  U  M     A  U  L  D
O     T     T     B     S     D     C  D
R  H  U  B  A  R  B     S  P  A  R  K  L  E
E     R     T     I     L     R     L  N
   R  E  G  A  I  N     E  I  T  H  E  R
```

**4**

```
C  A  V  I  L  S     A  S  P  I  R  A  N  T
R     I     E        Q     N     D     Y
A  C  A  C  I  A     B  U  T  T  E  R  U  P
Z     T     T     C     A     E     O     I
I  D  I  O  M     O  R  D  E  R  L  I  E  S
E     C     O  W  N     M        T     T
S  H  U  N  T     D  E  M  U  R  E
T     M     I     O     A     O     M     P
      A  F  F  R  A  Y     V  O  U  C  H
A     D           I     H  O  I     C  A
R  E  I  T  E  R  A  T  E     N  O  I  S  E
C     S     N     B     M     G     L  T
H  U  M  A  N  E  L  Y     D  E  L  A  N  O
E     A     U        E        Y     G  N
S  O  L  D  I  E  R  S     S  E  V  E  R  S
```

**5**

```
M  Y  S  T  E  R  I  E  S     K     L     H
E     R     A     X     S  A  L  I  V  A
C  O  L  O  N  I  S  E        R     B     R
M     O     S     R     S  A  L  A  A  M
S  A  M  P  L  E     T  A  C  T     T     O
N     S  I  D  L  E     R  E  G  I  O  N  I
S        E     D           A     O     I
T  R  A  I  N  E  D     A  P  P  E  N  D  S
A     T     N     T        E        E
M  O  R  A  L  S     R  A  T  E  D     C
M     O     A  U  R  A     E  L  I  C  I  T
E  N  C  O  R  E     V     N     L     R
R     I     D     A  N  N  O  U  N  C  E
E  N  T  R  E  E     I     I     T     L
D     Y     R     F  L  U  S  T  E  R  E  D
```

**6**

```
   M     S     F     M     C     I     R
S  U  B  P  O  E  N  A     R  E  C  K  O  N
   S     O     A     S        O     L  L
S  E  C  T  O  R     S  I  C  K  C  A  L  L
   U     W     L     I     U     L     N
I  M  P  E  D  E     F  A  S  T  E  N  E  D
      L     S  A  S  H              C
S  A  W  D  U  S  T     E  E  L  L  I  K  E
E           O  H  M  S           I
G  R  U  E  S  O  M  E     C  U  T  L  E  T
O     Q     R     R     A     E     D
I  N  N  U  E  N  D  O     P  E  R  M  I  T
A     A     A     I     I     A     B
T  U  T  T  U  T     N  O  S  T  R  I  L  S
T     E     E     N     M     Y     E
```

**7**

```
C  H  A  R  L  A  T  A  N     I     T     T
O     A     B     N     I  N  C  I  S  E
S  Y  M  B  O  L  I  C        S     N     D
D     I     A     I     M  I  N  C  E  D
R  E  J  E  C  T     E  D  I  T     T     Y
N     S  H  E  E  N     S  U  B  U  R  B
S        A     T        E     R     O
T  R  A  M  P  L  E     T  R  A  C  E  R  Y
A     N     E     A        M        S
M  A  T  U  R  E     L  I  V  E  N     S
P     E     E  K  E  D     A  N  I  M  U  S
E  Y  R  I  E  S     E     C     N     D
D     I     K     N  E  A  P  T  I  D  E
E  X  O  C  E  T     T     N     H     E
S     R     D     J  E  T  T  I  S  O  N  S
```

**8**

```
   K     T     M     P     L     C     G
F  I  D  E  L  I  T  Y     A  P  I  A  R  Y
   B     A     S     R        U     T  A
T  O  M  C  A  T     A  I  R  C  R  A  F  T
   S     H     A     M     E     O     F
S  H  R  I  E  K     I  L  L  I  N  O  I  S
      N     E  D  D  Y           T
I  M  A  G  I  N  E     R  A  C  C  O  O  N
N           F  R  E  T        O
V  E  N  D  E  T  T  A     T  O  U  C  A  N
M     E     E     T        I     N     L
C  O  S  M  E  T  I  C     T  I  T  B  I  T
N     A     H        H     U     E     E
F  I  A  N  C  E     E  N  D  U  R  I  N  G
C     D     R     T        E     S     S
```

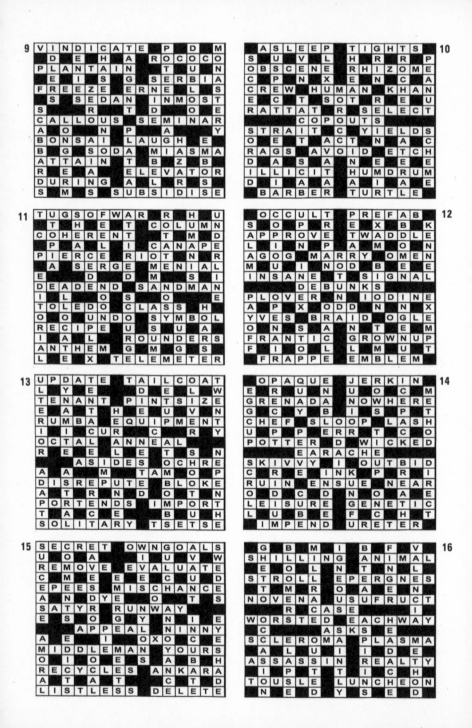

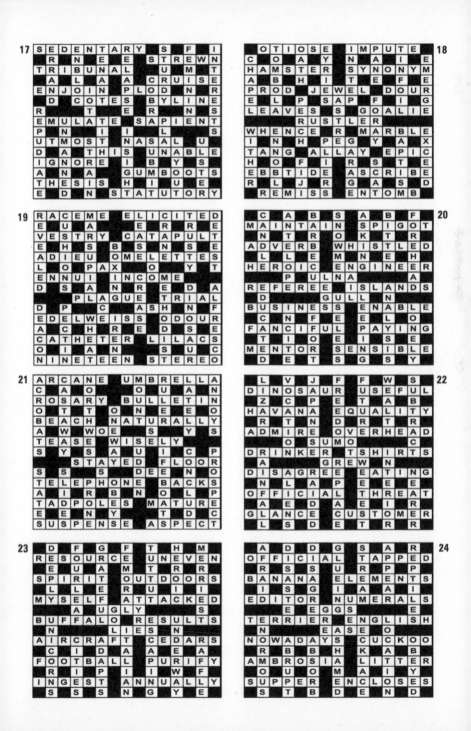

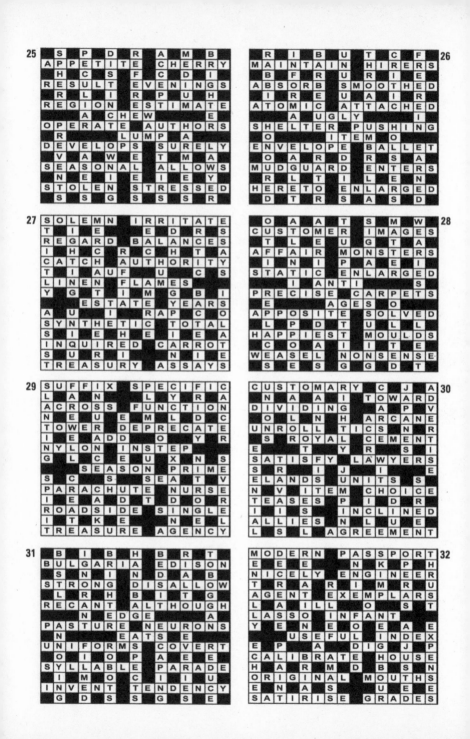

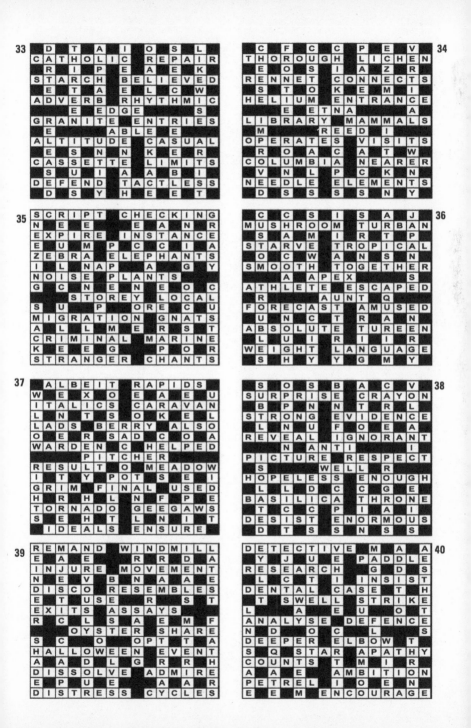

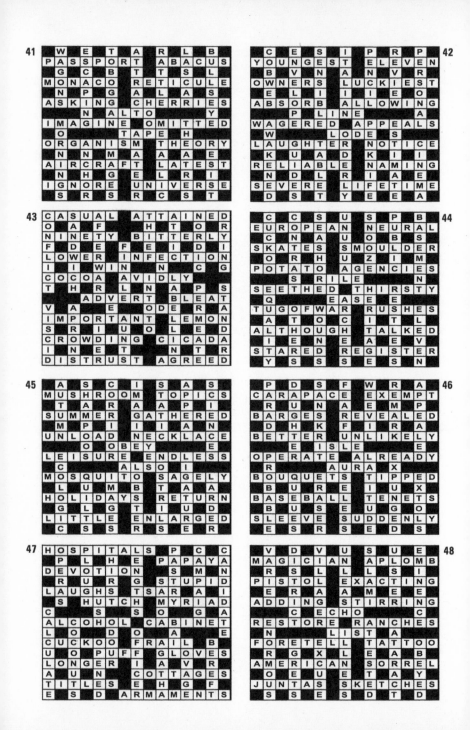

**49**

```
  L A S D S M D
M U L T I P L E   U N E V E N
  X H E   L N D S
P U B L I C   I N S P I R E D
  R E I   V E U R
S Y S T E M   E S T I M A T E
    I   E C R U       E
V O L C A N O   R E C O R D S
  L     W H E N     N
M E M O R I S E   T I C K E T
  A R N   R E U L
I N T A G L I O   R A P I D S
  D C A   I I I E
F E L L O W   N O N S E N S E
  R E S   E G D T
```

**50**

```
T E R R I T O R Y   C   V   G
  A   A   H   E   C O L O U R
P R O B L E M S   A   L   E
  N   B   M   C   T R O I K A
D E C I D E   U F O S   T   T
    D   T A S T E   R E S I G N
C     T   D   C   O   E
O R C H A R D   A S S E N T S
N   O   O   T   P   S
N O R M A L   O C C U R   S
E   R   F L O W   A D U L T S
C H I E F S   A   N   S   U
T   D   A   R H A P S O D Y
E X O T I C   D   D   I   I
D   R   R   E S C A L A T O R
```

**51**

```
  B B T L R R L
J A V A N E S E   E C H O E S
  M S X T C Y A
O B J E C T   T R A C T O R S
  O B B U L H N
P O T A T O   C O L O M B I A
    L   O P E N       N
D I S L I K E   C A B B A G E
  S       A G E S   I
M O I S T U R E   S I S T E R
  L A N T U C I
E A R L I E S T   M O U L T S
  T A V I I I H
N E E D L E   N I N E T E E N
  D S N G G S R
```

**52**

```
C R I S P Y   E D U C A T E D
O   N   R     R A   A R   I
M O V I E S   C A R R Y I N G
P   E   S   C F G B   I
O U N C E   A S T R O N A U T
S   T   N O D   O   L   S
E V E N T   E N A B L E
R   D L   T R   I T   S
    G Y P S U M   M O R A L
I   S   I   I C E   O   I
S I T U A T I O N   S T U N G
L   A   L D G T   B   H
A D M I T T E D   G O B L E T
N   P   E A   N E L
D I S T R E S S   D E A D L Y
```

**53**

```
  V D S H R C S
M A J O L I C A   E P O C H S
  C W X N N S O
C A T N I P   D I N O S A U R
  N C E B E E L
A T T A I N   A L T I T U D E
    S   C A G E       E
A N O T H E R   G A L L E R Y
  A       I R O N   U
S T O C K A D E   C U C K O O
  I   R M P H K W
M O D E R A T E   O N I O N S
  N A Z A R E E
B A T T L E   T R E A S U R E
  L E D S D T S
```

**54**

```
D I R E C T   A C C L A I M S
I   E   E   Y   E   N   E
R E A L L Y   U N I V E R S E
E   L   N   I   E   O   I
C L I M B   A S C E R T A I N
T   S   R I B   G   D   G
O P E R A   B U R G E E
R   D   T E A   V   R D
    G E N D E R   I M A G E
O   S   I   E N D   T   C
P O T E N T I A L   E L I D E
E   I   E   S Y   N O   A
N O N S E N S E   S T U N T S
E   T   D U   L   A   E
D I S A S T E R   E Y E L I D
```

**55**

```
S T R A N G E S T   A   K   R
  A   C R   A   O C T A V E
P R U R I E N T   C   N   F
  P   O A   I   L E A G U E
H O I S T S   S A I D   A   R
  N   S H E L F   N E A R E R
I   E   Y E   O   I
S H R I N K S   U N K N O W N
L   E   I   A   E       G
A U T U M N   M I M E S   E
M   U   I D E A   U N I O N S
A P R O N S   T   S S   J
B   N   C   E L E C T I O N
A L E V E L   U   U E   I
D   D   D   T R I M A R A N S
```

**56**

```
  M   P   R   S   S   F
M A R R I A G E   A U T H O R
  N   G   R   F   M   E   U
B A N A N A   E X P L A I N S
  N   N   L   R   L D   T
D A N I E L   E V E R Y D A Y
    S   E P E E       I
F O R M U L A   R A I S I N G
  R     L A Y S   P
P I L G R I M S   S T E A M S
  G   R   C   S   E   A
L I F E T I M E   M O D E R N
  N   E   C   R   B   I   T
S A N D A L   T A L E N T E D
  L   Y   E   S   E   G   N
```

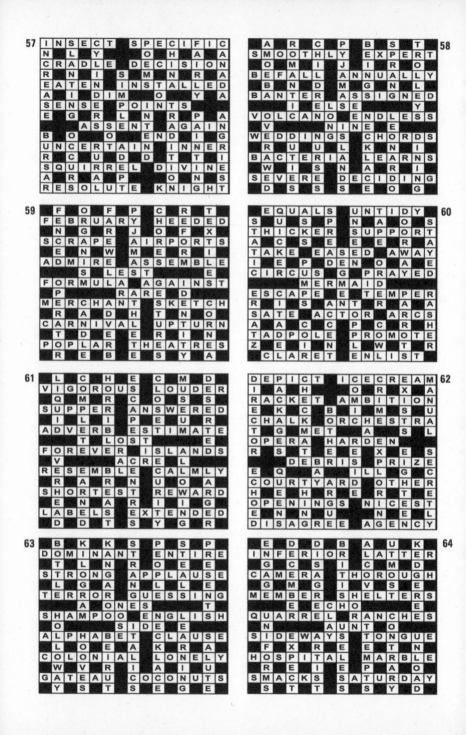

Crossword solutions 65–72

**65**
```
E N C O U R A G E   F   I   I
  A   R   O   R   T A N N I N
G R A D U A T E   C   S   T
  R   E   R   E   C I R C L E
C O A R S E   T O O L   R   R
  W   S E D G E   C E R I S E
P   E   D   O   B   S
A T T E M P T   T A L L E S T
R   W   I   S   A   S
A N I M A L   T O R C H   S
C   L   S O L O   H E A R T S
H E I G H T   M   Y   W   O
U   G   O   A C T U A L L Y
T S H I R T   C   H   I   E
E   T   E   C H A M P I O N S
```

**66**
```
  S   H   B   D   P   S   L
D E L I C A T E   R A P I E R
  V   G   C   C   E   A   B
R E D H O T   I N F O R M A L
  R   B   E   M   E   K   N
T E R R O R   A R R E S T E D
    O   I D L E       S
C R O W B A R   N A T I V E S
E       E A T S   N
S W A L L O W S   S E C U R E
A   I   R   P   U   L   E
P R O V I N C E   M O U L D S
D   E   A   C   I   D   U
P E L L E T   T E N D E N C Y
D   Y   E   S   G   S   E
```

**67**
```
V A R I E T I E S   C   O   A
  B   S   O   A   S O R R O W
C O R R I D O R   F   G   A
  A   A   D   N   A F F A I R
O R D E A L   E D G E   N   E
  D   L E E K S   R E G I O N
A   O   T   E   S   E
D E F U N C T   H E A V E N S
D   I   R   P   D   S
R E S C U E   L O R D S   S
E   S   G A L A   E S T E E M
S Q U E A K   T   T   Y   E
S   R   N   E Q U A L I T Y
E M E N D S   A   R   E   H
D   S   A   F U R N I S H E D
```

**68**
```
E   C   A   A   C   S   F
E N R O L L E D   A B H O R S
O   N   F   V   M   R   I
S U F F E R   E V E N I N G S
G   L   E   R   R   N   H
T H E I R S   B L A N K E T S
  C   C A S E       E
G L U T T O N   A N C I E N T
A     N U D E   D
A U T O C R A T   C R E E P S
N   B   O   T   K   N   I
S C H E D U L E   L I T T L E
H   Y   B   R   A   I   L
R E V E A L   L O C A T I O N
S   D   E   Y   E   Y   W
```

**69**
```
  A   S   B   D   S   P   E
A C C U R A T E   C H O R U S
  T   N   C   F   R   T   R
V I O L E T   E L E V A T O R
  V   I   E   N   A   T   P
L E D G E R   C O M P O S E R
  H   I T E M       A
P L A T E A U   I R O N I N G
  I   R A T E       O
A C C I D E N T   P O I S O N
  E   N   R   H   U   S   T
O N E H O R S E   B R I G H T
  S   A   A   I   L   E   E
Z E A L O T   S C I S S O R S
  D   E   A   T   C   T   S
```

**70**
```
S E R A P H   A C R O B A T S
O   E   R   U   C   D   P
M E T H O D   O B S E R V E R
E   U   C   F   I   A   E
W O R S E   E C C E N T R I C
H   N   S U M   Y   T   E
A R E A S   A P P E A R
T   D   E   L   U   N   F   S
  A S L E E P   S E R V E
W   E   I   P A W   I   V
R E S I D E N C E   E A G L E
I   T   R   U   T   R   H   R
G L A C I E R S   V I R T U E
H   T   E   S   N   E   L
T R E A D L E S   A G E N C Y
```

**71**
```
S C A T T E R E D   R   T   I
  H   H   X   A   R E F O R M
R E T R A C T S   G   X   A
  Q   I   E   I   B A K I N G
G U I L D S   E V I L   C   I
  E   L O S E S   R E T A I N
A   O   T   T   N   A
D E S E R T S   C H A P T E R
M   U   U   O   L   Y
I N D I A N   F L A S H   S
S   D   S E L F   R O A M E D
S L E E P S   I   C   W   V
I   N   E   C O T T A G E S
O B L O N G   E   I   I   R
N   Y   S   P R A C T I S E D
```

**72**
```
  U N I T E S   F L O R A L
B   U   I   O   I   P   U   C
E S C A P E D   S A T I S F Y
L   L   S   I   H   S   T   C
I C E S   T U B E S   O R A L
E   A   L   M R S   B   I   E
F O R G E T   U   O R G A N S
      M I S S I L E
G A L L O P   H   D A R T E D
L   A   N   S E T   M   E   E
A C R E   U P S E T   P L U S
N   G   D   I   N   C   L   I
C L E A R E R   N E E D I N G
E   L   A   A   I   D   N   N
  S Y M B O L   S L E D G E
```

**73**

```
  B K   A D B M
DOMINANT ERASER
  T L N H N R R
STRONG LITERARY
  L G A E A E I
NEARER TALENTED
    A OVER   S
SHAMPOO ABILITY
  O   TUBE  A
SPECIMEN RUBIES
  E A O B A E N
CLAVICLE TOLEDO
  E I K N I L I
ESCAPE DUNGEONS
  S R D S G D G
```

**74**

```
CHANGE STRESSED
H R U   H L T I
ACTUAL DEIGNING
R I R P M I N I
COCOA OVERNIGHT
O L NAP  E S S
ADEPT LARVAE
L S E I E U D M
  LEANED SCENE
A A P EAT M A
DETECTIVE ROARS
U T A N M A N U
LEARNING GLIDER
T C A E   I E E
SCHOLARS LAUDED
```

**75**

```
P R G A S P C
CARAVANS TERROR
N T N S R I M
HAVING AWAKENED
M O S Y I S D
WALNUT EINSTEIN
A ENDS  A
DECLARE NAPPING
L WITS  I
WEAKNESS SHANDY
V I R L I I I
CANBERRA GENEVA
T B O N N E I
BOWLER DRESSING
R E S S D T E
```

**76**

```
B S N A P A M
MUSHROOM ABROAD
R O N E P C I
GROUPS REACHING
O L E I Y E T
SWEDEN CHAIRMAN
  E STAY  I
MERRIER MACHINE
N AUNT  O
NOWADAYS TALKED
R D S U E S G
UMBRELLA MATURE
O O E L P E E
FUTILE LITERATE
S T P Y S S S
```

**77**

```
M P B F C R C
CARRIAGE LEEWAY
L O C A O F S
RABBIT RESPONSE
W A E F E R E
TIMBER ULTIMATE
L IDLE  T
VINEGAR ASHAMED
G AUNT  T
INKLINGS RETURN
O I I E A I I
CRITICAL NOTICE
A R E E G U H
UNLESS STEADILY
T S T S R E Y
```

**78**

```
D S C A S A C
HECTORED INDIAN
B R I V N V S
VACANT ANGRIEST
T I E N E S E
BEGGAR CORRECTS
H ITEM  T
PLATEAU INJURED
A NOTE L
CUSTOMER COTTON
G A E A K I W
CHILDREN LEMONS
T K E G A A I
REVEAL EXCITING
R R R Y S E E G
```

**79**

```
MEADOW BEASTS
B R A I E T E A
AVOIDED ADORNED
L S S E T M D D
LAIR ASHES COTE
E O W TON O N R
TENNIS L PURSES
    DESIRES
SHADOW D TENURE
I D W FAR L S L
SAVE LAYER RUED
T I S S M S R E
EASIEST OCTOPUS
R E N E T O E T
EDITOR EMPIRE
```

**80**

```
A G E T P G B
ALTITUDE ISAIAH
C G G R A C L N
POTATO CONCLUDE
V N P H I O A
METTLE ESCAPING
I ACRE  A
VOLCANO AGAINST
P IDLE  N
MEDICINE SOVIET
R N N F T I N
CASSETTE UNTIDY
T I E N R I U
LESSON CLEANERS
D T T E S G E
```

**81**

ESTABLISH · SLEAZE · DISCOVER · RUNNER · SOLEMN · AXIS · DEPART · RIGID · TUESDAY · REGULAR · EARNED · URBAN · VEIN · AMAZED · WAIVED · IMAGINED · SIGHTS · ORDAINING

**82**

HITHERTO · NOISES · MOSAIC · OCCASION · SALAMI · EASTWARD · OWLS · FORTUNE · KNOCKED · EASE · DEVELOPS · CAMEOS · PATIENCE · LOOSEN · BOTTLE · TACKLING

**83**

SCRATCHED · FLEECE · DESTROYS · LOUISE · DILUTE · APED · LANES · ASPECT · RESTORE · BETWEEN · COBWEB · READS · LOGO · RETAIN · FORMAT · REINDEER · RACKET · EMOTIONAL

**84**

ORDINARY · SORROW · SUPERB · IDENTITY · STATIC · ATTACKED · UGLY · BARRIER · RUSHING · ITEM · ENVELOPE · BYLINE · PARDONED · ENTERS · GLANCE · ENLARGED

**85**

PASTRY · COMPLAIN · OBTAIN · PEDANTIC · PALLS · AWARENESS · CURIA · ANYWAY · TIN · REPEAL · VOWEL · LYE · INTRODUCE · ROLLS · EPIDEMIC · SINGLE · ATTENDED · DEATHS

**86**

MINOTAUR · SANDAL · THIEVE · GRADUATE · RHYTHM · AUDIENCE · ARMS · VOLCANO · ESCAPES · LAST · REFERRED · RUGGED · CALENDAR · GUILTY · LOATHE · SPLASHES

**87**

REMARK · RELIES · STATION · DECRIES · EATS · ALLOW · BIER · YES · PICNIC · MURDER · MATTERS · MAGNET · STRAWS · DROP · SHREW · ASIA · SEW · STIRRED · PLANNED · AGREES · NUDGED

**88**

CONCRETE · LOOKED · SALADS · UPSTAIRS · DESIGN · RATIONAL · AGED · TWINKLE · DROPPED · ALSO · PLEASURE · METHOD · COMMERCE · NIECES · REVEAL · DRIFTING

**89**

```
S H O U T S   C O N F U S E D
T   V   R       D   O   L   I
U N E V E N   W O R R Y I N G
D   R   A   C   U   C   V   I
E X A C T   A G R E E M E N T
N   W   M E N     N     R   S
T H E R E   N E E D L E
S     D   N O X   I D   R
    S T A T I C   T R O V E
G   K   X     I R E   O   A
O I N T M E N T S   R U R A L
A   O   O   O   E   A   B   I
D E L I V E R S   F L E E T S
E   L   E   S     L   L   E
D I S A S T E R   C Y C L E D
```

**90**

```
  I   L   I   S   D   S   D
A N N O U N C E   O U T W I T
  F   C   V   V   R   R   R
S A V A G E   E X A M I N E D
  N   T   N   N   D   N   C
S T R I C T   T H O U G H T S
  O   E C H O       O
T O R N A D O   W E S T E R N
  I     O I L S   W
S N O W B A L L   C L I M B S
  T   A   L   L   A   L   O
A M B I T I O N   P O I S O N
  E   T   E   E   I   G   I
U N S E E N   S U N S H I N E
  T   D   S   S   G   T   G
```

**91**

```
N E C E S S A R Y   D   E   S
  X   X   U   U   C O L L I E
R E C O R D E D   C   E   N
  T   T   D   D   P I S C E S
V E N I C E   I D O L   T   A
  R   C A N O E   L E A R N T
S   N   R   I   I
T A U T E S T   T O B A C C O
R   N   T   C   E   N
A V E R S E   A S H E S   S
N   A   C R A B   A R C H E D
G E R M A N   B   V   H   V
E   N   R   A W A K E N E D
S P E E C H   G   N   M   R
T   D   E   H E X A M E T E R
```

**92**

```
  P   U   P   S   G   M
C R A N K I E R   A M A Z E D
  A   I   R   E   F   L   A
C I R C L E   C R A W L I N G
  S   O   C   I   R   O   I
F E R R E T   S K I P P I N G
      N   O P E N       G
C E N S U R E   E N D L E S S
  M       A R E A   I
M O I S T U R E   T I G E R S
  T   E   N   N   I   H   O
D I V E R T E D   O U T P U T
  O   S   I   E   N   E   N
E N G A G E   R H A P S O D Y
  S   W   D   S   L   T   S
```

**93**

```
P R E D I C T E D   D   P   S
  A   E   O   A   S E A R C H
C R Y S T A L S   C   E   A
  E   I   S   I   E R A S E D
F L I G H T   E I R E   E   O
  Y   N E S T S   R E D R A W
S   R   T   O   V   B
C O W B O Y S   A R T D E C O
A   A   O   P   Y       X
T U R K E Y   R A S P S   V
T   N   S O L O   T O I L E D
E X I S T S   G   E   E   L
R   N   A   R E N E G A D E
E I G H T S   A   C   E   T
D   S   E   E M P H A S I S E
```

**94**

```
  P   K   B   S   S   R   R
P L E A S A N T   T R A C E D
  U   N   C   R   U   T   S
K N I G H T   A D D I T I O N
  G   A   E   N   I   L   U
T E R R O R   G E O M E T R Y
  O   I D E A           C
S C H O L A R   S H E L T E R
  H   U N T O   I
B E G R U D G E   M O T O R S
  A   A   A   U   O   E   O
O P T I M I S T   N O R M A L
  E   D   N   R   Y   A   M
A S S E N T   A R M O R I E S
  T   D   Y   L   S   D
```

**95**

```
  C O M M A S   U N L I K E
R   V   E   P   N   U   I   A
A M A T E U R   E X C I T E S
Z   T   T   A   A   K   C   C
O M I T   G Y P S Y   S H O E
R   O   M   S A Y   O   E   N
S E N D E R   I   I R O N E D
        R U I N I N G
G O V E R N   F   N A T I O N
R   E   Y   M U M   N   N   A
A C R E   P I L O T   S T O P
V   S   S   D   M   S   E   L
E X I S T E D   E X P E N S E
L   O   A   A   N   I   S   S
  E N E R G Y   T I T T E R
```

**96**

```
  L   P   P   A   S   L   U
F I N I S H E D   T H U M P S
  T   Z   O   V   A   M   S
A M A Z O N   A C R O B A T S
  U   E   E   N   V   E   R
E S P R I T   C H E R R I E S
  I   I D E A           A
J A M A I C A   R H Y T H M S
  B   R I D E   A
P A R A L L E L   A L L O W S
  C   L   I   L   R   E   A
B U L L E T I N   I G N O R E
  S   I   T   E   N   T   M
S E V E R E   S E G M E N T S
  S   S   R   S   S   D   H
```

**97**

```
S T R E S S _ P R E S U M E S
U   E   H     U   E   A   Y
D E F E A T _ A M B I T I O N
D   L   T   S   B   N   N   O
E V E N T _ T R A V E L L E D
N   C   E R A   E   Y   S
L A T E R _ N E A T E R
Y   S   E   C   S   N   S   D
_ _ I D L E R S _ C A P E R
W   C   E     E A R   E   E
A L L U S I O N S _ Y U C C A
G   I   M   R   S   P   I   M
O R C H A R D S _ S T Y M I E
N   H   R   E     E   E   R
S W E A T E R S _ A D O N I S
```

**98**

```
_ I   D   D   P   S   V   T
I N T E R I O R _ T H E I R S
  H   S   S   O   A   L   A
D A R I N G _ T H R I V I N G
  L   G   R   E   V   E   S
H E R N I A _ I D E N T I F Y
  E   C A N E       E
S T U D I E S _ A P P E A R S
  E     K I L L   N
O R G A N I S M _ A C T U A L
  R   S   D   I   U   I
P I T H I E S T _ D U R E S S
  B   O   A   A   I   E   L
P L U R A L _ T O T A L L E D
  E   E   S   E   S   Y   S
```

**99**

```
A S T H M A _ P A R T I C L E
B   R   I     R   R   R   N
S P A R S E _ O R N A M E N T
I   P   E   S   O   M   E   E
N A D I R _ N E W S P A P E R
T   O   A R E   E   S   S
H B O M B _ E X P A N D
E   R   L   Z   I   O   S   G
_ _ R E V E A L _ S P E L L
S   C   A   O P T   N   A
P R O M I N E N T _ A N T I C
I   A   L   D   S   L   R   I
C U R L I C U E _ I G N I T E
E   S   A   C   I   E   R
S T E A D I E R _ R A I S E S
```

**100**

```
_ B E L I E F _ S T R E S S
U   N   D O   A   A   H   B
S T A B L E S _ I N G R A T E
E   B   E   S   L   E   M   I
F O L K _ D I M E S _ O P E N
U   E   W   L I D   U   O   G
L A S T E D _ S _ E N V O Y S
  _ I R E L A N D
M E M O R Y _ E _ D I T H E R
E   E   D   B A R   D   A   A
R U N G _ E I D E R _ C R O P
E   T   B   P   V   A   N   I
L E I S U R E _ E N F I E L D
Y   O   L   D   R   A   S   S
_ U N C L E S _ E G R E S S
```

**101**

```
S T A T U E _ C H U R C H
S   A   H   C   R   O   A
K I B B U T Z _ E N G I N E S
I   L   S   E D   E   Q   S
F L E E _ E M A I L _ T U N E
F   A   R   A C T   P   E   R
S T U D I O _ C _ P A R R O T
_ _ F L O O D E D
S H O U L D _ U _ A D V E R B
L   R   E   I N K   Y   X   I
E N D S _ A T T I C _ B A L I
E   E   C   H   L   D   M   D
P E R G O L A _ L E A S I N G
Y   L   O   C   E   T   N   E
_ M Y O P I A _ D I A D E M
```

**102**

```
_ C   A   M   M   U   T   W
M I G R A I N E _ N O U G H T
  C   O   S   A   R   T   E
M A R M O T _ S C O O T E R S
  D   A   A   U   L   U   E
B A R T O K _ R E L A T I V E
  I   E Y E D   E         E
V O L C A N O _ G A T H E R S
  V     U S E S   E
R E C O V E R Y _ S A S H E S
  R   R   L   S   U   I   R
A C C I D E N T _ M E T E R S
  O   G   V   E   I   A   O
E M P I R E _ M O N S T E R S
  E   N   N   S   G   E   S
```

**103**

```
_ P   S   F   U   M   R   D
C O M P L A I N _ I B E R I A
  L   E   R   C   N   V   S
C I R C L E _ O R I G I N A L
  S   T   W   V   M   E
C H A R G E _ E A S T W A R D
  U   L O R D       E
F O R M U L A _ D R O W N E D
  V     R U S H   E
R E S T L E S S _ Y E A R L Y
  R   E   F   E   T   K   U
T H A N K F U L _ H O N E S T
  E   D   O   E   M   E   T
C A R E E R _ S C I S S O R S
  D   D   T   S   C   S   E
```

**104**

```
S U S P E C T E D _ C _ R _ N
  N   R   O   L   P H O E B E
R E S E M B L E _ A   S   C
  V   F   W   C   S P H E R E
D E F A M E _ T Y P E _ A   S
  N   B I B L E _ A L A R M S
E   _ N   D   I   C   A
V I C T I M S _ A N O T H E R
E   A   I   F   V   Y
R U S S E T _ L I V E D _ P
Y   U   S T O A _ O R I G I N
B R A C T S   V   I   P   G
O   L   E   O C C U P I E D
D I T H E R _ U   E   E   O
Y   Y   M   P R E S I D E N T
```

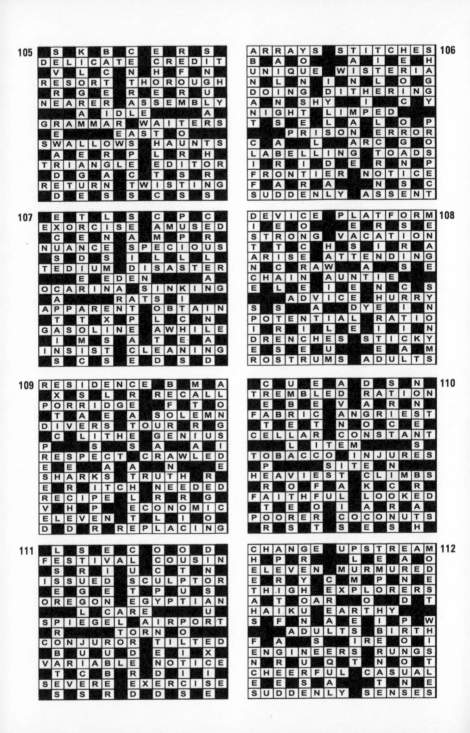

**105**

| S | | K | | B | | C | | E | | R | | S |
| D | E | L | I | C | A | T | E | | C | R | E | D | I | T |
| | V | | L | | C | | N | | H | | F | | N | |
| R | E | S | O | R | T | | T | H | O | R | O | U | G | H |
| | R | | G | | E | | E | | R | | E | | R | U |
| N | E | A | R | E | R | | A | S | S | E | M | B | L | Y |
| | A | | I | D | L | E | | | | | | | A | |
| G | R | A | M | M | A | R | | W | A | I | T | E | R | S |
| | E | | | E | A | S | T | | O | | | | | |
| S | W | A | L | L | O | W | S | | H | A | U | N | T | S |
| | A | | E | | R | | P | | L | | R | | H |
| T | R | I | A | N | G | L | E | | E | D | I | T | O | R |
| | D | | G | | A | | C | | T | | S | | R |
| R | E | T | U | R | N | | T | W | I | S | T | I | N | G |
| | D | | E | | S | | S | | C | | S | | S |

**106**

| A | R | R | A | Y | S | | S | T | I | T | C | H | E | S |
| B | | A | | O | | A | | I | | E | | H |
| U | N | I | Q | U | E | | W | I | S | T | E | R | I | A |
| N | | L | | N | | I | | N | | L | | O | | G |
| D | O | I | N | G | | D | I | T | H | E | R | I | N | G |
| A | | N | | S | H | Y | | I | | | C | | Y |
| N | I | G | H | T | | L | I | M | P | E | D | |
| T | | S | E | | L | A | | L | | O | | P |
| | | | P | R | I | S | O | N | | E | R | R | O | R |
| C | A | | L | | | A | R | C | | G | | O |
| L | A | B | E | L | L | I | N | G | | T | O | A | D | S |
| I | R | | I | | D | E | | R | N | | P |
| F | R | O | N | T | I | E | R | | N | O | T | I | C | E |
| F | | A | | R | | A | | N | | S | | C |
| S | U | D | D | E | N | L | Y | | A | S | S | E | N | T |

**107**

| E | | T | | L | | S | | C | | P | | C |
| E | X | O | R | C | I | S | E | | A | M | U | S | E | D |
| C | | E | | N | | A | | M | | P | | R |
| N | U | A | N | C | E | | S | P | E | C | I | O | U | S |
| | S | | D | | S | | I | | L | | L | | L |
| T | E | D | I | U | M | | D | I | S | A | S | T | E | R |
| | E | | | E | D | E | N | | | | | A |
| O | C | A | R | I | N | A | | S | I | N | K | I | N | G |
| | A | | R | | R | A | T | S | | I | |
| A | P | P | A | R | E | N | T | | O | B | T | A | I | N |
| | T | | T | X | | P | | L | | C | | N |
| G | A | S | O | L | I | N | E | | A | W | H | I | L | E |
| | I | | M | | S | | A | | T | E | | A |
| I | N | S | I | S | T | | C | L | E | A | N | I | N | G |
| | S | | C | | S | | E | | D | | S | | D |

**108**

| D | E | V | I | C | E | | P | L | A | T | F | O | R | M |
| I | | E | | O | | E | | R | | S | | E |
| S | T | R | O | N | G | | V | A | C | A | T | I | O | N |
| T | | T | | C | H | S | | I | | R | | A |
| A | R | I | S | E | | A | T | T | E | N | D | I | N | G |
| N | | C | | R | A | W | | A | | | S | | E |
| C | H | A | I | N | | A | U | N | T | I | E | |
| E | | L | | I | E | | N | | C | | S |
| | | A | D | V | I | C | E | | H | U | R | R | Y |
| S | S | | A | | D | Y | E | | I | | N |
| P | O | T | E | N | T | I | A | L | | R | A | T | I | O |
| I | R | | I | L | | E | | I | | I | | N |
| D | R | E | N | C | H | E | S | | S | T | I | C | K | Y |
| E | S | | S | | E | U | | E | | A | | M |
| R | O | S | T | R | U | M | S | | A | D | U | L | T | S |

**109**

| R | E | S | I | D | E | N | C | E | | B | | M | | A |
| X | | S | | L | | R | | R | E | C | A | L | L | L |
| P | O | R | R | I | D | G | E | | F | | T | | O |
| | T | | A | E | A | | S | O | L | E | M | N | |
| D | I | V | E | R | S | | T | O | U | R | | R | G |
| C | | L | I | T | H | E | | G | E | N | I | U | S |
| P | | S | | S | A | A | | I |
| R | E | S | P | E | C | T | | C | R | A | W | L | E | D |
| E | | E | | A | A | | N | | E |
| S | H | A | R | K | S | | T | R | U | T | H | R |
| E | R | | I | T | C | H | | N | E | E | D | E | D |
| R | E | C | I | P | E | | L | R | R | G |
| V | H | P | | E | C | O | N | O | M | I | C |
| E | L | E | V | E | N | | T | L | I | O |
| D | D | R | | R | E | P | L | A | C | I | N | G |

**110**

| C | | U | | E | | A | | D | | S | | N |
| T | R | E | M | B | L | E | D | | R | A | T | I | O | N |
| E | | B | E | | V | A | | R | | N |
| F | A | B | R | I | C | | A | N | G | R | I | E | S | T |
| | T | | E | T | | N | | O | | C | | E |
| C | E | L | L | A | R | | C | O | N | S | T | A | N | T |
| L | | | I | T | E | M | | | S |
| T | O | B | A | C | C | O | | I | N | J | U | R | E | S |
| P | | | S | I | T | E | | N |
| H | E | A | V | I | E | S | T | | C | L | I | M | B | S |
| R | O | | F | A | K | | C | R |
| F | A | I | T | H | F | U | L | | L | O | O | K | E | D |
| T | E | O | | I | A | R | A |
| P | O | O | R | E | R | | C | O | C | O | N | U | T | S |
| R | S | T | | S | E | S | H |

**111**

| L | | S | | E | | C | | O | | O | | D |
| F | E | S | T | I | V | A | L | | C | O | U | S | I | N |
| S | R | I | | U | C | T | N |
| I | S | S | U | E | D | | S | C | U | L | P | T | O | R |
| E | G | E | | T | P | U | S |
| O | R | E | G | O | N | | E | G | Y | P | T | I | A | N |
| L | | C | A | R | E | U |
| S | P | I | E | G | E | L | | A | I | R | P | O | R | T |
| R | | | T | O | R | N | O |
| C | O | N | J | U | R | O | R | | T | I | L | T | E | D |
| B | U | U | D | E | I | X |
| V | A | R | I | A | B | L | E | | N | O | T | I | C | E |
| T | C | B | R | D | I | I |
| S | E | V | E | R | E | | E | X | E | R | C | I | S | E |
| S | S | R | D | D | S | E |

**112**

| C | H | A | N | G | E | | U | P | S | T | R | E | A | M |
| H | | P | R | L | E | A | O |
| E | L | E | V | E | N | | M | U | R | M | U | R | E | D |
| E | R | Y | C | M | P | N | E |
| T | H | I | G | H | | E | X | P | L | O | R | E | R | S |
| A | T | | O | A | R | O | D | T |
| H | A | I | K | U | | E | A | R | T | H | Y |
| S | F | N | A | E | I | P | W |
| | A | D | U | L | T | S | | B | I | R | T | H |
| F | A | S | I | R | E | O | I |
| E | N | G | I | N | E | E | R | S | | R | U | N | G | S |
| N | R | U | Q | T | N | O | T |
| C | H | E | E | R | F | U | L | | C | A | S | U | A | L |
| E | E | S | A | T | N | E |
| S | U | D | D | E | N | L | Y | | S | E | N | S | E | S |

## 113

```
A S S I S T   T A D P O L E S
D   U   U     B   R   E   K
M E N A G E   P A T I E N C E
I   D   G   M   F   A   G   T
T E R S E   A U T O M A T I C
T   I   S O L   W   H   H
E V E N T   A F F E C T
D   S   E   W   I   O   M   T
    A D D I N G   M O U T H
V   S   A   H O P   L   I
E Q U I P M E N T   A F T E R
G   B   U   S   S   N   I   T
A S T E R I S K   S I M P L E
N   L   S   E   O   L   E
S H E B E E N S   I N T E R N
```

## 114

```
  S   N   A   I S   T   B   D
M E T A L L I C   T A R G E T
  E   P   P   E   U   E   M
S M O O T H   B A R B A D O S
  E   L   A   E   D   C   T
A D V E R B   R H Y T H M I C
      O   E R G O       O
G R A N I T E   W R I T I N G
  E       A B L E   W
P L E A S U R E   C R I S P S
  E   G   N   N   O   L   O
L A B E L L E D   V O I C E D
  S   N   E   I   E   G   T
D E U C E S   N O R T H E R N
  D   Y   S   G   Y   T   Y
```

## 115

```
  M   T   B   B   V   E   J
D E T O N A T E   A B R O A D
  M   B   R   D   C   A   V
A B S O R B   T H U R S D A Y
  E   G   E   I   U   E   N
T R A G I C   M E M O R I E S
      A   U S E D       S
C H A N N E L   G U E S S E S
  O       I T E M   H
E S T I M A T E   B O E I N G
  P   B   C   D   R   L   U
D I R E C T E D   E S T A T E
  T   R   O   I   L   E   M
C A V I A R   E N L A R G E D
  L   A   S   S   A   S   G
```

## 116

```
  S C I O N S   M I N I N G
S   A   W   I   E   O   E   P
T U R T L E S   D E S P A I R
A   C   S   T   I   Y   R   A
N O A H   J E S U S   D E F Y
Z   S   Y   R I M   D   S   E
A I S L E S   M   B I T T E R
      M I N I M U M
K I T T E N   L   S L A T E S
N   R   N   P A T   Y   H   E
I R O N   M U R A L   A I D E
G   T   T   N   N   F   N   M
H A T C H E D   K N O W A L L
T   E   O   I   E   N   I   Y
  A D J U S T   R E T I R E
```

## 117

```
S E S A M E   C A N T I C L E
O   U   O   L   O   O   L
M U S E U M   C O M P O U N D
E   T   S   W   N   E   R   E
T R A I T   A N E U R I S M S
I   I   A L L   L   E   T
M A N I C   L I S T E D
E   S   H   O   T   X   T   C
    D E E P E R   P I A N O
L   S   R   I L L   L   N
A S T H M A T I C   O M E N S
S   R   I   E   T   S   N   I
C L E A N I N G   J I L T E D
A   E   O   S   V   E   E
R E T U R N E D   R E N D E R
```

## 118

```
  N   M   D   F   S   S   D
F A M I L I A R   T I C K E R
  T   S   R   A   A   O   B
C I R C L E   N A T I O N A L
  O   H   C   T   E   P   R
I N S I S T   I N D U S T R Y
      E   O N C E       E
B O N F I R E   A L R E A D Y
  R       R A R E   Q
F I R E W O O D   M O U L D S
  G   S   U   V   O   A   R
D I S T A N C E   N E T T E D
  N   A   C   R   A   I   A
B A T T L E   B E D R O O M S
  L   E   S   S   E   N   S
```

## 119

```
C L I F F S   A D V A N C E S
E   N   R   R   G   O   U
R E T A I N   B O R R O W E D
E   E   G   U   N   E   B   D
M A R C H   T H E R E F O R E
O   I   T O O   A   Y   N
N O O N E   P O T T E R
Y   R   N   I   H   F   A   M
    E S C A P E   F I B R E
A   E   U   I R E   S   N
D I S R E P A I R   C L E A T
D   C   V   B   S   T   N   A
U X O R I O U S   P I S T O L
C   R   C   S   V   E   L
E N T I T L E D   H E R E B Y
```

## 120

```
S A F E S T   B A S S O O N S
U   R   I   E   C   P   C
S W I N G S   A S T O N I S H
P   C   N   P   O   U   A   I
E X T R A   A P P A R A T U S
N   I   L A P   X   E   M
S P O I L   A B S E N T
E   N   E   Y   Y   A   A   P
    I D E A L S   U N C L E
S   A   A   T A G   C   A
M A R G A R I N E   H E I R S
A   C   G   T   M   T   D   A
C O T T A G E S   P I G E O N
K   I   I   M   E   N   T
S I C K N E S S   W R I T E S
```

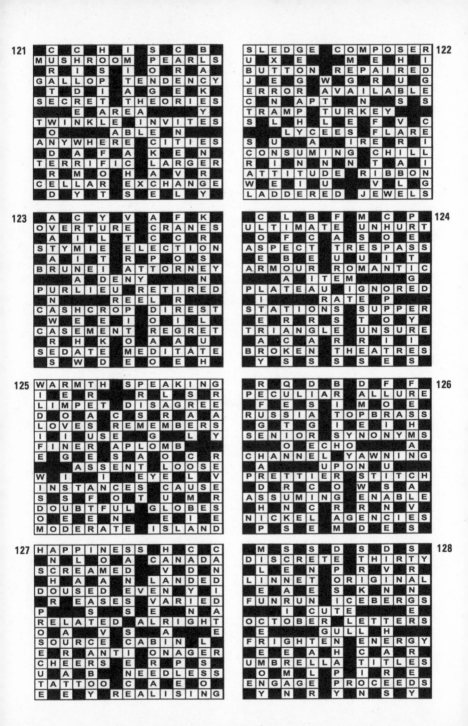

**121**

```
  C C H I S C B
MUSHROOM PEARLS
  R I S O R A
GALLOP TENDENCY
  T D I A G E K
SECRET THEORIES
      E AREA   Y
TWINKLE INVITES
  O     ABLE  N
ANYWHERE CITIES
  D A F A K E N
TERRIFIC LARGER
  R M O H A V R
CELLAR EXCHANGE
  D Y T S E L Y
```

**122**

```
SLEDGE   COMPOSER
U X E     M E H I
BUTTON REPAIRED
J E G W G R U G
ERROR AVAILABLE
C N   APT N S S
TRAMP   TURKEY
S L H L E F V C
    LYCEES FLARE
S U   A IRE R E
CONSUMING CHILL
R I N N N T A I
ATTITUDE RIBBON
W E I U   V L G
LADDERED JEWELS
```

**123**

```
  A C Y V A F K
OVERTURE CRANES
  A I L T C C R
STYMIE ELECTION
  A I T R P O S
BRUNEI ATTORNEY
    A DENY     N
PURLIEU RETIRED
  N     REEL  R
CASHCROP DIREST
  W E E I O I L
CASEMENT REGRET
  R H K O A A U
SEDATE MEDITATE
  S W D E O E H
```

**124**

```
  C L B F M C P
ULTIMATE UNHURT
  O F C A S O E
ASPECT TRESPASS
  E B E U U I T
ARMOUR ROMANTIC
    A ITEM     G
PLATEAU IGNORED
  I     RATE  P
STATIONS SUPPER
  E R R S T O Y
TRIANGLE UNSURE
  A C A R R I I
BROKEN THEATRES
  Y S S S S E S
```

**125**

```
WARMTH   SPEAKING
I E R     R L S R
LIMPET DISAGREE
D O A C S R A A
LOVES REMEMBERS
I I   USE G L Y
FINER APLOMB
E G E S A O C R
  ASSENT LOOSE
W I I EYE I L V
INSTANCES CAUSE
S S F O T U M R
DOUBTFUL GLOBES
O E E N   E I E
MODERATE ISLAND
```

**126**

```
  R Q D B D F F
PECULIAR ALLURE
  F E S I M O E
RUSSIA TOPBRASS
  G T G I E I H
SENIOR SYNONYMS
    O ECHO    A
CHANNEL YAWNING
  A     UPON  U
PRETTIER STITCH
  D R C O W S A
ASSUMING ENABLE
  H N C R R N V
NICKEL AGENCIES
  P S E M D E S
```

**127**

```
HAPPINESS H C C
  N L O A CANADA
SCREAMED V D N
  H A A N LANDED
DOUSED EVEN Y I
  R EASES VARIED
P   S   S E N A
RELATED ALRIGHT
O A V S A E
SOURCE CABIN L
E R ANTI ONAGER
CHEERS E R P S
U A B NEEDLESS
TATTOO C A E O
E E Y REALISING
```

**128**

```
M S S D S D S
DISCRETE THIRTY
L E N P R V R
LINNET ORIGINAL
E A E S K N N
FUNRUN ICEBERGS
    I CUTE    E
OCTOBER LETTERS
E     GULL H
FRIGHTEN ENERGY
E E A H C A R
UMBRELLA TITLES
O M L P I E
ENGAGE PROCEEDS
Y N R Y N S Y
```

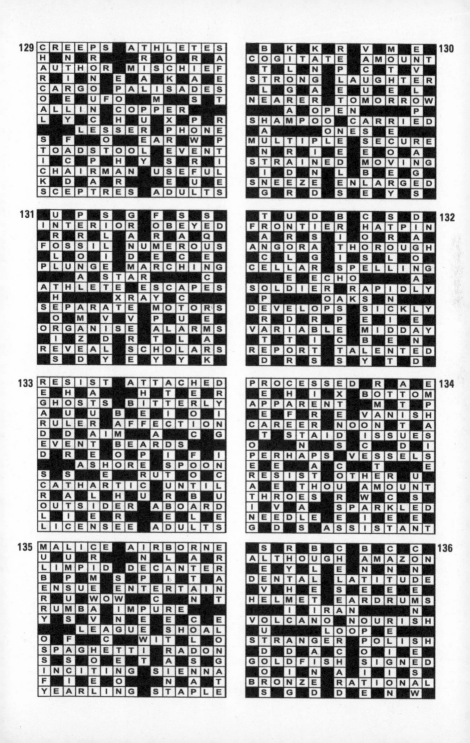

**129**
```
C R E E P S   A T H L E T E S
H   N   R     R   O   R   A
A U T H O R   M I S C H I E F
R   I   N   E   A   K   A   E
C A R G O   P A L I S A D E S
O   E   U F O   M     S   T
A L L I N   C O P P E R
L Y   C   H   U   X   P   R
    L E S S E R   P H O N E
S   F   O   E A R   W   P
T O A D S T O O L   E V E N T
I   C   P   H   Y   S   R   I
C H A I R M A N   U S E F U L
K   D   A   R     E   U   E
S C E P T R E S   A D U L T S
```

**130**
```
  B   K   R   V   M   E
C O G I T A T E   A M O U N T
  T   L   N   C   T   V
S T R O N G   L A U G H T E R
  L   G   A   E   U   E   L
N E A R E R   T O M O R R O W
  A   O P E N         P
S H A M P O O   C A R R I E D
  A   O N E S   E
M U L T I P L E   S E C U R E
  N   R   I   E   E   O   A
S T R A I N E D   M O V I N G
  I   D   N   L   B   G
S N E E Z E   E N L A R G E D
  G   R   D   S   E   Y   S
```

**131**
```
  U   P   S   G   F   S   S
I N T E R I O R   O B E Y E D
  R   R   L   A   R   A   Q
F O S S I L   N U M E R O U S
  L   O   I   D   E   C   E
P L U N G E   M A R C H I N G
  A   S T A R         C
A T H L E T E   E S C A P E S
  H   X R A Y   C
S E P A R A T E   M O T O R S
  O   M   V   V   P   U   E
O R G A N I S E   A L A R M S
  I   Z   D   R   T   L   A
R E V E A L   S C H O L A R S
  S   D   Y   E   Y   Y   K
```

**132**
```
  T   U   D   B   C   S   D
F R O N T I E R   H A T P I N
  A   R   S   I   O   R   A
A N G O R A   T H O R O U G H
  C   L   G   I   S   L   O
C E L L A R   S P E L L I N G
  E   E C H O         A
S O L D I E R   R A P I D L Y
  P   O A K S   N
D E V E L O P S   S I C K L Y
  R   D   R   P   E   I   E
V A R I A B L E   M I D D A Y
  T   T   I   C   B   E   N
R E P O R T   T A L E N T E D
  D   R   S   S   Y   T   D
```

**133**
```
R E S I S T   A T T A C H E D
E   H   A   H   T   E   R
G H O S T S   B I T T E R L Y
A   U   U   B   E   I   O   I
R U L E R   A F F E C T I O N
D   D   A I M   A   C   G
E V E N T   B E A R D S
D   R   E   O   P   I   F   I
    A S H O R E   S P O O N
S   S   E   R U T   O   C
C A T H A R T I C   U N T I L
R   A   L   H   U   R   B   U
O U T S I D E R   A B O A R D
L   I   E   R     E   L   E
L I C E N S E E   A D U L T S
```

**134**
```
P R O C E S S E D   R   A   E
E   H   I   X   B O T T O M
A P P A R E N T   M   T   P
E   F   R   E   V A N I S H
C A R E E R   N O O N   T   A
T   S T A I D   I S S U E S
O   N   S   C   D   I
P E R H A P S   V E S S E L S
E   E   A   C   T   E
R E S I S T   O T H E R   U
A   E   T H O U   A M O U N T
T H R O E S   R   W   C   S
I   V   A   S P A R K L E D
N E E D L E   E   I   E   E
G   D   S   A S S I S T A N T
```

**135**
```
M A L I C E   A I R B O R N E
U   U   R     N   L   A   R
L I M P I D   D E C A N T E R
B   P   M   S   P   I   T   A
E N S U E   E N T E R T A I N
R   U   W O W   C   N   T
R U M B A   I M P U R E
Y   S   V   N   E   E   C   E
    L E A G U E   S H O A L
O   F   C   W I T   L   O
S P A G H E T T I   R A D O N
S   S   O   E   T   A   S   G
I N C I T I N G   S I E N N A
F   I   E   O   N   A   T
Y E A R L I N G   S T A P L E
```

**136**
```
  S   R   B   C   B   C   C
A L T H O U G H   A M A Z O N
  E   Y   L   E   N   N   N
D E N T A L   L A T I T U D E
  V   H   E   S   E   E   E
H E L M E T   E A R D R U M S
  I   I R A N         N
V O L C A N O   N O U R I S H
  U   L O O P   E
S T R A N G E R   P O L I S H
  D   D   A   C   O   I   E
G O L D F I S H   S I G N E D
  O   I   N   A   I   S
B R O N Z E   R A T I O N A L
  S   G   D   D   E   N   W
```

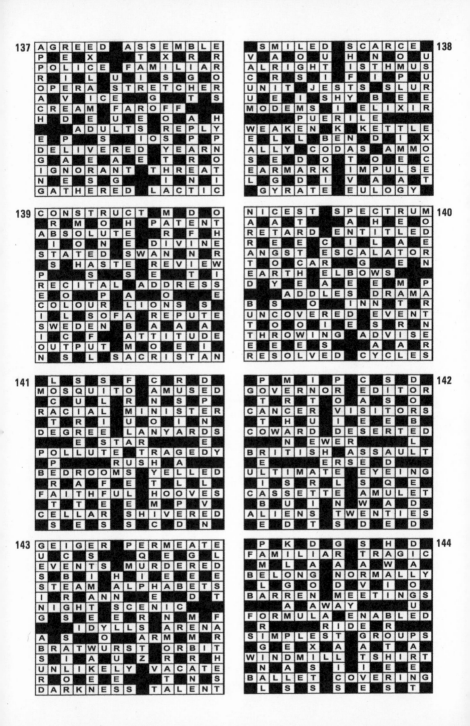

**145**
```
. C . A . W . P . R . D . T
M A N D R I L L . E A R T H Y
. N . D . R . A . P . A . A
S T R I F E . . T R A P P I N G
. O . T . L . E . I . E . K
U R S I N E . A I R C R A F T
. . O . S T U N . . . . U
G A R N I S H . C H I E F L Y
. D . . E C H O . A
N O C T U R N E . M O S T L Y
. P . R . U . N . O . T . O
S T R A I G H T . N E W E S T
. I . D . G . R . Y . A . I
S N E E Z E . A D M I R I N G
. G . R . D . L . S . D . G
```

**146**
```
. S T I G M A . D R O O P S
E . I . R . L . A . U . I . A
G I M M I C K . M I R A G E S
R . P . M . A . A . S . T . S
E X A M . S L U S H . M A G I
S . N . C . I N K . S . I . S
S M I T H Y . B . P E L L E T
. . . A E R O B I C
C O M F I T . W . E T H I C S
O . A . R . V E T . S . N . T
D I N E . S O D O M . E S P Y
I . A . T . Y . M . B . P . L
F U C H S I A . C O R T E G E
Y . L . A . G . A . A . C . S
. D E C R E E . T I G H T S
```

**147**
```
. M . F . S . S . T . A . E
M O T O R I S T . U N R U L Y
. R . U . D . R . N . D . E
C O E R C E . A U D I E N C E
. S . L . R . U . R . N . T
R E N E G E . S P A T T E R S
. A . A P S E . . . . O
B U F F A L O . R A I N I N G
P . . O N U S . E
A S S E M B L E . T U G G E D
. T . S . A . R . U . A . R
P A R T E R R E . T U T O R S
. I . H . R . I . E . I . O
G R E E C E . D E L I V E R S
. S . R . L . S . Y . E . S
```

**148**
```
S U B S T A N C E . M . K . R
. N . E . U . A . D A M A G E
V I L L A G E S . N . N . A
. Q . E . U . H . R A N G E S
Q U A C K S . I R O N . A . O
. E . T I T L E . B A R R E N
S . . T . R . I . O . I
C O N F E R S . U N K N O W N
R . I . A . S . E . G
A U T U M N . H O T E L . S
T . R . I D E A . E N A M E L
C L O W N S . R . A . B . V
H . G . U . P U S H O V E R
E V E N T S . L . E . U . R
S . N . E . M Y S T E R I E S
```

**149**
```
. B . A . T . T . W . G
S O M B R E R O . R E A S O N
. N . R . S . R . A . R . V
A S L A N T . N O V E M B E R
. A . S . R . A . E . T . R
B I K I N I . D O L P H I N S
. O . C H O P . . . . O
G R A N I T E . E A S T E R N
E . . R I N G . H
B A T H R O O M . E N E R G Y
. L . O . U . M . N . A . A
V I O L E N C E . C A T T L E
. S . L . C . N . I . R . L
B E C O M E . S K E L E T O N
. D . W . S . E . S . S . N
```

**150**
```
A S T R O N O M Y . S . T . I
. P . A . I . A . B A R R E N
C O N N E C T S . F . E . T
. O . D . E . T . B E H A V E
I N G O T S . E A R S . T . N
. S . M O T O R . A T T I C S
P . G . S . V . S . I
E S T U A R Y . D E E P E S T
S . O . E . P . X . Y
S Y M B O L . A N T I C . F
I . O . T A X I . A T O M I C
M A R S H Y . N . M . U . E
I . R . E . T R E A S U R E
S C O U R S . E . S . I . C
M . W . S . P R E T E N D E D
```

**151**
```
. S . O . K . C . K . O . M
C A R R I A G E . A M U S E D
. M . G . N . N . B . T . A
S P R A N G . T H U M P I N G
. L . N . A . I . K . U . T
S E N I O R . M A I N T A I N
. . S . O P E N . . . . M
S H A M P O O . T R U M P E T
. U . . E A S E . O
P R O D U C T S . P O N I E S
. R . O . A . P . L . S . A
S Y L L A B L E . A C T O R S
. I . L . L . C . C . E . N
E N G A G E . T H E O R I E S
. G . R . S . S . S . D . S
```

**152**
```
. T . T . B . A . S . B . E
D I N O S A U R . T U R T L E
. M . B . R . R . U . E . E
A B S O R B . A U D I E N C E
. E . G . E . N . I . Z . T
T R A G I C . G E O M E T R Y
. . A . U S E D . . . . O
C H A N N E L . G E T T I N G
. A . . I T E M . E
E N V E L O P E . P A R A D E
. D . M . B . N . L . M . R
S L I P P E R S . O R I G I N
. I . T . Y . I . Y . N . V
I N C O M E . O P E R A T E S
. G . R . D . N . D . L . S
```

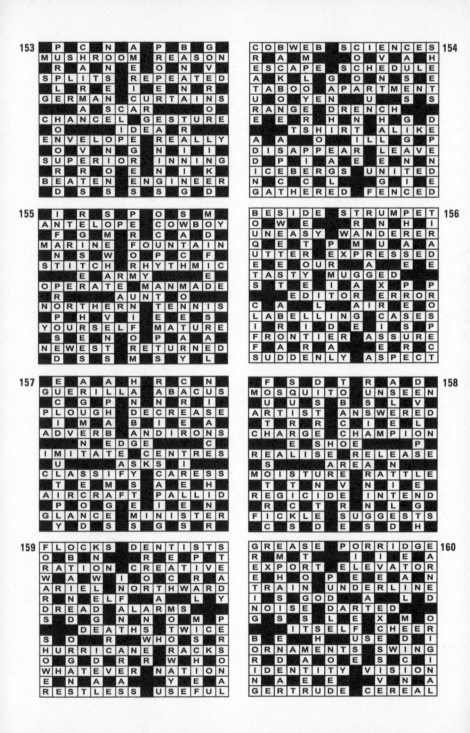

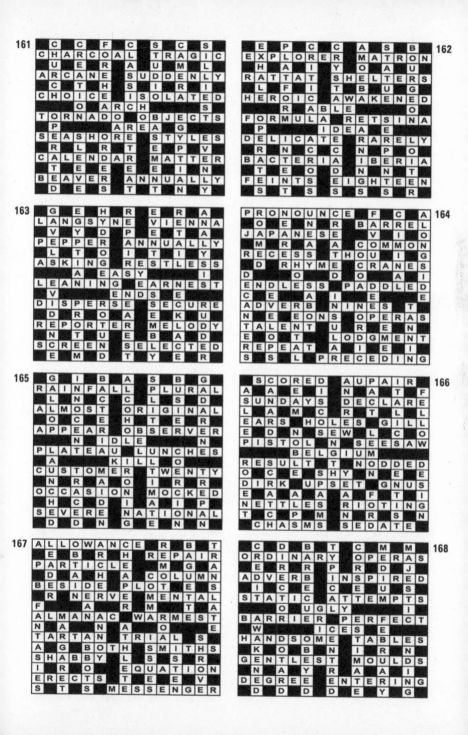

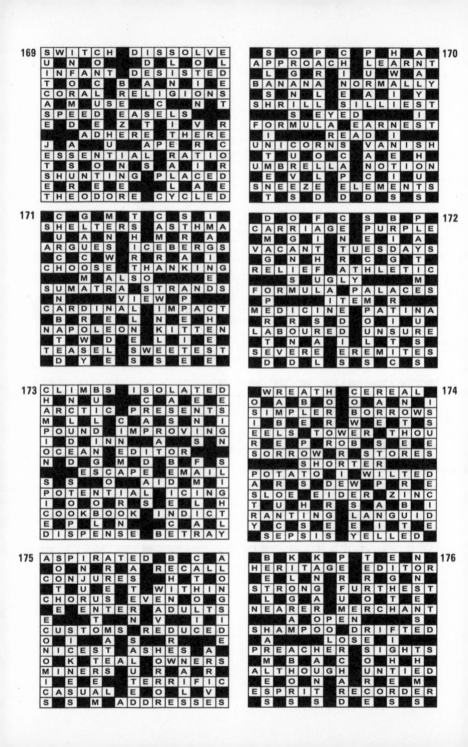

**169**
```
S W I T C H . D I S S O L V E
U . N . O . . D . L . O . . L
I N F A N T . D E S I S T E D
T . O . C . B . A . N . I . E
C O R A L . R E L I G I O N S
A . M . U S E . C . . N . . T
S P E E D . E A S E L S . . .
E . D . E . Z . T . I . V . R
. . A D H E R E . T H E R E .
J . A . . U . A P E . R . C .
E S S E N T I A L . R A T I O
T . S . O . N . S . A . I . R
S H U N T I N G . P L A C E D
E . R . E . E . . L . A . E .
T H E O D O R E . C Y C L E D
```

**170**
```
. S . O P . C . P . H . A .
A P P R O A C H . L E A R N T
. L . G . R . I . U . W . A .
B A N A N A . N O R M A L L Y
. S . N . L . E . A . I . Y .
S H R I L L . S I L L I E S T
. . . S . E Y E D . . . I . .
F O R M U L A . E A R N E S T
. I . . R E A D . I . . . . .
U N I C O R N S . V A N I S H
. T . U . O . C . A . E . H .
U M B R E L L A . N O T I O N
. E . V . L . P . C . I . U .
S N E E Z E . E L E M E N T S
. T . S . D . D . D . S . S .
```

**171**
```
. C . G . M . T . C . S . . I
S H E L T E R S . A S T H M A
. U . A . N . H . M . R . A .
A R G U E S . I C E B E R G S
. C . C . W . R . R . A . I .
C H O O S E . T H A N K I N G
. . . M . A L S O . . . . E .
S U M A T R A . S T R A N D S
. N . . . V I E W . P . . . .
C A R D I N A L . I M P A C T
. B . R . E . L . N . E . H .
N A P O L E O N . K I T T E N
. T . W . D . E . L . I . E .
T E A S E L . S W E E T E S T
. D . Y . E . S . S . E . E .
```

**172**
```
. D . O F . C . S . B P . P .
C A R R I A G E . P U R P L E
. M . G . I . N . E . I . A .
V A C A N T . T U E S D A Y S
. G . N . H . R . C . G . T .
R E L I E F . A T H L E T I C
. . . S . U G L Y . . . . M .
F O R M U L A . P A L A C E S
. P . . . I T E M . R . . . .
M E D I C I N E . P A T I N A
. R . R . S . D . O . I . U .
L A B O U R E D . U N S U R E
. T . N . A . I . L . T . S .
S E V E R E . E R E M I T E S
. D . D . L . S . S . C . S .
```

**173**
```
C L I M B S . I S O L A T E D
H . N . U . . C . A . E . E .
A R C T I C . P R E S E N T S
M . L . L . C . A . S . N . I
P O U N D . I M P R O V I N G
I . D . I N N . A . . S . . N
O C E A N . E D I T O R . . .
N . D . G . M . D . B . F . S
. . . E S C A P E . E M A I L
S . S . O . . A I D . M . . I
P O T E N T I A L . I C I N G
I . O . O . R . S . E . L . H
C O O K B O O K . I N D I C T
E . P . L . N . . C . A . L .
D I S P E N S E . B E T R A Y
```

**174**
```
. W R E A T H . C E R E A L .
O . A . B . O . O . A . N . I
S I M P L E R . B O R R O W S
I . B . E . R . W . E . T . S
E E L S . T O W E R . T H O U
R . E . P . R O B . S . E . E
S O R R O W . R . S T O R E S
. . . S H O R T E R . . . . .
P O T A T O . I . W I L T E D
A . R . S . D E W . P . R . E
S L O E . E I D E R . Z I N C
T . U . H . R . S . A . B . I
R A N T I N G . L A N G U I D
Y . C . S . E . E . I . T . E
. S E P S I S . Y E L L E D .
```

**175**
```
A S P I R A T E D . B . C . A
. O . N . R . A . R E C A L L
C O N J U R E S . H . T . O .
. T . U . E . T . W I T H I N
C H O R U S . E V E N . O . G
. E . E N T E R . A D U L T S
E . . T . N . V . I . I . . .
C U S T O M S . R E D U C E D
O . I . A . S . R . . . . . E
N I C E S T . A S H E S . A .
O . K . T E A L . O W N E R S
M I N E R S . U . R . A . R .
I . E . E . T E R R I F I C .
C A S U A L . E . O . L . V .
S . S . M . A D D R E S S E S
```

**176**
```
. B . K . K . P . T . E . N .
H E R I T A G E . E D I T O R
. E . L . N . R . R . G . N .
S T R O N G . F U R T H E S T
. L . G . A . U . O . T . E .
N E A R E R . M E R C H A N T
. . . A . O P E N . . . . S .
S H A M P O O . D R I F T E D
. A . . . L O S E . I . . . .
P R E A C H E R . S I G H T S
. M . B . A . C . O . H . H .
A L T H O U G H . U N T I E D
. E . O . N . A . R . E . M .
E S P R I T . R E C O R D E R
. S . S . S . D . E . S . S .
```

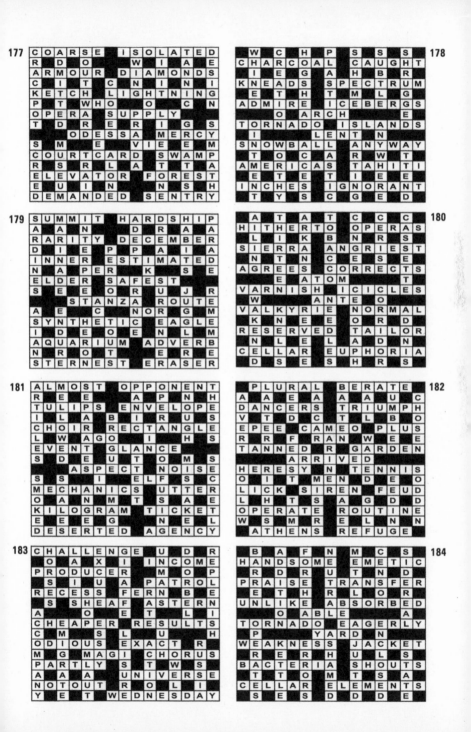

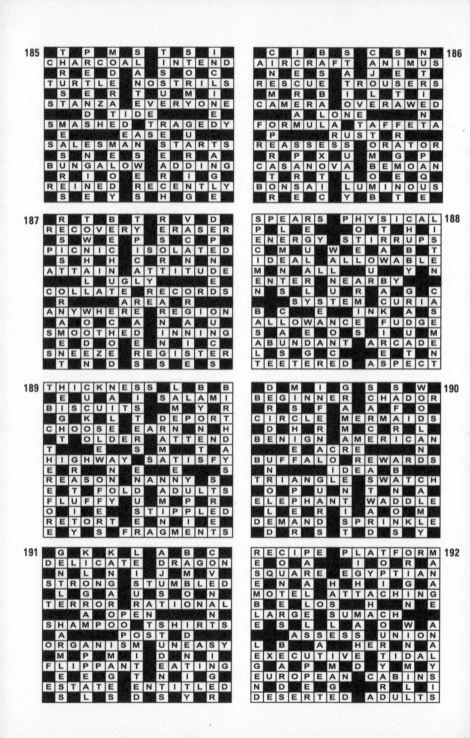

**185**

Across: CHARCOAL · INTEND · TURTLE · NOSTRILS · STANZA · EVERYONE · TIDE · SMASHED · TRAGEDY · EASE · SALESMAN · STARTS · SERA · BUNGALOW · ADDING · REINED · RECENTLY

**186**

Across: AIRCRAFT · ANIMUS · RESCUE · TROUSERS · CAMERA · OVERAWED · ALONE · FORMULA · TAFFETA · RUST · REASSESS · ORATOR · CASANOVA · BEMOAN · BONSAI · LUMINOUS

**187**

Across: RECOVERY · ERASER · PICNIC · ISOLATED · ATTAIN · ATTITUDE · UGLY · COLLATE · RECORDS · AREA · ANYWHERE · REGION · SMOOTHED · INNING · SNEEZE · REGISTER

**188**

Across: SPEARS · PHYSICAL · ENERGY · STIRRUPS · IDEAL · ALLOWABLE · ENTER · NEARBY · SYSTEM · CURIA · ALLOWANCE · FUDGE · ABUNDANT · ARCADE · TEETERED · ASPECT

**189**

Across: THICKNESS · SALAMI · BISCUITS · DEPORT · CHOOSE · EARN · OLDER · ATTEND · HIGHWAY · SATISFY · REASON · NANNY · FOLD · ADULTS · FLUFFY · STIPPLED · RETORT · FRAGMENTS

**190**

Across: BEGINNER · CHADOR · CIRCLE · MERMAIDS · BENIGN · AMERICAN · ACRE · BUFFALO · REWARDS · IDEA · TRIANGLE · SWATCH · ELEPHANT · WADDLE · DEMAND · SPRINKLE

**191**

Across: DELICATE · DRAGON · STRONG · STUMBLED · TERROR · RATIONAL · OPEN · SHAMPOO · TSHIRTS · POST · ORGANISM · UNEASY · FLIPPANT · EATING · ESTATE · ENTITLED

**192**

Across: RECIPE · PLATFORM · SQUARE · EGYPTIAN · MOTEL · ATTACHING · LARGE · SUMACH · ASSESS · UNION · EXECUTIVE · TIDAL · EUROPEAN · CABINS · DESERTED · ADULTS

## 193

```
G E O G R A P H Y . S . P . O
. L U . M . A . R E P O R T .
V I G I L A N T . V . R . H .
. C . T . Z . C . D E G R E E
P I R A T E . H A I R . I . R
. T . R I D G E . M E A D O W
P . M . D . L . G . . . I . .
R E F L E C T . O Y S T E R S
I . O . O . G . O . . . E . .
M A R G I N . I S S U E . A .
A . E . N E A R . E L D E S T
R E C E S S . A . C . I . L .
I . A . E . F O U R T E E N .
L O S E R S . F . R . O . E .
Y . T . T . T E L E G R A P H
```

## 194

```
H I S T O L O G Y . S . S . P
. M . H . A . A . A P P E A R
O P E R A T O R . I . P . O .
. A . I . E . L . B R E A S T
S C A L E S . A R E A . R . E
. T . L A T I N . A L W A Y S
P . S . . D . S . T . . T . .
R E S P E C T . A T H L E T E
E . H . A . C . E . . . D . .
S W E D E N . L O L L S . R .
E . L . S O F A . E L E V E N
N O T I C E . S . S . R . L .
T . E . H . H O S P I T A L .
E A R N E D . E . E . E . T .
D . S . W . A D D R E S S E D
```

## 195

```
. C . U . P . C . S . E . . .
P R O P E R L Y . L I K E N S
. A . S . I . J . O . I . T .
S Y S T E M . A B S O R B E D
. O . R . I . M . E . T . R .
U N S E E N . A R T I S T I C
. A . A L S O . . . N . . . .
F O R M U L A . B I O L O G Y
. P . . . T O S S . A . . . .
D I S C O V E R . O R B I T S
. N . A . D . L . E . R . . .
V I O L E N C E . A S L E E P
. O . M . I . R . T . L . A .
A N G E L S . E L E M E N T S
. S . R . H . D . D . D . Y .
```

## 196

```
. P . D . E . P . B . M . P .
B A S E B A L L . O P E R A S
. M . C . R . A . A . D . R .
R E V E A L . T E R M I N A L
. L . M . I . E . D . U . L .
M A R B L E . A S S E M B L E
. E . S H U T . . . E . . . .
O P E R A T E . U S U A L L Y
. R . . . R E N T . P . . . .
F O R W A R D S . R E P E A T
. B . A . A . C . A . E . T .
B A C T E R I A . N O T I O N
. B . E . E . P . G . I . M .
P L U R A L . E L E C T R I C
. Y . Y . Y . D . R . E . C .
```

## 197

```
M E L O D Y . E L E P H A N T
A . A . A . E . H . F . U . .
G E N I U S . L A B O U R E R
I . G . G . R . S . T . A . N
C O U G H . A U T H O R I S E
I . A . T O M . O . . . D . R
A N G L E . B I G W I G . . .
N . E . R . L . E . N . L . I
. A S T E R N . T R A I N . .
F . C . A . T O E . T . . . H
U N I V E R S A L . R A I S E
R . R . M . K . Y . E . T . R
O C C U P I E D . A S S U R E
R . L . T . I . . . T . D . N
E V E R Y O N E . A S P E C T
```

## 198

```
. C . I . C . A . R . B . W .
D I S C L O S E . A B O A R D
. C . E . R . O . N . T . I .
B E A C O N . L I G H T I N G
. R . R . W . I . E . O . K .
N O V E N A . A S S E M B L Y
. A . . . L E N T . . . E . .
F O R M U L A . I N C L U D E
. R . . . S U R E . E . . . .
S I D E W A Y S . C H A N C E
. G . N . L . E . K . R . H .
W I N D M I L L . L O N D O N
. N . I . E . E . A . I . O .
C A N N O N . S I C K N E S S
. L . G . S . S . E . G . E .
```

## 199

```
. T . M . E . A . R . C . D .
G O V E R N E D . E L A T E D
. M . R . O . V . C . N . L .
S A U C E R . A N A L Y S I S
. T . H . M . N . L . O . C .
M O N A C O . C A L E N D A R
. N . U S E D . . . T . . . .
C O N T E S T . D R I L L E D
. N . . . E A S E . A . . . .
B L O S S O M S . F R U M P Y
. O . H . R . H . L . G . E .
C O L O M B I A . E C H O E S
. K . V . I . M . C . I . V .
N E W E S T . E X T E N D E D
. R . L . S . D . S . G . D .
```

## 200

```
. S . T . T . L . C . K . . .
H A C I E N D A . A B R O A D
. L . A . G . B . W . A . T .
C A L M E R . L I F E T I M E
. M . A . I . E . U . E . A .
F I E R C E . A I L E R O N S
. . I . S T U B . . . D . . .
D E F A C T O . I S T H M U S
. J . . . W E S T . . . . . .
S E M O L I N A . R A R E S T
. C . B . N . R . A . D . C .
S T A R T L E D . N E C T A R
. I . I . E . R . G . A . R .
I N V E N T . U N L I S T E D
. G . N . S . M . E . H . D .
```

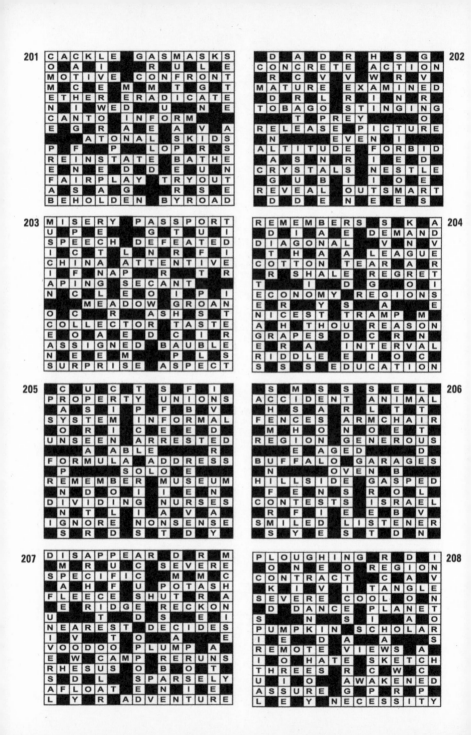

**209**

Across: MOSQUITO, INFANT, ASSIST, MULTIPLY, STARVE, LOWLANDS, SWAM, ENGLISH, EARNEST, INNS, ANTELOPE, TACTIC, PACIFIER, RELISH, RABIES, SUITCASE

**210**

SHRUBS, FOXHOUND, REMITS, REPLACES, RANGE, ELABORATE, RAG, STIFF, RAISES, MYSELF, POLAR, AIR, POLICEMEN, EXITS, NITROGEN, ASTUTE, DISTRESS, ASCENT

**211**

SYNTHETIC, DIGEST, ELECTION, TUNING, FOREST, ROUT, TASTE, NETTLE, RESULTS, ACHIEVE, CHOSEN, EAGLE, IDEA, LEARNT, SPLITS, INVENTED, LONGER, PRESIDENT

**212**

APPROACH, UNABLE, MIASMA, REPUBLIC, ANIMAL, NATIONAL, EGGS, GONDOLA, ICICLES, MEAL, MISCHIEF, ONIONS, DISAGREE, HEARTS, SNEEZE, TENDENCY

**213**

MIDDAY, STITCHED, RECIPE, TERMINAL, INDIA, AUSTRALIA, BOW, SINCE, ALLOWS, TSHIRT, NYLON, END, SPIRITUAL, EGYPT, AIRPORTS, FINISH, DISASTER, AGREED

**214**

UNUSUALLY, CHARGE, SALESMAN, WAITER, FLOATS, AXIS, WATER, DEPEND, CHEWING, WHITSUN, NATION, OILED, TEAR, EARTHY, MONTHS, ARRANGED, CHERRY, POSSESSED

**215**

REINDEER, DAPHNE, ROUTES, DRAMATIC, ACTION, ASSIGNED, TILE, BIGGEST, THEATRE, EASY, HOMONYMS, DEPART, PARTICLE, ORANGE, RESIST, TREASURE

**216**

FANTASIES, TOMATO, GANGRENE, RIBBON, SEVERN, EDIT, DISCS, PENCIL, STACKED, UNDRESS, RECESS, HOPED, TAXI, OPENED, NORWAY, EXAMINED, UNCLES, RECOGNISE

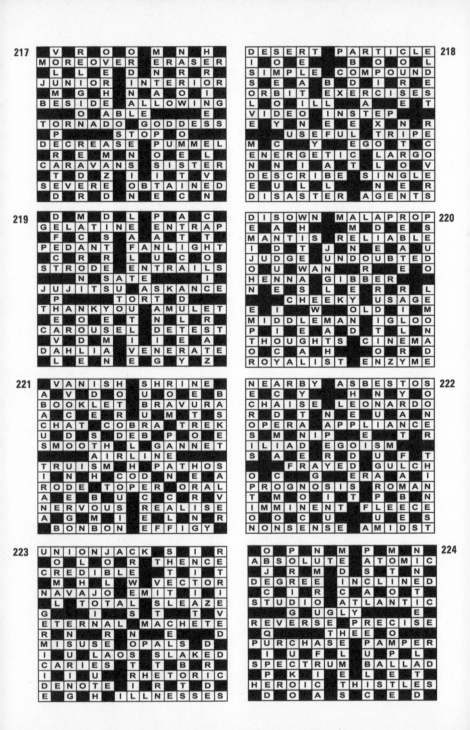

**225**

Row 1: C L I M B S · · G A L L O P E D
Row 2: H · N · E · · R · I · O · · A
Row 3: I N D I A N · S I N G U L A R
Row 4: L · I · N · H · S · H · I · K
Row 5: D U C K S · I D E N T I C A L
Row 6: R · A · T U G · O · · Y · Y
Row 7: E X T R A · H I D D E N · · ·
Row 8: N · E L E · E · C · P · A
Row 9: · · S K I R T S · O C E A N
Row 10: E · N · L · · I N N · R · G
Row 11: G R U E L L I N G · O C C U R
Row 12: G · G · A · M · N · M · E · I
Row 13: N I G E R I A N · D I V I N E
Row 14: O · E · G · G · C · V · S
Row 15: G A T H E R E D · A S P E C T

**226**

· M · D · F · A · · A · U · R
F I R E W O O D · F A S T E N
· R · M · R · D · R · E · A
G R O O V E · R A I N F A L L
· O · T · H · E · C · U · I
P R A I S E · S M A L L E S T
· O · A L S O · · E
T O R N A D O · A N G U I S H
· R · N I N E · N
E I G H T E E N · C A S U A L
· G · I · X · T · K · T · R
W I L D L I F E · L E A V E S
· N · D · S · N · A · B · N
S A F E S T · S I C I L I A N
· L · N · S · E · E · E · S

**227**

· S · B · D · A · T · H · M
A Q U A R I U M · W E A P O N
· U · R · E · E · W · D
R A B B I T · R E L E A S E D
· R · E · I · V · I · R
R E S C U E · C H E M I C A L
· U · S T A Y · T
B E N E A T H · M A R S H E S
· N · A U N T · T
C O N C E R T S · T H R U S T
· R · A · U · U · E · E · P
U M B R E L L A · M O N K E Y
· O · T · E · L · P · G · N
H U M O U R · L A T I T U D E
· S · N · S · Y · S · H · S

**228**

F I N A N C I A L · L · F · C
· S · F · H · S · T A K E T H
G L O R I O U S · U · S · E
· A · A · S · U · P R O T E M
E N G I N E · R A R E · I · I
· D · D E N S E · O L I V E S
C · A · D · B · A · T
O R D E R L Y · R E G U L A R
N · I · E · G · I · · Y
S C R E A M · A L A R M · S
T · E · T O U R · F L Y I N G
R E C K O N · B · F · S · E
U · T · M · A W A K E N E D
C R E D I T · G · I · L · Z
T · D · C · T E R R I F I E D

**229**

· S · E · D · S · P · O · P
C O N F L I C T · A N C H O R
· C · F · S · O · P · C · W
E C Z E M A · M E A S U R E D
· E · C · G · A · Y · R · R
C R A T E R · C L A S S I F Y
· E · E C H O · U
S O L D I E R · C E R E A L S
· V · · A S K S · Q
D E S C R I B E · C L U M S Y
· R · O · S · N · A · I · P
A C Q U I R E D · P U P I L S
· O · L · A · I · I · P · A
E M P I R E · N O N S E N S E
· E · S · L · G · G · D · H

**230**

P R O G R A M M E · S · D · A
· E · U · N · O · R E V E A L
O C C A S I O N · I · F · T
· I · V · M · D · S T R I P E
S T R A T A · A C H E · N · R
· E · S A L L Y · R E G I O N
S · C · S · U · T · A
T O P C O A T · U G L I E S T
R · E · T · S · I · · E
A N N U A L · H A R S H · W
N · K · C A S A · A T O M I C
G E N I U S · R · N · L · N
E · I · I · P A D D L I N G
S A F E T Y · E · O · O · E
T · E · Y · F R A M E W O R K

**231**

· Q U O R U M · N O R M A L
S · I · E · O · I · U · S
C O U P L E T · D E P O S I T
A · S · L · H · D · E · T · R
L O U D · W O M E N · T R E E
E · A · H · D A D · E · I · A
S E L D O M · R · A T T A C K
· · · R U B B I S H · · ·
V O T I N G · L · K E E P E R
I · A · S · R E D · R · L · E
S I L L · N O S E Y · W O L F
U · L · D · W · M · Y · U · U
A M E R I C A · O R A N G E S
L · S · M · N · T · R · H · E
· O T H E R S · E L D E S T

**232**

P R E D I C A T E · P · I · T
· E · E · L · O · D I N N E R
P A S S P O R T · L · T · A
· S · E · S · A · S O L E M N
C O A R S E · L E N T · R · S
· N · T O T A L · A S L E E P
B · · F · · Y · I · · S · O
A P P E A R S · P L A S T E R
R · E · O · O · L · · T
B U R S T S · F L A S H · S
E · S · R E E F · R O A R E D
C A U C U S · I · C · W · V
U · A · I · C O T T A G E S
E L D E S T · E · I · I · R
S · E · M · P R A C T I C E S

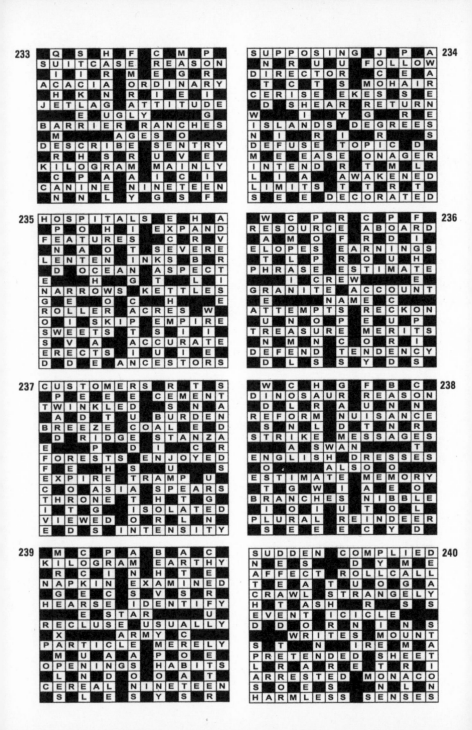

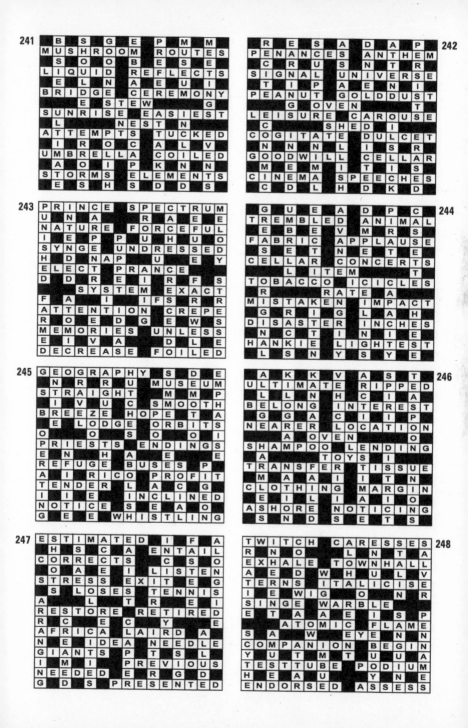

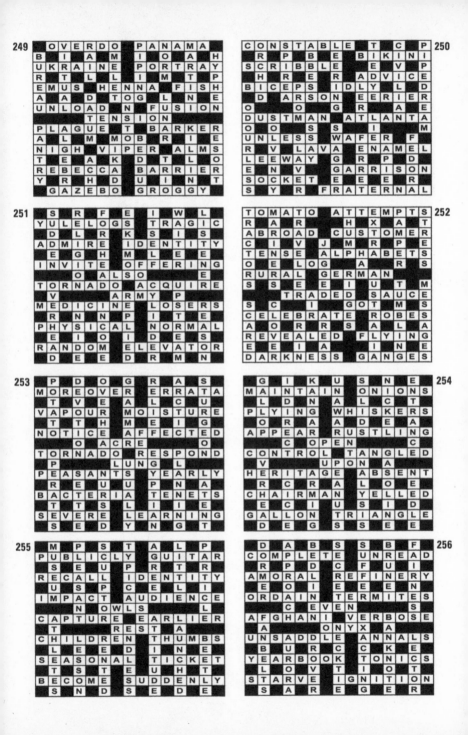

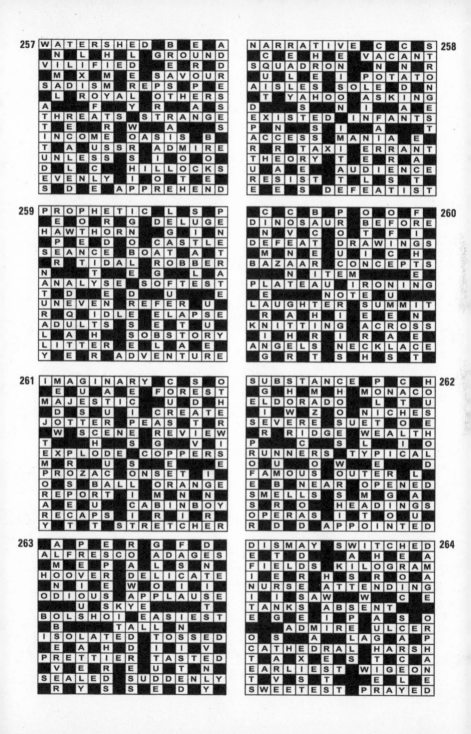

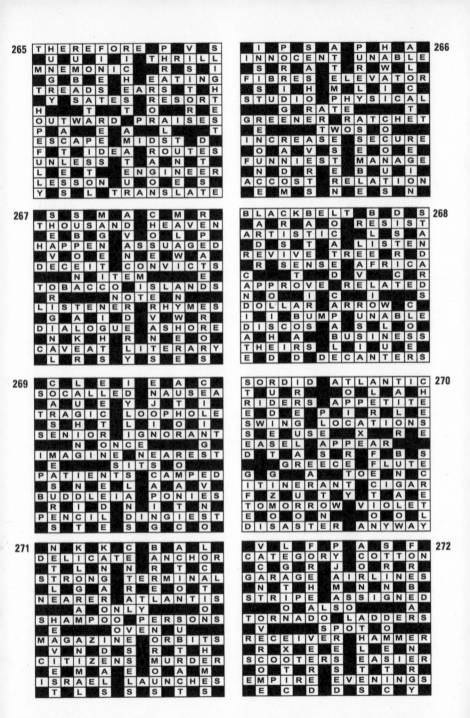

**273**

```
  M M C A   D F I
V A N I S H E S   O N I O N S
  R   S E   S   R E   V
C I R C L E   U P S T R E A M
N   H   R   A   E   C   D
R E L I E F   G A T H E R E D
    E   U S E D       R
B U F F A L O   D A R K E S T
N       L E S S   N
S K E L E T O N   S T I T C H
  I   A   H   G   U   T   O
S N O W B A L L   M E T A L S
  D   Y   M   I   I   I U
S L E E V E   S Y N O N Y M S
  Y   R   S   H   G   G   N
```

**274**

```
C H A R O N   S I N G U L A R
O   L   R     D   A   O   E
N O T I C E   S E X T A N T S
F   I   H   S   A   E   D   T
L I T R E   T E L E S C O P E
I   U   S E E   R     N   D
C A D E T   A L A R M S
T   E   R   L   N   E   I   W
    C A U S E S     N I N T H
K   O   S     W I T   F   I
I N F L U E N C E   I R O N S
S   F   N   O   R   O   R   T
S P E C I F I C   A N I M A L
E   R   T   S     E   A   E
D E S I S T E D   A D U L T S
```

**275**

```
  C O   C   C   S   R A
T H O R O U G H   T W E N T Y
  O   G   L   A   A   L   H
H O B A R T   N O R M A L L Y
  S   N   U   N   V   T   E
S E N I O R   E L E M E N T S
    S   A B L E       E
F O R M U L A   G L I M P S E
  B     S H O E   O
D E C R E A S E   G A I E T Y
  D   U   N   R   G   S   A
D I A M E T E R   I N T E N T
  E   P   L   I   E   U   G
U N G L U E   N O S T R I L S
  T   E   R   G   T   E   E
```

**276**

```
  E   B B   S   S   S M
O V E R C A S T   A U T H O R
  O   O   S   U   M   U   D
C L I C H E   D E P A R T E D
  V   C   B   I   L   D   R
S E N O R A   E V E R Y D A Y
      L   L O S E       T
G O R I L L A   I C I C L E S
  R         T U N E   A
M I D N I G H T   I N S I S T
  G   E   U   T   L   S   P
L I K E W I S E   I D E A L S
  N   D   L   R   N   T   A
B A L L E T   L I G H T E S T
  L   E   Y   Y   S   E   H
```

**277**

```
  B   I   P   A   I   U H
M E R C H A N T   C A N N O T
  R   E   R   H   I   I   M
F A S C I A   L O C A T I O N
  T   R   L   E   L   E   N
C E R E A L   T U E S D A Y S
  A   E V E R       M
F O R M U L A   G L I M P S E
  P       I D E A   U
M E M B R A N E   U N L E S S
  R   A   W   E   G   L   E
H A R D S H I P   H A I R D O
  T   G   I   E   I   O   U
R E V E A L   S Y N O N Y M S
  D   S   E   T   G   S   S
```

**278**

```
  M   D   N   R   R F   F
M O L E C U L E   E D I T O R
  N   L   M   S   P   A   U
M A N A G E   T H O U S A N D
  C   W   R   O   R   C   T
T O B A G O   R A T I O N A L
      R   U S E D       I
I M M E N S E   D R I V I N G
  O       E L S E   O
P U R C H A S E   S P L A S H
  N   A   N   N   P   C   I
S T I R R I N G   O R A N G E
  A   P   M   T   N   N   N
C I N E M A   H O S P I T A L
  N   T   L   Y   E   C   L
```

**279**

```
  D   S   B   C   S   I P
M O S Q U I T O   T I M B E R
  U   U   R   U   R   P   A
O B J E C T   N U I S A N C E
  L   E   H   C   K   C   E
S E I Z E D   I D E N T I F Y
  E   A B L E       U
G O O D B Y E   A W F U L L Y
  P       S I D E   N
R E F L E C T S   S T I T C H
  R   A   A   L   T   C   H
B A C T E R I A   W O O D E N
  T   T   I   N   A   R   E
G O V E R N   D A R K N E S S
  R   R   G   S   D   S E
```

**280**

```
  D   A   T   A   S   C P
B O U L D E R S   Q U A R R Y
  M   T   A   S   U   J   E
B I C E P S   U N I F O R M S
  N   R   P   A   R   L   I
B O L E R O   G A T H E R E D
  G   O P E N       R
H E R O I N E   T R I P P E D
  N       A L S O   E
M O I S T U R E   M O N T H S
  R   T   N   I   A   K   O
E M B R A C E S   N I N E T Y
  O   I   L   U   T   I   E
P U R P L E   R A I N F A L L
  S   E   S   E   C   E   S
```

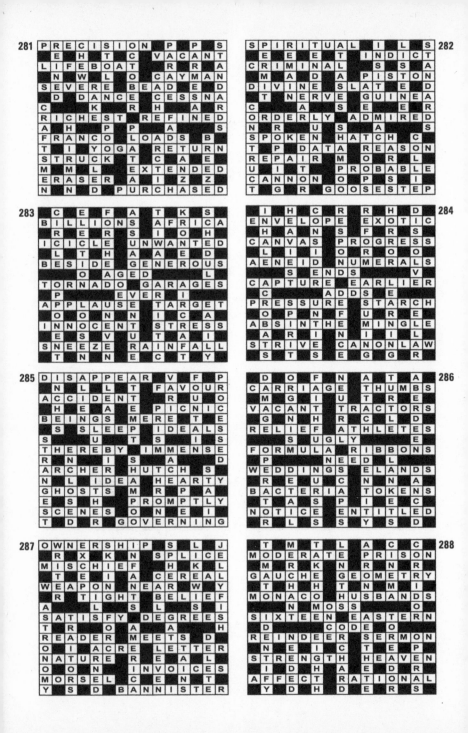

## 289

```
R E M O V E   C R O W D I N G
E   N   E     E   A   R   A
S L E D G E   C A R T O O N S
E   M   E   L   C   E   N   K
A B O U T   I N T E R F E R E
R   N   A R C   F   D     T
C L I M B   K E T T L E
H   C   L   E   U   A S   A
    L E A D E R   N O T E D
S   F   P   K I D   A   D
P R I M I T I V E   S E N S E
E   N   N   D   Y   C   D N
E N G I N E E R   C A N A R D
D   E   E   A     P   R   U
S U R P R I S E   S E L D O M
```

## 290

```
  T   H H   T   R   R   R
D I N O S A U R   E R A S E R
  R   R   N   A L   T   F
M A D R I D   F R I G H T E N
  N   I S   F   E   E   R
B A M B O O   I N F O R M E D
      L   M I C E       E
F I R E M E N   C L O S E S T
  N       T A K E   Q
A C T O F G O D   M O U L D S
  L   C   O   D O   I   E
C I R C U L A R   N U R S E D
  N   U   D   E A   R   P
P E O P L E   S U D D E N L Y
  D   Y   N   S E   L   Y
```

## 291

```
  H   S   P   M   S G   M
S U B P O E N A   T H A M E S
  M   E   N   N U L   A
F A L C O N   M I D D L I N G
  N   I   A   A I O   I
G E R M A N   D R O P P I N G
  E   T H E E       G
C H I N E S E   N E A R E S T
  E     E A T S   E
C A P I T A L S   C A S H E W
  R   N   N   S A T   N
V I O L E N C E   P R O N T O
  N   A   O   N I R   I
A G E N C Y   T E N D E N C Y
  S   D   S   S G D   E
```

## 292

```
  R   S E   S   O   H   L
M E C H A N I C   P L A N E T
  N   O   V   I P W   V
E N D U R E   E D U C A T E D
  E   L   L   N G I   R
S T U D I O   C O N F I D E D
  E   P O E M       T
S H O R T E N   I M M E N S E
  O     C U T E   N
F R I G H T E N   R E T A I N
  R   R   H K C   I   B
D I V I S I O N   H A T P I N
  B   L   R O A   L   D
C L O S E D   W A N D E R E D
  E   E S   N   T   D   M
```

## 293

```
P R O T E C T E D   C   T   R
  A   I   I   X   C A M E R A
A G I T P R O P   R   A   I
  G   L   C   E   S E A S O N
R E V E A L   C O T E   P   D
  D   S C E N T   A R B O U R
S       T   S   I   O   O
P L E A S E D   G R O W N U P
  A   X   R   S   M   S
G O P H E R   C H O I R   F
  H   L   L E G O   U T O P I A
E L A T E D   O   N   T E
  T   I   C   T A C I T U R N
T E N E T S   E   E E   C
  I   S   S   P R E S E N T E D
```

## 294

```
  M   M   B B   A   D   T
C A R E F R E E   S L I G H T
  R   R   O   T H V   I
C I T R I C   T E R R I E R S
  N   I   C   I A N   T
T E R E D O   N U M B E R E D
      S   L E G S       E
N O S T R I L   E V I D E N T
  P       S I D E   I
D I S A S T E R   L E S S E R
  N   N   R   O O T   N
S I C I L I A N   C H A N G E
  O   M   A   I I N   I
I N L A N D   N O T I C I N G
  S   L   S   G Y E   E
```

## 295

```
T R I A N G L E S   G   C   C
  E   S   A   X   G A L O R E
C A T H O L I C   T   C   L
  P   L   L   U   L E G A T E
L E G A T O   S O Y A   C   B
  R   R A N G E   R U M O U R
M   X   S   E   L   A
I T A L I C S   A S P H A L T
N   U   A   C   U   E
I N D I A N   R O A R S   A
A   I   D O M E   P E T A L S
T W E L V E   A   O   A   B
U   N   I   T A L E N T E D
R E C U S E   O   L   Z   I
E   E   E   A R G O N A U T S
```

## 296

```
  C   P   S   P O   H   T
S I L E N T L Y   C H O I R S
  N   R   U   J C   R   O
L E S S O N   A Q U A R I U M
  M   U   N   M R   O   S
M A L A W I   A B S O R B E D
  D   N O S E       R
F O R E I G N   E A S I E S T
  B       C A R S   N
S T A R T L E D   S O V I E T
  A   E   I   D E   I   X
V I L L A G E R   M E T H O D
  N   I   H   E B   I   T
C E M E N T   S P L E N D I D
  D   F   S   S E   G   C
```

**297**

```
O B J E C T I V E . S . N . P
. E . X . R . I . E A S I E R
S A M O V A R S . H . T . O
. K . T . D . I . C A R R O T
R E C I T E . T S A R . O . E
. R . C A R G O . B A D G E S
P . . . X . R . L . E . T
R E A L I T Y . D E F E N C E
I . P . . E . C . . L . . D
M E R M A N . A N D E S . S
A . I . P E L T . R E A S O N
R E C E N T . E . I . F . L
I . O . O . R E V E A L E D
L E T T E R . E . E . R . M
Y . S . A . B R I L L I A N T
```

**298**

```
. C . B . S . E . A . S . B
B I G A M O U S . R E E K E D
. C . S . M . C . C . P . A
F A M I N E . A C A N T H U S
. D . L . W . P . D . E . F
B A N I S H . E L E C T I O N
. . C . A L S O . . . . R
A T L A N T A . S P I R I T S
E . . . M A T E . O
D E S C R I B E . R E B U F F
. T . E . R . O . S . I . I
C H A R C O A L . O U N C E S
. I . E . N . I . N . S . N
E N R A G E . A N A C O N D A
. G . L . D . N . L . N . S
```

**299**

```
. T . O . N . E . A . E . N
T H I R T E E N . P I G E O N
. I . G . W . G . A . O . N
B R I A R S . L U C K I E S T
. S . N . R . I . H . S . E
S T R I F E . S T E A M I N G
. . S . E C H O . . . . S
F O R M U L A . O C T O B E R
. U . . . S E L L . F
S T R I C K E N . O F F I C E
. B . N . E . D . T . E . O
C O N C E R T O . H A R D L Y
. U . U . N . R . I . I . U
U N T R U E . S Y N O N Y M S
. D . S . L . E . G . G . N
```

**300**

```
. B . U . S . S . W . R . E
M A G N E T I C . R H E S U S
. N . I . U . H . I . L . P
C A R V E D . O U T R I G H T
. N . E . E . L . H . C . O
B A R R E N . A P E R T U R E
. . S . T A R E . . . . I
A T H E I S M . R E D C O A T
. H . . . I R I S . O
L E O N A R D O . T U N D R A
. A . U . E . A . I . S . E
A T T R A C T S . M E T A L S
. R . S . E . T . A . A . I
B E R E T S . E X T E N D E D
. S . S . S . D . E . T . F
```